Principles, Elements, and Types of Persuasion

Principles, Elements, and Types of Persuasion

JAMES BENJAMIN
University of Toledo

HARCOURT BRACE COLLEGE PUBLISHERS

Fort Worth   Philadelphia   San Diego   New York   Orlando   Austin   San Antonio
Toronto   Montreal   London   Sydney   Tokyo

Publisher	Christopher P. Klein
Senior Acquisitions Editor	Carol Wada
Developmental Editors	Laurie Runion and Diane Drexler
Senior Project Editor	Laura J. Hanna
Production Manager	Lois West
Art Director	Candice Johnson Clifford
Picture and Rights Editor	Sandra Lord
Photo Researcher	Lili Weiner

Harcourt Brace may provide complimentary instructional aids and supplements or supplement packages to those adopters qualified under our adoption policy. Please contact your sales representative for more information. If as an adopter or potential user you receive supplements you do not need, please return them to your sales representative or send them to: Attn: Returns Department, Troy Warehouse, 465 South Lincoln Drive, Troy, MO 63379.

Requests for permission to make copies of any part of the work should be mailed to: Permissions Department, Harcourt Brace & Company, 6277 Sea Harbor Drive, Orlando, Florida 32887-6777.

Address for Editorial Correspondence: Harcourt Brace College Publishers, 301 Commerce Street, Suite 3700, Fort Worth, TX 76102.

Address for Orders: Harcourt Brace & Company, 6277 Sea Harbor Drive, Orlando, FL 32887-6777. 1-800-782-4479, or 1-800-433-0001 (in Florida).

Printed in the United States of America

ISBN: 0-15-502355-1

Library of Congress Catalog Card Number: 96-76311

6 7 8 9 0 1 2 3 4 5   039   9 8 7 6 5 4 3 2 1

For Barbie, at last

ACKNOWLEDGMENTS

No book springs full grown from the mind of the author. The process is more like constructing a building or making a movie or building an automobile. The author may be the architect but the product is the result of collaboration. This prefatory material is an attempt to acknowledge some of the people who influenced the pages you are about to read.

First, and foremost, I would like to thank my students in persuasion courses at the University of Hawaii, at Southwest Texas State University, and at the University of Toledo. Together we learned about persuasion and refined the ideas in the following pages. The really great parts are the result of their interactions. The confusing or mistaken parts are mine alone.

Second, I would like to acknowledge the contributions of Dr. Barbaranne Benjamin. She patiently read every word of many drafts of this work. Her suggestions, as always, were gratefully incorporated into the work. In addition, I want to thank her for her unfailing good humor throughout the throes of the creative process.

Finally, the editors and reviewers of drafts of this manuscript deserve a special thank you. John Grashoff of Harcourt Brace encouraged the project from the start. Carol Wada, Senior Acquisitions Editor, was unflaggingly supportive. Laurie Runion and Diane Drexler, Developmental Editors, were graciously critical in the development of the work. Laura Hanna, Senior Project Editor, carefully supervised the editing and production of the book. Lili Weiner, Photo Researcher, contributed her talented vision to the final product. My colleagues Jerry Anderson, Concordia College; Vincent Bloom, California State University—Fresno; Jacquelyn Buckrop, Ball State University; Floyd Merritt, Eastern Illinois University; Ellen Arden-Ogle, Cosumnes River College; Dan Gross, Montana State University; Ferald Bryan, Northern Illinois University; and Anneke-Jan Boden, Eastern Montana College must be thanked for their insightful comments and careful critiques of the manuscript.

James Benjamin
University of Toledo

CONTENTS

Principles, Elements, and Types of Persuasion

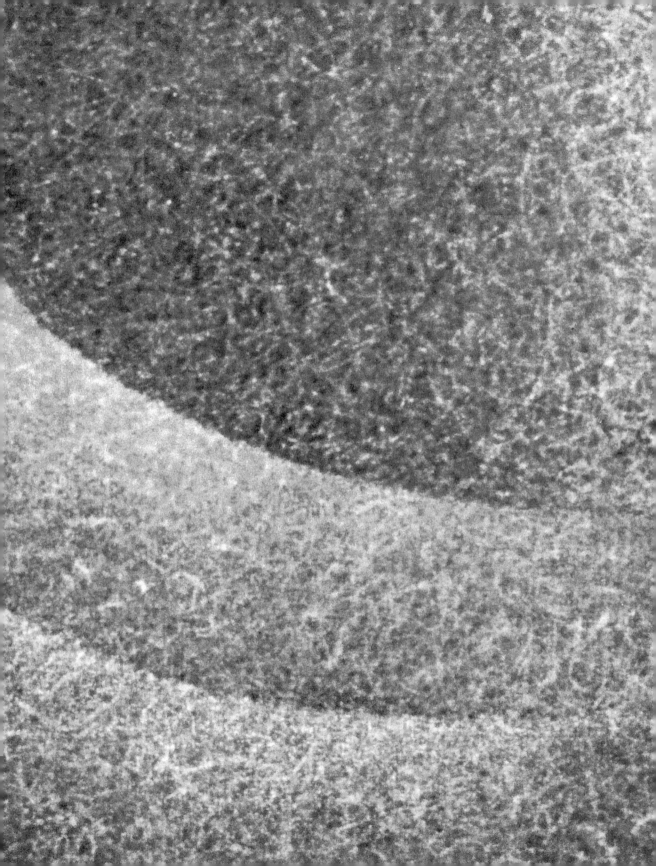

PART ONE

PRINCIPLES OF PERSUASION

INTRODUCTION

Persuasion pervades our lives. It surrounds us with attempts to influence us to feel, to think, and to act. And we use persuasion on a daily basis. We try to influence others to feel, to think, to act in accordance with our goals. In short, it is a defining characteristic of being a human. To be human is to persuade and to be persuaded.

This book is about persuasion. As such, it focuses on communication but does not assume that you are a major in communication. While the topic is persuasive communication, the book does not focus exclusively on public speaking since persuasion is a part of all aspects of human communication. Consider the following forums:

Intrapersonal communication centers on internal communication activities such as the role of communication in thinking and listening. Clearly, persuasion plays a role in our communication to ourselves—when we are getting ready for a test or a job interview, for example, we will psych ourselves up. To do that is to engage in self-persuasion, convincing ourselves that we can do well or that we are the best candidate for the job. Such self-persuasion is the basis of a modern approach to personal problem solving called Rational Emotive Therapy. We engage in self-persuasion in creating and in changing our emotional reactions to events. As noted psychologist Dr. David Burns observed, "If you want to feel better, you must realize that your thoughts and attitudes—not external events—create your feelings. You can learn to change the way you think, feel and behave in the here and now. That simple but revolutionary principle can help you change your life."[1]

What goes on within us as we are persuaded is also a topic of interest for intrapersonal communication. Concepts like attitude, belief, and value are central to an understanding of persuasion. Such concepts describe intrapersonal dimensions of human persuasion. Psychological factors such as attention, cognition, and emotional response are all intrapersonal elements of persuasion.

By contrast, **interpersonal communication** is concerned with dyadic communication, with discourse between two parties rather than within a single individual. Persuasion plays a major role in this type of communication as well. From the relatively formal interactions in a sales interview to the very informal conversations between friends, we engage in persuasion. We seek to sell a product or service; we seek to negotiate the best price for that product or service. We seek to influence a friend to try a new restaurant; we choose to agree or to suggest an alternative place to eat.

Persuasion also operates at the interpersonal level in the professional world. We try to influence a candidate to join our company; we seek to convince an employer that we are the best candidate for a job. In short, our interactions with others are directed toward goals and to accomplish those goals we must persuade and be persuaded.

In **group communication,** several people interact and here again persuasion is omnipresent. In problem-solving groups, for example, we must advocate a specific solution we believe best meets the criteria for the optimal course. We may try to convince a campus review board to excuse a parking ticket. In a business setting we may seek to get a committee to approve our proposed budget.

Leadership in groups or organizations also requires persuasion. In *Presidential Power* Richard Neustadt wrote that of all of the powers (the power as commander-in-chief of the Armed Forces, the power to appoint and receive foreign ambassadors, the power to make treaties, the power to execute the laws), the ultimate power of the president is "the power to persuade."[2] Whether one is the president of the United States, the chief executive officer of a corporation, or the leader of a discussion group, effective leadership is a matter of persuasive communication.

Persuasion is also vital to **public communication.** Preachers, teachers, and politicians influence us through public speaking. Architects propose designs; sports figures pitch products and ideas in public appearances; lawyers address judges and juries. We speak before City Council to put more police officers on the street; we address the school board to improve the educational system; we talk to employees to motivate them to try a new procedure.

Persuasion in public communication also applies to our efforts to listen critically to public discourse. As audiences, we are exposed to the public presentation of information and ideas on a daily basis. We must listen and decide our positions on public issues constantly. As we shall see in Chapter Two, the origins of rhetoric—persuasive communication—grew from a social need to present public issues effectively. Much of what we know about the psychology of decision making has developed from our need to know about how to influence those decisions, whether it be in the law courts, political assemblies, or other public gatherings.

Mass communication also provides paradigms of persuasion. Whether we use electronic media like radio or television; print media like newspapers, magazines, or direct mail; or newer technologies like the fax or computer networks, persuasion pervades the media. Advertising agencies and public relations firms are clearly groups that attempt to persuade using mass communication channels. Some of our most vivid memories are of a favorite commercial. Every magazine and newspaper we open is filled with advertisements, all vying for our attention. Streets and highways are lined with billboards competing for our attention. We attend movies and see coming attractions. Sports stadiums are filled with ads and race cars and their drivers are plastered with product logos.

Mass persuasion through mass communication is evolving with the newer technologies. Facsimile machines crank out sales pitches on a daily basis. Log onto a computer network and you soon encounter billboards in cyberspace. Each new development in mass communication brings with it opportunities to persuade and to be persuaded.

Even the field of **intercultural communication** is concerned with persuasion. Since the dawn of time, communication among cultures has been a priority. Nations have conducted trade and diplomatic relations through persuasive communication. As a result, nations have needed to adapt their messages to each other in an attempt to influence the beliefs, values, attitudes, and behaviors of receivers. In explaining the "rules" for selling products overseas, the World Trade Press suggests that advertisers avoid "lazy and culturally biased thinking. A foreign country has official regulations and cultural preferences that differ from those of your own. Learn about these differences, respect them, and adapt your product accordingly. Often it won't even take that much thought, money, or effort. Kentucky Fried Chicken offers a salmon sandwich in Japan, fried plantains in Mexico, and tabouleh in the Middle East—and 450 other locally specific menu items worldwide. And even the highly standardized McDonald's serves pineapple pie in Thailand, teriyaki burgers and tatsuda sandwiches (chicken with ginger and soy) in Japan, spicy sauces with burgers in Malaysia (prepared according to Muslim guidelines), and a seasonal durian fruit shake in Singapore."[3] As the European Economic Community continues to develop, the United Nations takes on expanded roles in world affairs, the North American Free Trade Alliance expands, it is becoming increasingly important for businesses and citizens to understand what motivates members of other cultures.

Even within our own country, the cultural demographics are changing, and those changes mandate that we all understand how to persuade and how to respond to persuasion on an intercultural level. Effective persuasion is the best hope for enriching the mix that constitutes American society.

At all levels, then, from within ourselves to among our nations, we are persuaded and we persuade. To understand how persuasion works and how to make persuasive communication effective in all of these arenas require the study of three dimensions that form the outline for what follows in this book: principles, elements, and types of persuasion.

PRINCIPLES OF PERSUASION : Fundamentals, Basic, Common patterns, theorize

First, we must understand the principles of persuasion. While we can drive a car without understanding the principles of mechanics, we drive a car more effectively if we understand why things happen. It is similar with persuasion. Naturally gifted communicators can persuade without studying the principles of persuasion, but knowing why persuasion works and not just how to create a persuasive message will make us more effective communicators.

Abraham Kaplan in *Conduct of Inquiry* defines theory as "a cognitive device for interpreting, criticizing, and unifying established laws, modifying them to fit data unanticipated in their formulation, and guiding the enterprise of discovering new and more powerful generalizations."[4]

By cognitive device, Kaplan means a mental construct; theories of persuasion are principles about persuasion rather than persuasion itself. Theories help us to interpret, critique and draw together established principles. Theories also help us to modify those principles to fit data that have not been anticipated in their formulation. Just as freedom of the press has been modified to include electronic media the founding fathers could not be expected to foresee, our principles of persuasion should be modified to fit new persuasive situations. Theories also help us to uncover new and more powerful generalizations. The principles of persuasion are intended to be generalizations that should apply whether the discourse is oral or written, whether the speech is done in ancient Greece or contemporary England.

Part One is devoted to Principles of Persuasion. In Chapter One we shall examine key ideas in persuasion and from these we shall build a model of persuasion to better grasp what happens in the process. Chapter Two will examine the historical foundations of the study of persuasion. Here we shall explore the central ideas we can use stemming from rhetoricians like Aristotle, Cicero, and Kenneth Burke. In Chapter Three we explore empirical and psychological theories of persuasion. Here we shall look for the principles of persuasion that we can draw from modern psychology and sociology. Chapter Four will address a special concern in the principles of persuasion: ethics. The power to persuade is also the power to mislead, and this chapter will examine the ethical underpinnings of the power of persuasion as reflected in propaganda, the intentions of sources, message ethics, and the relationship of ethics to channels.

ELEMENTS OF PERSUASION

Theory represents general principles that inform our research, but research in persuasion extends further than the generalizations that apply to all persuasion. For decades, research has also focused on specific facets of the persuasive process. In other words, in addition to understanding principles of persuasion, we must also understand the elements of persuasion. Part Two provides an in-depth examination of key elements that will help us to improve both our persuasive efforts and our responses to efforts to persuade us. Chapter Five will examine the impact of the source as a key element in persuasion. Here we shall develop ways to enhance credibility and learn what to look for in assessing an attempt to persuade. Chapter Six will consider the message factors that influence communication. Aspects such as logic, emotion, and structure will provide a firm foundation for putting together persuasive messages. Channels for persuasion will be considered in Chapter Seven. Since persuasion is multisensory, the various channels for writing and speaking persuasively and for reading and listening to persuasion will be examined. Finally, in Chapter Eight we shall explore the critical component of receivers. Here we shall learn about both demographic and psychological features that motivate people and how those features can be used in persuasion.

TYPES OF PERSUASION

My father used to say that he graduated from the school of hard knocks and the university of adversity. What he meant, I think, was that practical application is just as important as theory. Part Three considers persuasion in specific practical contexts, the types of persuasion. Chapter Nine looks at persuasive presentations. As mentioned earlier, public presentations are familiar forums for persuasion. Drawing on the principles and elements of previous chapters, we shall look at how to put together an effective persuasive presentation for diverse listeners. In addition, we shall explore persuasive presentations from the consumer's point of view by exploring how to analyze and evaluate persuasive messages. Chapter Ten will apply the principles and elements of persuasion in the critically important context of a sales setting. We shall explore sales in the form of a persuasive interview with an emphasis on analyzing the prospect and the product for effective sales. We shall also consider sales from the consumer's standpoint by exploring what to look for and what to look out for in sales situations. The marketing and advertising context of persuasion is examined in Chapter Eleven. Learning how the principles of persuasion apply in print, radio, television, as well as direct mail will make us more effective persuaders and consumers. Chapter Twelve addresses persuasive campaigns. Since a single attempt at persuasion usually is not enough for success, it is vital that we explore how to apply the elements and principles of persuasion in a campaign effort. Here we shall examine the process of campaigning as well as the means for overcoming resistance and the methods for countering competing campaigns.

Principles, elements, and types of persuasion are, then, the three mainstays of this book. In the pages that follow, we shall seek to combine theory and practice so that we learn both why and how persuasion works in our lives. It is a fascinating world to explore, and the rewards of mastering the subject are great.

Notes

[1] David Burns, *The Feeling Good Handbook* (New York: William Morrow and Company, Inc, 1989), p. 4.

[2] Richard E. Neustadt, *Presidential Power: The Politics of Leadership* (New York: John Wiley and Sons, 1976), pp. 33–58.

[3] Edward G. Hinkleman, et al. *Japan Business* (San Rafael, CA: World Trade Press, 1994), p. 182. © 1994 World Trade Press. All rights reserved.

[4] Abraham Kaplan, *The Conduct of Inquiry* (San Francisco: Chandler Publishing Company, 1964), p. 32.

Chapter One

ASPECTS OF PERSUASION

Definitions are like diamonds—the greater the clarity, the greater the value. Definitions give us starting points for understanding, so it is important that we begin by clearly defining key terms in our study of persuasion.

✳ DEFINITIONS OF PERSUASION

comm. process (act)
symbolism
Deliberate
influences

Like all central aspects of human life, persuasion has been variously defined. Consider the following examples:

"Persuasion is a transactional process among two or more persons whereby the management of symbolic meaning reconstructs reality, resulting in voluntary change in beliefs, attitudes, and/or behaviors."[1]

"Persuasibility refers to situations in which a source gives his position on an issue and . . . presents various arguments, based on emotional or rational considerations, why this position is correct."[2]

Persuasion is "the co-creation of a state of identification or alignment between a source and a receiver that results from the use of symbols."[3]

Persuasion may be defined as "communication intended to influence choice."[4]

Persuasion is also defined as a "process of communication designed to modify the judgments of others, and . . . success at modifying the judgments of others in intended directions."[5]

Persuasion is considered to be "a change process resulting mostly from shared, symbolic thinking activity."[6]

Persuasion is "the process or art of influencing, or seeking to influence, an individual's opinions or actions, ostensibly by reasoning or

Persuasion: the strategic construction of symbols designed to influence others.

intellectual appeal, though depending for its effectiveness in most cases on non-rational factors."[7]

What do these diverse, yet related, definitions have in common? There seems to be general agreement that, however persuasion is defined, it involves the strategic construction of symbols designed to influence others. Exactly what *that* means requires further elaboration.

First, it is clear that persuasion is a **communication process.** Process means that persuaders are engaged in an activity. Persuasion is not static. It is dynamic and can be shaped by a variety of forces. Consider, for example, a typical persuasive situation. A sales agent is going door-to-door with magazine subscriptions. The sales agent is influenced by a variety of factors including experience in sales, past successes and failures at selling, how critical it may become to meet sales goals, and so on. There are also a variety of factors that influence the people answering the doors: past experience with the company or companies like it, how interested they are in reading, whether they are already subscribing through some other means, how they regard the sales agent, the availability of their favorite periodicals, the price of the subscription, the variety of potential messages that may be exchanged, and so on. In addition, there are situational features that may influence the process: whether the day is clear or rainy, the local ordinances on soliciting, whether the client was just interrupted in an important task by the sales agent, and so on. Any of these factors and a host of other forces shape the exchange and the outcome of the persuasive interaction.

Second, persuasion involves **symbolism.** A defining characteristic of human beings is the ability to manipulate symbols. We use the concept of symbols rather than words because the process of persuasion is not carried out by words alone. Tone of voice, appearance of typeface, photographs, icons and images— all can play a part in persuasion. Consider the advertisement that appears in Figure 1.1.

The appeal of this ad is more than just the words used to describe the product. The images of Benjamin Franklin as an adventurous innovator at the top and as a wise founding father in the logo, the size and shading of the lettering, the appeal of growth potential with the stability of a steady income provide more than the appeal of words alone.

Third, persuasion is **deliberate.** We intentionally manipulate symbols to accomplish our persuasive goals. While it is true that we may, from time to time, unintentionally influence others, persuasion has connotations of a conscious effort. From the standpoint of the consumer, we may talk about "subliminal persuasion" but the vast majority of the time the receiver is well aware of the source's effort and responds with a conscious decision.

Figure 1.1
Sample Persuasive Message

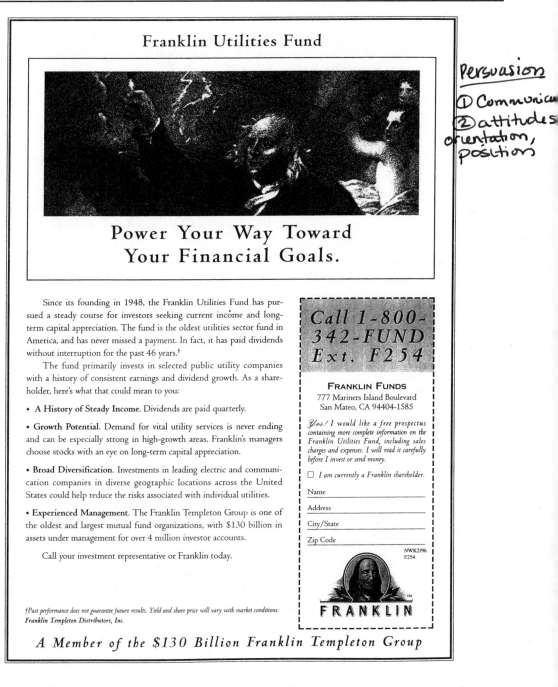

Persuasion involves symbolism. Notice how this ad uses both words and images in its appeal.

Often our goal in persuasion is to effect change, to alter the beliefs, values, attitudes, and behaviors of our receivers. But persuasive outcomes do not always imply change. Sometimes our goal is to reinforce existing views and actions. A public television station's campaign, for example, may seek to renew membership rather than to gain new members.

Finally, persuasion **influences.** Those who are suspicious of the power of persuasion sometimes suggest that persuasion is the evil manipulation of a naïve, gullible person. In reality, the manipulation is a manipulation of symbols, not of people. The motivation of persuaders is to try to gain the receiver's cooperation because the issue cannot be resolved by the persuader alone. The ultimate power rests not with the source but the receiver, to attend or ignore, accept or reject, remember or forget, act or not act on the persuasive effort. All that a persuader really does is to try to influence the decisions of the receiver. Persuasion is not coercion; influence is not control. Persuasion may influence our decision to marry but it does not make for a shotgun wedding. Persuasion may influence us to vote for a politician but it does not control our behavior in the voting booth. Persuasion may influence our decision to buy an automobile but it does not force us to sign the sales contract.

This deliberate communicative process of persuasive influence depends upon a conceptualization of key terms in persuasion. These terms, often used interchangeably when talking about persuasion, are: beliefs, values, attitudes, and behaviors.

KEY TERMS IN PERSUASION

Benjamin Bloom in *Taxonomy of Educational Objectives*[8] suggested an interesting concept of human activity. He indicated that we live concurrently in three domains:

The **cognitive domain** is the domain of thought. We have ideas, concepts, and rational processes for connecting thoughts. In short, we are thinking creatures.

The **affective domain** is the realm of feelings. We are not just thinking creatures; we are also feeling creatures. We feel pity, fear, anger, love, sympathy, loneliness, happiness, and a myriad of other emotions. Figure 1.2 identifies some of the emotional states controlled by the limbic system of the brain.

Our affective domain provides a counterbalance to the coldly rational part of our existence.

Figure 1.2
The Affective Domain

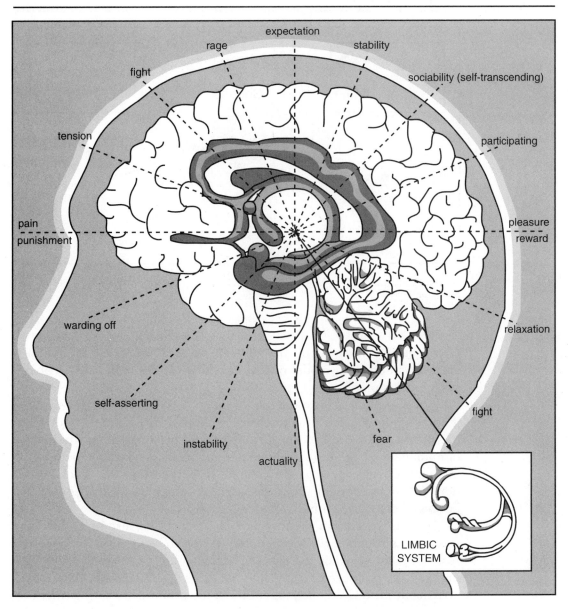

The third realm is the **psychomotor domain.** Using this domain, we act on the basis of our thoughts and feelings. This is the realm of behavior—behavior that is shaped and influenced by the affective and cognitive domains and behavior that also reflects these domains. Stephen

Figure 1.3
Stephen Covey's Proactive Model

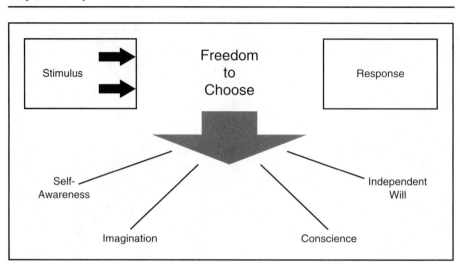

SOURCE: Stephen R. Covey, *Seven Habits of Highly Effective People* (New York: Simon and Schuster, 1989), p. 71.

Covey, basing his ideas on the work of psychiatrist Victor Frankl, provided an interesting model of the psychomotor domain. Covey's proactive model is pictured in Figure 1.3.

Covey explained his model in this way: "In the midst of the most degrading circumstances imaginable, Frankl used the human endowment of self-awareness to discover a fundamental principle about the nature of man: *Between stimulus and response, man has the freedom to choose.*"[9] To apply Covey's ideas to our interest in persuasion, the psychomotor domain offers thought processes such as imagination and conscience between persuasive stimuli and our responses.

In fact, we exist in these realms all at once. For example, when we take an examination we are thinking (trying to remember the material, reasoning about which choices to eliminate, etc.), but we are also feeling (anxiety, pressure to complete within the specified time, elation over arriving at the answer, etc.) and at the same time we are acting (marking our answer, turning the page of the examination booklet, glancing at the clock on the wall, etc.).

Bloom's taxonomy provides a useful model for considering the relationship of beliefs, values, attitudes, and behaviors. Generally speaking, beliefs are cognitive constructs; values are affective relations; attitudes

Box 1.1
THE RELATIONSHIP OF BELIEFS, VALUES, ATTITUDES, AND BEHAVIORS

Belief	Value	Attitude	Behavior
I think the car meets my criteria for value.	I like the styling and the color.	I'm inclined to get this automobile.	I sign a check for the down payment.
I believe our schools need more money.	I feel that education is crucial.	I am ready to support higher taxes.	I mark the ballot for the levy.
I calculate my checking and savings balances.	I desperately need a source of additional income.	I decide to try to get part-time job.	I fill out an application and submit my résumé.

represent psychomotor readiness to respond; and behaviors are the observable actions. Persuasion involves all of these elements. Consider Box 1.1.

Each of these examples shows how the combination of rational thought and emotion leads us to be inclined to take a particular action and the resultant behavior. Persuasion, then, is a communicative effort to influence our beliefs, values, attitudes, and behaviors. Let's examine each of these elements in more detail.

BELIEFS

As we have indicated, a belief is a cognitive construct. Psychologists identify beliefs as views that we take to be true or real. In other words, beliefs are cognitive constructs that we consider to be true or valid. For example, I believe that the economy is essentially sound, that perspective influences perception, that the shortest distance between two points is a straight line, that the future holds lots of surprises, that I cannot fly without mechanical assistance, and so on.

Milton Rokeach suggested that beliefs can also be organized along a continuum from central to peripheral. In other words, some of our beliefs are central to our personalities (e.g., the belief that freedom of speech is critically important) while other beliefs are much more peripheral (e.g., the belief that we look better in blue than in green).

Rokeach structured the beliefs into five categories.[10] These are arranged in a hierarchy of importance with Type A being the most central and Type E the least central.

The most central beliefs (Type A) are "primitive beliefs, 100 percent consensus," beliefs that one holds and that have social consensus as well. Type A beliefs constitute a person's "'basic truths' about physical reality, social reality, and the nature of the self." For example, to believe the object you are holding is a book is a primitive belief that could be confirmed by anyone you might ask.

Type B beliefs are "primitive beliefs, zero consensus." Type B beliefs are still very central, but they are not supported by others. An anorexic person, for example, may have a self-image of being fat even though that belief is not supported by anyone else.

Type C beliefs are "authority beliefs." These are beliefs that are based on people we deem to be important, like our parents, teachers, and peers we respect. According to Rokeach, "[S]uch beliefs, while important and generally resistant to change, are nevertheless conjectured to be less important and easier to change than Types A and B beliefs." For example, we may believe it is sophisticated to drink alcohol because our peers imbibe.

Type D beliefs are "derived beliefs" that we take on faith from authorities rather than direct experience. For example, we may believe that Winston Churchill said, "I have nothing to offer but blood, sweat, and tears" because we read about it, even though the actual sentence from his speech on May 13, 1940, was "I have nothing to offer but blood and toil, tears and sweat."

Finally, there are Type E or "inconsequential beliefs." These are "more or less arbitrary matters of taste. . . ." As such, they are the easiest to change because they are not linked to other beliefs. According to Rokeach, advertisers focus on inconsequential beliefs and attempt to change them by linking the inconsequential belief with a more central belief.[11]

There are three characteristics about beliefs that we should bear in mind as we explore persuasion. Beliefs are learned; they are interrelated; beliefs have structure.

First, beliefs are **learned.** This means that we enter the world without any particular set of beliefs but that our interaction with the world and the people in it establishes and shapes our beliefs. For example, there are those who believe in magic, who believe that it is possible to make objects appear or disappear through mystical powers. Others believe that while magic is entertaining, Houdini did not actually make an elephant disappear nor did magician David Copperfield actually make the Statue of Liberty disappear. There were, in fact, very clever mechanisms for making the audience believe the objects had disappeared. Once the gimmick is revealed, we no longer believe such magical occurrences, though we may still admire the magician's ability to conjure.

Because beliefs are learned, it is important to know the sources of people's beliefs. What in their experience led them to hold those particular beliefs? Was the source of a belief direct experience and therefore harder to change than beliefs derived from things we have been told? How deeply held is this belief? People who deeply believe in some proposition are less likely to be persuaded than those who hold a belief to be inconsequential. For example, we once believed that blue and brown clashed and that a brown jacket could not be worn with blue pants; but such beliefs are usually inconsequential unless the person is deeply fashion-conscious.

Second, beliefs are **interrelated.** Just as the systems of the body interrelate (the muscle system providing motion for the skeletal system, which provides structure; both of these systems nourished by the circulatory system), so are our beliefs interrelated. Beliefs do not ordinarily exist in isolation. We should more properly talk about belief systems rather than a belief. For example, we may believe that cigarette smoking is hazardous because of our own experience with a relative who suffered from emphysema caused by smoking, and from having heard authorities like the several surgeons general who have warned us of the medical dangers, and from conversations with our parents, who feel concern. All of these systems interact to uphold our belief.

Because beliefs are interrelated, they are remarkably difficult to influence. Even if a tobacco company were able to refute the surgeon general's medical report, we would still be concerned about smoking based on our own experiences and the beliefs derived from our parents.

Because beliefs are interrelated, we work to maintain a consistent belief system. When new experiences are encountered, we seek to integrate them with our existing belief structure. So when we learn of a new product, we will seek information from *Consumer Reports*, we'll discuss the product with trusted friends, and we'll try out the product ourselves as we integrate the new information into the contents of our belief system to form a coherent whole. If our experience contradicts the claims of our friends or the reports of unbiased tests, we will seek to adjust to such dissonance by discounting our experience as a fluke, by doubting

Hard to believe you ever lived without it...

Beliefs are cognitive constructs. Using home computers to pay bills accurately and inexpensively appeals to our rational selves.

Figure 1.4

Vertical and Horizontal Belief Structures

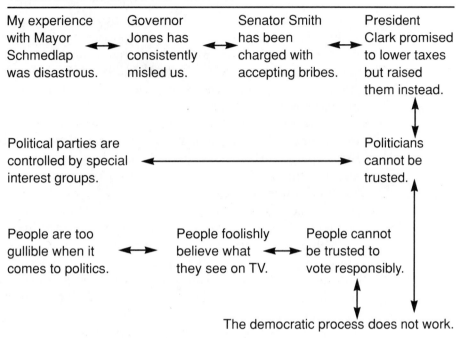

the veracity of our friends, by deciding to live with the contradiction, or perhaps by engaging in some psychological defense mechanism in order to hold a consistent belief system.

Third, beliefs have vertical as well as horizontal **structures.** As we have seen, beliefs are interrelated and therefore reinforce each other, but the structure is vertical as well as horizontal. Beliefs combine in intricate patterns. Figure 1.4 suggests some possible relationships.

Our experience with a variety of politicians may lead us to generalize that distrust to other politicians (a horizontal belief structure). This distrust of politicians combined with other beliefs may lead us to lose confidence in the government or in the democratic system (vertical structure).

Because belief systems combine in intricate relations, we tend to find that the more experienced a person is, the more difficult it is to persuade him or her. Experienced travelers, for example, have learned to look for the special restrictions that apply to advertised ticket prices and are therefore more resistant to travel advertisements; they have also learned to shop around for the best price on tickets and will resist attempts at persuasion by travel agents.

VALUES

A value has been defined as "the relative worth of an object; a quality that makes something desirable or undesirable; an ideal or custom about which we have emotional responses, whether positive or negative."[12] From this definition we note that a value has an affective dimension. In other words, values are **evaluative.** "Honesty is the best policy," "Chocolate is good," "The Bears are better than the Bengals" are all expressions of values.

According to Milton Rokeach, value systems concern "preferable modes of conduct or end-states of existence along a continuum of relative importance."[13] He suggested that values could be considered as instrumental (i.e., serving as a means) or terminal (i.e., end state). Terminal values are ultimate goals like a comfortable life, inner happiness, or pleasure. Instrumental values, on the other hand, are "modes of conduct" such as honesty, politeness, and responsibility.

Values, then, are affective constructs that offer assessments. For example, a person may feel responsible for minimizing air pollution by automobile emissions. Such a person will be more susceptible to automobile ads that emphasize the value of catalytic converters and other exhaust control systems.

Values function by offering a perspective on experience. We inevitably make evaluative judgments about our experiences based on our value systems. For example, we will argue that a particular movie is a waste of time and money because it is boring; we may select a car because it has a pleasing style; we may purchase from a particular store because it has a comfortable layout; we may select a major because it is more enjoyable, easier for us, and more important as a potential career.

Values are intimately linked to our **culture.** From our cultural background we derive a value system that can influence our reactions to relatively superficial things like food preferences and relatively significant decisions like a marriage partner. What is important, what is unimportant—what is good, what is evil—what is desirable, what is repulsive—are often determined by the underlying culture. In Rubens' era, for example, hefty people were considered more attractive than in our current culture where thin is "in." In Eastern cultures, white is a color of mourning. Punctuality is treated as critical in Japan, as important in the United States, and as relatively unimportant in Mexico.

Cultural values have a significant impact on how people think, feel, and behave. Consider, for example, this passage about the importance of family in American ethnic groups. "Hispanics are more likely than other Americans to believe that the demands and needs of the family should

LET NATIONWIDE'S FINANCIAL PLANNING HELP MAKE YOUR FUTURE THIS HAPPY.

Happiness comes in many different forms. For some, it may mean a steady income for retirement. For others, it may mean providing a financial mainstay for loved ones in the event of death. And for many, it may just mean ensuring that the farm you've worked so hard to build will be around for your children.

Whatever your dream for the future, our Nationwide® Insurance Agents can provide solid answers. They have a comprehensive portfolio of insurance products and financial services to help meet every need, from the fairly simple to the complex. They'll provide understandable solutions and knowledgeable advice with the same friendliness you've come to expect from Nationwide Insurance.

So talk to your Nationwide Insurance Agent today. And find out how we can help make your future something worth smiling about.

N A T I O N W I D E   I S   O N   Y O U R   S I D E®

Values are affective constructs. Many forms of happiness are used to appeal to receivers in this ad.

take precedence over those of the individual. In an earlier age this attitude was common among other ethnic groups— Italians, for example. Today, however, it runs counter to the dominant culture of individualism characteristic of American life and may even impede individual success. This perhaps explains why so many young Hispanics drop out of school to take jobs, a decision that has some immediate financial benefits for the family but is detrimental to the individual in the long run."[14]

Values are also **linked to beliefs.** In fact, Milton Rokeach argued that values are a type of belief. He wrote that a value "is an enduring belief that a specific mode of conduct or end-state of existence is personally or socially preferable to an opposite or converse mode of conduct or end-state of existence."[15]

We do not exist in a purely contemplative, rational world of cognition nor do we exist in purely emotional, irrational bundles of feelings. Our thoughts and our feelings are connected in a marvelous mixture of wisdom and wonder. When we select a candidate, we may be persuaded by the insight and ideas that candidate expresses, but at the same time, we may get a feeling that the person is trustworthy and honest. In short, persuasion must be aimed at the person as a whole, not just at convincing with evidence or at moving with emotion.

ATTITUDES

An attitude is a relatively enduring inclination to respond, favorably or unfavorably, toward a person, object, or event.[16] This means that an attitude is a predisposition to respond, a readiness to respond, but not an overt response. Attitudes are relatively enduring. Once established, our attitudes are ongoing but not necessarily unchangeable. And our attitudes are always about something, whether that something is a person, an object, an idea, or an event.

Attitudes have **direction.** They are positive or negative. For example, a Republican may have a positive attitude toward the Republican nominee, an urban resident may have a negative attitude toward rural towns, and a Catholic may have a negative attitude toward abortion. In fact, Rokeach suggested that attitudes, values, and beliefs are closely related. "An attitude differs from a value in that an attitude refers to an organization of several beliefs around a specific object or situation. . . . A value, on the other hand, refers to a single belief of a very specific kind."[17]

Attitudes have **stability.** Because attitudes are linked to belief and value systems, they have an enduring quality. For example, we are

American
Red Cross

Public Service Television Commercials

1 "X " :30
SFX: Music "Love Spreads" by The Stone Roses throughout.
Anncr. (VO): They've given our generation a label. X.
(X appears on the screen and dissolves into various X shapes and colors)
Anncr. (VO): Generation nothing.
(X continues to change)
Anncr. (VO): They say we have no sense of purpose.
(X continues to move)
Anncr. (VO): They say we have no war to fight and no cause to believe in. Who are they?
(X changes into a cross)
Anncr. (VO): Join the thousands of us who are making a difference.
(Red cross appears)
Anncr. (VO): And wear a label that does mean something.
Super: American Red Cross. Volunteer. Call your local chapter.

Whitney Pillsbury, art director
William Gelner, writer
J.J. Jordan, creative director
Rich Rosenthal, producer
Tomato London/Graham Wood, directors
Curious Pictures, production company
J. Walter Thompson Company (New York), agency
American Red Cross, client

2 "Policeman" :30
(Various supers scroll up the right side of the screen, one after another, as the camera pans slowly across the face of a black man)
SFX: Music under. As supers appear, they are accentuated by a sharp, staccato-like thud.
Super: Michael Conrad.
Super: Male. Age 28.
Super: Armed Robbery.
Super: Assault and Battery.
Super: Rape. Murder.
Super: Apprehended August 1994 by
Super: Police Lieutenant Joseph Cruthers,
Super: shown here.
SFX: Music under stops abruptly. One last thud.
Logo: Urban Alliance on Race Relations.

Benjamin Vendramin, art director
Robert McDougall, writer
Paul Hains, creative director
Audrey Telfer, producer
Drew Jarvis, director
Stripes Film, production company
Bozell Palmer Bonner (Toronto), agency
Urban Alliance on Race Relations, client

Urban Alliance
on Race Relations

Attitudes are predispositions to respond. These public service commercials illustrate how such predispositions influence our perceptions.

inclined to vote for candidates in our political party, unless persuaded otherwise. We are inclined to give to our favorite charity regularly, but we might be persuaded that a competing charity is more worthy of our contributions.

Attitudes have **salience.** The more a part of our core personality an attitude is, the more relevant we consider the attitude, the more difficult it is to change. For example, a devoutly religious person who identifies strongly with a church, who considers the church's teachings to be salient and closely related to his or her own life, is much less susceptible to arguments about atheism than an agnostic would be. A person who has grown up in Detroit is much more likely to favor American-made cars than a person raised in Hawaii.

Attitudes have **degree.** Attitudes may range on a continuum from strongly positive to strongly negative. When surveys attempt to determine our attitudes, they usually employ a Likert-type scale that ranges from Strongly Agree to Agree to Undecided to Disagree to Strongly Disagree. Our attitude about a test product may fall somewhere along that scale. This is an important factor because extreme attitudes are more difficult to change and because an extreme attitude may be used to motivate an individual in a particular direction.

BEHAVIORS

Some scholars have argued that we have no measure of people's beliefs, values, or attitudes except behavior, that is, observable activity by the person. This is certainly true, but does not mean that all attempts at persuasion are aimed solely at influencing behavior.

Often persuasion is directed at changing, shaping, or reinforcing behavior. We may seek to get a customer to sign a sales contract; we may seek to reinforce the charitable contribution made by a donor. But persuasion may be aimed at influencing beliefs, or values, or attitudes. Perhaps we want to have people remember our product name, or to improve the image of our company, or to incline them to vote for our proposal when the time is right.

Communication theorist Gerald Miller identified "three different behavioral outcomes served by the persuasion process."[18] Miller's first type is response shaping, which involves generating new responses. For example, a political campaign may shape our responses to an unknown candidate. Response reinforcing means shoring up currently held views. "Rather than aiming at changes in attitudes and behaviors, much persuasive communication seeks to reinforce currently held convictions

Persuasion connects beliefs, values, and attitudes with behaviors. Notice how beliefs, values, and attitudes symbolically interact to urge consumers to "pump some iron."

and to make them more resistant to change."[19] A minister, for example, may be seeking to reinforce good behavior among congregants rather than seeking to get them to repent. Finally, there are response-changing outcomes. These involve altering responses, the usual focus of persuasion. Convincing someone to give up smoking, for example, is a response-changing outcome.

Clearly persuasion may have ultimate behavioral outcomes, but a given persuasive message may be more limited and directed at influencing beliefs, values, or attitudes with the intent that changes in beliefs, values, or attitudes will result in observable behaviors at some relevant time in the future.

With this background in mind, refer back to Box 1.1. The examples should remind us of the cognitive, affective, and psychomotor domains as well as the characteristics and relationships of beliefs, values, attitudes, and behaviors.

MODELS OF PERSUASION

Having examined the various definitions of persuasion and with an understanding of the key elements of beliefs, values, attitudes, and behaviors, it is time to put the ideas together by creating some models of persuasion.

We make models for a variety of reasons. Models describe. Models can help us to "see" a complicated or abstract process. For example, by building a physical model of the molecule, noted scientists Crick, Watson, and Wilkins were able to identify the complicated double helix of DNA. Models explain. By constructing models we are able to explain the relationships among the parts of the event. For example, an organization chart is a model of relationships within the organization. An organization chart explains who reports to whom and how the parts of the organization are formally related. Models simulate. Models are frequently used to recreate events. Flight simulators, for example, are models that recreate specified events and allow pilots and computer pilots to train for unexpected conditions. Models of persuasion, then, can describe the critical elements in persuasion, can explain the relationship among those elements, and can be used to simulate persuasive events.

This section will be primarily concerned with the functions of describing and explaining. Classroom projects and experiences are often models that simulate persuasive processes. To understand how to create models, we shall begin by showing how a description of persuasion can be made into a model.

MODEL OF BITZER'S RHETORICAL SITUATION

In 1968 Professor Lloyd Bitzer published a seminal essay called "The Rhetorical Situation," which he defined as "a complex of persons, events, objects, and relations presenting an actual or potential exigence which can be completely or partially removed if discourse, introduced into the situation, can so constrain human decision or action as to bring about a significant modification of the exigence."[20]

In Bitzer's view, the rhetorical situation consisted of three main elements. First, the rhetorical exigence was some problem that called for someone to address an audience in order to resolve the difficulty. Second, the rhetorical audience was defined as those who could do something about the exigence or problem—the receivers who could resolve the problem addressed by the rhetor. Third, there were constraints, forces that had the power to shape "the decision and action needed to modify the exigence."[21]

To illustrate Bitzer's concepts we might consider an example. A sales agent wants to persuade a client to buy an encyclopedia. The problem (exigence) is that there is a need for a sale and a need for the encyclopedia. The sales agent cannot resolve the exigence, only the client (rhetorical audience) is capable of modifying the exigence. Finally, there are constraints that influence both the sales agent and the rhetorical audience: the Green River Ordinances that prohibit door-to-door solicitation, whether the client can afford the encyclopedia, and so on.

Bitzer did not develop a model of the rhetorical situation, but we can do so to demonstrate how to make a visual representation of the abstract process defined by Bitzer. Figure 1.5 shows how one could picture or model Bitzer's rhetorical situation.

Note that by drawing a picture, by creating a model, we can see the concepts and examine the relationships among the key elements.

MODEL OF BURKE'S DRAMATIC PENTAD

Another key figure in contemporary rhetorical theory is Kenneth Burke. Burke's *A Grammar of Motives* introduced his concept of the dramatic pentad. Burke wrote: "We shall use five terms as generating principle of our investigation. They are: Act, Scene, Agent, Agency, Purpose. In a rounded statement about motives, you must have some word that names the *act* (names what took place, in thought or deed), and another that names the *scene* (the background of the act, the situation in which it occurred); also, you must indicate what kind of person (*agent*) performed the act, what means or instruments he used (*agency*), and the

Figure 1.5
A Model of Bitzer's Rhetorical Situation

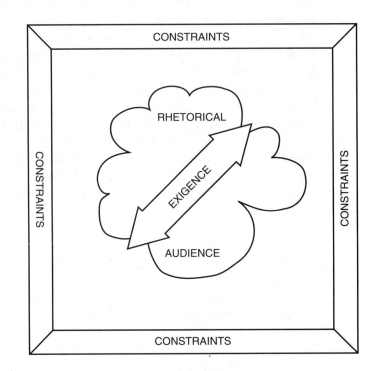

purpose."[22] Burke, like Bitzer, offered careful verbalizations of his concept. He did not draw a model of the dramatic pentad, but we may choose to do so in order to gain a clearer understanding of the elements. Figure 1.6 provides a model of Burke's dramatic pentad.

Because Burke emphasized the concept of ratios among the terms, the model uses overlapping circles to show the various interconnections possible among the key elements. In some cases the setting is proportionately more important. For example, in Martin Luther King's "I Have a Dream" speech, part of the effectiveness is based on the scene—the steps of the Lincoln Memorial. King's words reflected the impact of the scene when he said, "Five score years ago, a great American, in whose symbolic shadow we stand today, signed the Emancipation Proclamation." Once again, models can help us to see an abstract concept and explain the relationship among its parts.

Figure 1.6
A Model of Burke's Dramatic Pentad

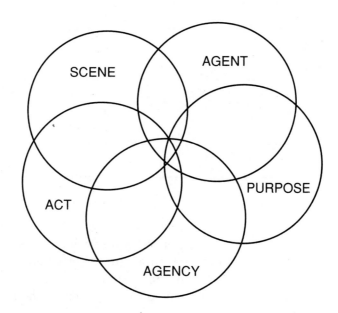

Berlo's Model of Persuasion

David Berlo developed a model of communication that emphasized sources, channels, messages, and receivers. He indicated that the key ingredients in communication were source–message–channel–receiver.[23] Berlo's model has been elaborated on by many communication scholars. Today we generally accept that the process of communication involves a source, who encodes a message and sends it out along a channel where it is picked up and decoded by a receiver who provides feedback and that all of this works well unless noise interferes with the production or reception of the messages. Furthermore, all of this takes place within a specific setting or context.

We can adapt the elaborated version of Berlo's model of communication to provide a picture of persuasion. Figure 1.7 offers one such model of persuasion.

In our model of persuasion we find a Source, the originator of persuasive messages. This individual operates in cognitive, affective, and psychomotor domains as a complex of beliefs, values, attitudes, and

Figure 1.7
A Model of Persuasion

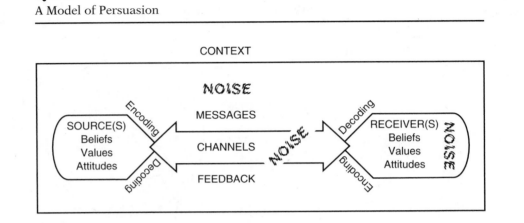

abilities. The source encodes his or her views into a message by selecting and structuring symbols (both verbal and nonverbal) into a persuasive message. The message or messages are sent out along channels, the media through which messages pass. The receiver is also a complex of beliefs, values, attitudes, and abilities. The receiver, or rhetorical audience, decodes the speaker's messages by listening to and observing the messages.

Because communication is a "two-way street" that offers the possibility of interaction between sources and receivers, the element of "feedback" is added to indicate that the receiver may encode responses to the source's messages. The feedback may, in turn, be decoded by the source in an ongoing process of interaction.

Noise, which is usually thought of as physical noise, is actually anything that can interfere with the production, reception, or interpretation of messages. Therefore, noise may be physical, like the competing sound of a lawn mower interfering with a lecture, but it may also be psychological, like the internal distractions of a listener disturbed by a fight with her roommate right before class. Noise may also be semantic, like the ambiguous meaning of a job recommendation: "You will be lucky if you can get this candidate to work for you."

Finally, all of this takes place within a specific context that may influence the persuasive process. The context, or situation, offers both constraints and opportunities to persuaders. The fact that an overhead projector may not work may constrain how a persuader presents a message. The insignia of a company on a lectern, for example,

Figure 1.8
An Alternative Model of Persuasion

may offer a persuader a theme for helping the audience to identify with the proposal.

Of course, the models presented so far are not the only ways to look at persuasion. Figures 1.8 and 1.9 offer two alternative views constructed by groups of students assigned the task of developing their own model of persuasion.

Figure 1.8 uses the image of a fisherman to represent the persuasive process. The source casts a message out to receivers and the receiver's feedback is represented by the fishing bob. Figure 1.9 offers a different image. Here the source is portrayed as the pedals of a bicycle that propel the receiver along a path to a goal. These images display the creativity in developing a model of an abstract process like persuasion.

Figure 1.9
Another Model of Persuasion

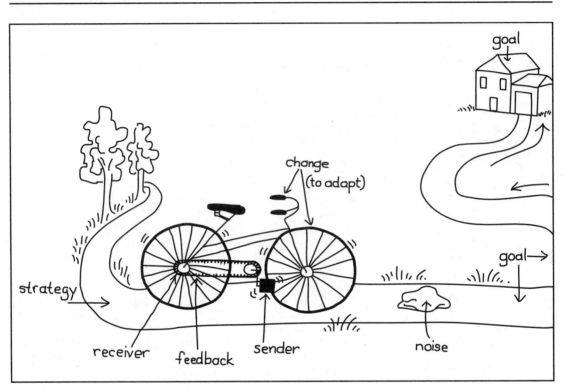

Summary

In summary, persuasion is a form of communication that is pervasive in our society. The process of persuasion is an attempt by a persuader to manipulate symbols in order to influence the beliefs, values, attitudes, and behaviors of others.

Beliefs are learned cognitive constructs about what one believes to be true or real. Beliefs are interrelated in vertical and horizontal structures that serve to reinforce each other in a consistent view.

Values are affective systems that reflect the worth of the object, idea, or person. Values provide an assessment and a perspective on experience. Rooted in one's culture and linked to beliefs, values provide an important addition to the cognitive process of human persuasion.

Attitudes are psychological states of readiness to respond, positively or negatively, toward objects, events, people, or ideas. These states have direction, stability, salience, and degree. Each of these qualities has important ramifications for persuasion.

Linked to beliefs and values, attitudes reflect a readiness to act; behavior is the act itself. In this chapter we have seen how beliefs, values, attitudes and behaviors are related to each other. They serve to reinforce one another, making the process of persuasion more understandable.

Finally, we examined a variety of models that depict aspects of persuasion. Bitzer's model introduced the important notions of exigences, constraints, and rhetorical audiences. Burke's model provided a view of how act, scene, agent, agency, and purpose interact in persuasive events. The Berlo model identified the key elements of source, channel, messages, receivers, feedback, noise, and context and reflected their relationship in a model of the persuasive process.

In the next chapter, we shall journey back through time to examine the key ideas that scholars of persuasion have developed in the history of ideas. We shall begin with the ancient Greek philosophers and trace a brief history of rhetoric up to contemporary times.

Notes

[1] Deirdre D. Johnston, *The Art and Science of Persuasion* (Dubuque, IA: Brown and Benchmark, 1994), p. 7.

[2] William J. McGuire, "Personality and Susceptibility to Social Influence," in *Handbook of Personality Theory and Research*, eds. Edgar F. Borgatta and William W. Lambert (Chicago: Rand McNally and Company, 1968), p. 1134.

[3] Charles Larson, *Persuasion: Reception and Responsibility* (Belmont, CA: Wadsworth Publishing Company, 1994), p. 9.

[4] Winston L. Brembeck and William S. Howell, *Persuasion: A Means of Social Influence* (Englewood Cliffs, NJ: Prentice-Hall: 1976), p. 19.

[5] Herbert W. Simons, *Persuasion: Understanding Practice, and Analysis* (New York: Random House, 1986), p. 24.

[6] Raymond S. Ross, *Understanding Persuasion* (Englewood Cliffs, NJ: Prentice-Hall, 1994), p. 7.

[7] James Drever, *A Dictionary of Psychology* (Baltimore, MD: Penguin Books, 1960), p. 205.

[8] Benjamin S. Bloom, et al. (eds.) *Taxonomy of Educational Objectives: The Classification of Educational Objectives* (New York: David McKay Company, Inc. 1956), pp. 7–8.

[9] Stephen R. Covey, *Seven Habits of Highly Effective People* (New York: Simon and Schuster, 1989), pp. 69–70.

[10] Milton Rokeach, *Beliefs, Attitudes, and Values: A Theory of Organization and Change* (San Francisco, Jossey-Bass Publishers, 1975), pp. 6–12.

[11] Ibid., pp. 183–184.

[12] Joseph A. DeVito, *The Communication Handbook: A Dictionary* (New York: Harper & Row, 1986), p. 332.

[13] Milton Rokeach, *The Nature of Human Values* (New York: The Free Press, a division of Simon & Schuster, 1973), p. 5.

[14] Linda Chavez, *Out of the Barrio* (New York: HarperCollins, 1991), p. 109.

[15] Rokeach, *The Nature of Human Values*, p. 5.

[16] This definition is derived from Rokeach, *Beliefs, Attitudes, and Values*, Chapter 6.

[17] Rokeach, *The Nature of Human Values*, p. 18.

[18] Gerald Miller, "On Being Persuaded: Some Basic Distinctions" in *Persuasion: New Directions in Theory and Research*, Michael E. Roloff and Gerald R. Miller, eds. (Beverly Hills, CA: Sage Publications, 1980), p. 16. Reprinted by permission of Sage Publications, Inc.

[19] Ibid., p. 19.

[20] Lloyd Bitzer, "The Rhetorical Situation," *Philosophy and Rhetoric*, 1 (1968), p. 6. Copyright 1968 by Pennsylvania State University.

[21] Ibid., p. 8.

[22] Kenneth Burke, *A Grammar of Motives* (Los Angeles: University of California Press, 1969), p. xv.

[23] David Berlo, *The Process of Communication* (New York: Holt, Rinehart and Winston, 1960), pp. 30–32.

For Further Thought

1. Interview someone who does a job you would like to do someday. Ask him or her about the kinds of persuasive situations that occur in this line of work. Seek ideas on constructing effective persuasive messages.

2. Find an example of an advertisement that appeals to values. Which values are being tapped in the ad? Would other values work better for the advertised product or service?

3. The model in Figure 1.7 shows one source and one receiver. Redraw the model to represent a persuasive situation of one source communicating with several receivers.

4. To experience the importance of channels, close your eyes during a television program and notice the limitation of a message created for sight and sound when it is presented solely through sound. Next watch the rest of the program with the sound off and experience the limitation of a visual channel alone. Discuss how the experience of listening to a television program differs from listening to a radio program. Discuss how the experience of watching a muted television program differs from reading.

5. Draw your own model of persuasion. Be sure to represent the elements discussed in the chapter but add any other concepts you consider important.

For Further Reading

Cialdini, Robert B. *Influence: The Psychology of Persuasion.* New York: William Morrow, 1993.

Ehninger, Douglas. *Influence, Belief, and Argument.* Glenview, IL: Scott, Foresman Publishing, 1974.

Reardon, Kathleen K. *Persuasion in Practice.* Newbury Park, CA: Sage Publications, 1991.

Smith, Mary John. *Persuasion and Human Action.* Belmont, CA: Wadsworth, 1982.

Suedfeld, Peter. *Attitude Change: The Competing Views.* Chicago, IL: Atherton Publishing, 1971.

Zimbardo, Philip G. *Influencing Attitudes and Changing Behavior.* Reading, MA: Addison-Wesley Publishing Company, 1977.

Chapter Two

RHETORICAL THEORY

Rhetoric is the art of persuasion, the art of using symbols to adjust ideas to people and people to ideas.[1] Historically rhetoric has been a fundamental part of civilization. It was one of the original seven liberal arts (rhetoric, dialectic, grammar, music, arithmetic, geometry, and astronomy) that formed the basis for higher education for centuries. In this chapter we shall survey the development of the theory of persuasion from its origins in ancient Greece to its contemporary contributors. Because our overview spans nearly two and a half millennia, we shall only be able to touch on the highlights in the development of rhetorical theory. The list of suggested readings at the end of the chapter provides some ideas for further reading in this field.

ANCIENT RHETORIC

The rocky soil of the Mediterranean country we call Greece gave rise to the core of Western civilization. An important area of education for the ancient Greeks was the study of persuasion. They emphasized this study, called rhetoric, because success in Athenian society was based on the ability to convince other people in the courts, in political settings, and in social settings. Because citizens in legal disputes were expected to plead their own cases, the ability to use rhetoric effectively was crucial if justice was to prevail. Because citizens were expected to participate in their governments, the skill of using rhetoric was necessary if government was to follow the best course of action. Because effective discourse encompassed both intellectual development and entertainment, rhetoric also came to be associated with the social functions of

The Bettmann Archive

Historically, rhetoric has been a fundamental part of civilization.

persuasion. In short, rhetoric flourished for very practical purposes. In the following pages we shall consider the main contributions of rhetorical theory to persuasion, beginning with ancient Athens.

The Pre-Socratics

Socrates was a central figure in ancient Athens because his ideas and his skill as a teacher heavily influenced his student Plato, who in turn influenced his student, Aristotle, and later generations. But Socrates was also a central figure in the early development of the study of persuasion. Prior to Socrates, the *practice* of rhetoric was emphasized in the earliest writings of the Greeks, and we classify these earliest rhetoricians as Pre-Socratics.

Homer

In Homer's famous works the *Odyssey* and *Iliad*, composed around 800 B.C., we find many examples of the importance of effective rhetoric. The rhetorical speeches in these works served not only as examples of persuasion but also as sources of the cultural heritage to be passed down

Box 2.1

And Helen answered, "He is Ulysses, a man of great craft, son of Laertes. He was born in rugged Ithaca, and excels in all manner of stratagems and subtle cunning."

On this Antenor said, "Madam, you have spoken truly. Ulysses once came here as envoy about yourself, and Menelaus with him. I received them in my own house, and therefore know both of them by sight and conversation. When they stood up in presence of the assembled Trojans, Menelaus was the broader shouldered, but when both were seated Ulysses had the more royal presence. After a time they delivered their message, and the speech of Menelaus ran trippingly on the tongue; he did not say much, for he was a man of few words, but he spoke very clearly and to the point, though he was the younger man of the two; Ulysses, on the other hand, when he rose to speak, was at first silent and kept his eyes fixed upon the ground. There was no play nor graceful movement of his sceptre; he kept it straight and stiff like a man unpracticed in oratory—one might have taken him for a mere churl or simpleton; but when he raised his voice, and the words came driving from his deep chest like winter snow before the wind, then there was none to touch him, and no man thought further of what he looked like."

SOURCE: Homer, *Iliad*, trans. Samuel Butler. New York: Longman, Green, 1898. Book III.

through the generations of listeners. Skill in the art of rhetoric was given as much respect as skill in the art of war. Consider, for example, the description of Ulysses, the hero of the *Iliad*, found in Box 2.1.

Note that heroes were defined not only by their physical ability but also by their eloquence.

Corax and Tisias

Because rhetoric was so critical to the ancient Greeks, people taught the subject of persuasion on a regular basis, but the study also had its critics. People were suspicious of any art that could confuse as easily as it could clarify, that could deceive as easily as it could motivate. Both sides of the question are illustrated in the story of one of the early teachers, Corax, and his student Tisias.

Corax, around 470 B.C., had composed a handbook on rhetoric in which he had emphasized that rhetoric deals with issues of probability, not issues of certainty. We do not argue, for example, that ice forms at 32 degrees Fahrenheit under standard atmospheric conditions. That is a matter that we demonstrate. We *do* argue whether O. J. Simpson murdered Nicole Brown Simpson and Ronald Goldman because whether he did the deed is a matter of greater or lesser probability. Rhetoric cannot prove that ice forms, but it can convince people of Simpson's innocence or guilt. That was a significant contribution of Corax to the history of rhetoric. The subject matters of persuasion are always matters of probability, matters of contingency, matters that can be argued.

Corax also illustrates why people are suspicious of persuasion. Young Tisias contracted with Corax to learn the art of persuasion. After the study, Tisias refused to pay Corax so they went to court. Tisias pleaded his case this way: "If Corax has fulfilled his contract to make me persuasive, then I can convince you that I do not owe him the money. On the other hand, if you find against me, then he has not fulfilled his contract and I do not owe him the money. Therefore if you find for me, I do not owe him the money, but if you find against me, then I do not owe him the money because he did not fulfill his contract to make me a persuasive person." The jury was angered by the shenanigans of such rhetors, and they threw the case out of court.

Protagoras

Despite the misgivings of many, the art of rhetoric flourished in the fourth century B.C. Another of the Pre-Socratic contributors was Protagoras, who lived from 481 to 411 B.C. Protagoras made two main contributions to rhetoric. One was the concept that "man is the measure of all things." This is important because it places an emphasis on human decision making. In a court case, for example, it is the jury who decides guilt or innocence. In a legislative assembly, it is the members who decide what form of action will be taken. In the marketplace, it is the customer who determines the success of a product or service. In other words, how human beings decide and what motivates them make up the central concern of rhetoric.

Protagoras also suggested that in any rhetorical encounter there are at least two sides. This is important because rhetoric is an art that can be used by either party in a dispute—it can be used by the Bradys to advocate stricter gun control and it can be used by the National Rifle Association to advocate the right to bear arms. Protagoras is often called the father of debate because he advanced this rhetorical principle.

Gorgias

Another ancient Greek was the long-lived Gorgias of Leontini (483–375 B.C.). Gorgias was a truly masterful teacher of rhetoric. His major contribution came in the form of emphasizing style or language choices in the art of rhetoric. He wrote that "speech is a powerful lord, which by means of the finest and most invisible body effects the divinest works: it can stop fear and banish grief and create joy and nurture pity."[2] But just as language can produce important results, Gorgias also warned that language can be deceptive. He argued that if anything can be known, it cannot be communicated because "that by which we reveal is *logos* (the word), but *logos* is not substances and existing things. Therefore we do not reveal existing things to our neighbors, but *logos,* which is something other than substances. Thus, just as the visible would not become audible, and vice versa, similarly, when external reality is involved, it would not become our *logos,* and not being *logos,* it would not have been revealed to another."[3]

SOCRATES AND PLATO

Socrates was Plato's teacher and appeared as a central character in the dialogues written by Plato (428–348 B.C.). In many of his dialogues Plato reviles the Pre-Socratics because they do not teach truth, but only the appearance of truth. To Plato, the art of rhetoric was a sham art that could make the good appear bad, the important seem unimportant, the guilty appear innocent. The Pre-Socratic rhetoricians were merely verbal wranglers who were not teaching an art at all but only the knack of verbal chicanery.

In later dialogues, Plato offered a more moderate position. He suggested that rhetoric might have some use but only if it were preceded by a careful inquiry into the truth of the position being advocated. He also placed an emphasis on audience psychology and organizing ideas to meet the type of audience. In the dialogue called "Phaedrus," Plato had Socrates say, "Until a man knows the truth of the several particulars of which he is writing or speaking, and is able to define them as they are, and having defined them again to divide them until they can be no longer divided, and until in like manner he is able to discern the nature of the soul, and discover the different modes of discourse which are adapted to different natures, and to arrange and dispose them in such a way that the simple form of speech may be addressed to the simpler nature, and the complex and composite to the more complex nature—until he has accomplished all this, he will be unable to handle arguments according to rules of art, as far as their nature allows them to be subjected to art, either for the purpose of teaching or persuading."[4] In other words, acceptable rhetoric is based on truth and is adapted to the specific nature of the audience.

ARISTOTLE

Plato's student Aristotle (384–322 B.C.) was more tolerant of the art of rhetoric. Aristotle suggested that far from being a sham art, it was a useful art that had four important values. First, he argued that truth will prevail if given an equal chance, and it is the art of rhetoric that gives both sides an equal chance. Second, he claimed that rhetoric could teach people who are not trained to follow the complicated syllogisms and close dialectical argumentation advocated by Plato. In other words, rhetoric could be used to popularize important issues. Third, he suggested that rhetoric is valuable because it does not judge a case—it is an art that can be used by both sides in a dispute. Finally, he argued that rhetoric is useful in defending yourself against attack. The art of verbal self-defense was as necessary in ancient Athens as it is today.

Aristotle defined rhetoric as "the art of discovering, in any given case, the available means of persuasion." In Aristotle's view, there were two broad classes of proof. One class was inartistic proof, support for a position that was not created by the art of rhetoric. Inartistic proof included such aspects as physical evidence. For example, the bloodstains at a murder scene are persuasive evidence, but they are inartistic proof because the art of rhetoric did not create them.

The second broad classification of means is artistic proof. This consisted of three types: the character of the source (*ethos*), the emotions of the audience (*pathos*) and the logic of the case (*logos*). It should be recognized that the Greek word *logos* can be translated as "the word" as it was used in the passage from Gorgias, but it can also mean the logic of the case as Aristotle uses the term.

According to Aristotle, "Of the modes of persuasion furnished by the spoken word there are three kinds. The first kind depends on the personal character of the speaker; the second on putting the audience into a certain frame of mind; the third on the proof, or apparent proof, provided by the words of the speech itself. Persuasion is achieved by the speaker's personal character when the speech is so spoken as to make us think him credible. We believe good men more fully and more readily than others; this is true generally, whatever the question is, and absolutely true where exact certainty is impossible and opinions are divided. This kind of persuasion, like the others, should be achieved by what the speaker says, not by what people think of his character before he begins to speak. It is not true, as some writers assume in their treatises on rhetoric, that the personal goodness revealed by the speaker contributes nothing to his power of persuasion; on the contrary, his character may almost be called the most effective means of persuasion he possesses."[5]

Aristotle's view of *ethos* will be explored in more detail in Chapter Five on "Sources of Persuasion." For the moment, be aware that the perceived character of the source of persuasion clearly influences the receiver's response to the message. In other words, the persuader should come across to the receiver as a knowledgeable, trustworthy, and friendly person.

Aristotle spent a considerable amount of time detailing the issue of *pathos* or emotional proof. Anger, mildness, love or friendship, hatred, fear, confidence, shame, shamelessness, benevolence, pity, indignation, envy, emulation, and contempt received specific attention. He also suggested that audiences can be analyzed according to age groups. For example, he suggested that young people have strong desires, are trustful, prefer honor to expediency, and have lofty aspirations. People in their prime, by contrast, will try to adhere to both honor and expediency, are neither excessively confident nor too timid, and use economy in all endeavors. Aristotle clearly believed that persuasion is more than a matter of presenting a logical case; persuasion also involves invoking the emotions of the audience.

Aristotle's third element, *logos*, was an extension and adaptation of his writings on logic. We shall consider his ideas on logical argumentation in Chapter Six. In this brief summary, we should note that Aristotle suggested that there are two logical types of rhetorical reasoning. One type is reasoning by *enthymeme*, a rhetorical form of deductive reasoning in which an audience is asked to start with a generalization and draw a conclusion about a specific instance. The second type is reasoning by example, a rhetorical form of inductive reasoning in which receivers would be asked to begin with a specific case and derive a generalization. For example, an audience might be asked to deduce that a successful welfare program that has worked in New York, San Antonio, Minneapolis, and Los Angeles will also work in Detroit, or they might be asked to conclude that because a neighborhood watch program reduced crime in a Brooklyn neighborhood, it is reasonable to

---

Box 2.2
SAMPLE OF SYLLOGISMS AND ENTHYMEMES

Syllogisms	Enthymemes
Human beings are basically selfish. John is a human being. Therefore, John is basically selfish.	Human beings are basically selfish, and so is John.
Detective novels are enjoyable. *A Study in Scarlet* is a detective novel. So, *A Study in Scarlet* will be enjoyable.	Detective novels are enjoyable, so *A Study in Scarlet* will be enjoyable.
Work-at-home ads are scams. "Addresses Are Us" is a work-at-home ad. Therefore, "Addresses Are Us" is a scam.	Work-at-home ads are scams, and so is "Addresses Are Us."

---

conclude that neighborhood watch programs will reduce crime in any metropolitan area.

Reasoning by enthymeme was a rhetorical adaptation of syllogistic reasoning, the formal method for arriving at conclusions based on deduction. In syllogistic reasoning we begin with a generalization called a major premise. We also have a specific instance called the minor premise. If our reasoning follows the rules of a valid syllogism, we can derive a conclusion based on the major and minor premise. For example, we might argue that big businesses exploit their workers (major premise) and that MegaCorp is a big business (minor premise). Therefore, MegaCorp exploits its workers (conclusion). An enthymeme, a rhetorical form of this syllogistic reasoning, is an abbreviated syllogism in which the receiver is expected to supply the missing links. In other words, rather than spelling out the syllogism, persuaders are likely to say, "We should control big business, so we should control MegaCorp." In presenting an enthymeme, the audience is expected to participate in the reasoning process by "filling in the gaps" that the enthymeme leaves out of the fully developed syllogism.

Box 2.2 illustrates the difference between a syllogism and an enthymeme. It offers examples of the two forms using the same concepts in each form.

In reasoning by example, Aristotle developed a rhetorical form of inductive reasoning. In inductive reasoning, we take note of a series of specific instances and derive a generalization based on those instances. This involves making an "inductive leap" that purports that what is true of a series of instances will also be true of other, unexamined instances of the same class. For example, in the paleontologist's study of fossils, there is a debate about whether certain dinosaurs are ancestors of birds or reptiles. Those who favor the claim that dinosaurs are forerunners of birds argue that hollow bones, the dense network of fossilized blood vessels, and other features are general characteristics of warm-blooded birds rather than cold-blooded reptiles. Persuaders frequently use examples to generalize about a situation. Here is an example of how Hillary Clinton used a specific example to persuade members of the American Medical Association about health care reform:

> Dr. Bob Barrinson, one of the practicing physicians who spent hours and hours working with us while also maintaining his practice, told us recently of an experience that he had as one of many. He admitted an emergency room patient named Jeff. Jeff suffered from cirrhosis of the liver. Dr. Barrinson put him in the hospital and within 24 hours received a call from Jeff's insurance company. The insurance company wanted to know exactly how many days Jeff would be in the hospital and why. Dr. Barrinson replies that he couldn't predict the precise length of stay. A few days later the insurance company called back and questioned whether Jeff would need surgery. Again, Dr. Barrinson said he wasn't yet sure.
>
> And what was Dr. Barrinson's reward for his honesty and his professionalism? He was placed on the insurance company's special exceptions list. You know, that's a list of troublesome doctors who make the insurance company wait a few days or a few weeks to determine the bottom line on a particular patient. From that point on, the insurance company called Dr. Barrinson six times in two weeks. Each time he had to be summoned away from the patient to take the call. Each time he spoke to a different insurance company representative. Each time he repeated the same story. Each time his role as the physician was subverted. And each time the treatment of the patient was impeded.
>
> Dr. Barrinson and you know that medicine, the art of healing, doesn't work like that. There is no master checklist that can be administered by some faceless bureaucrat that can tell you what you need to do on an hourly basis to take care of your patients; and, frankly, I wouldn't want to be one of your patients if there were.[6]

In Aristotle's view, argument by example is a particularly useful technique for persuasion because it provides a sense of specificity to the process—"they have the effect of witnesses giving evidence, and this always tells."[7]

ROMAN RHETORIC

Following the lead of the Greeks, the Romans adopted and adapted the emphasis on rhetoric as a central part of both education and public life.

While there are many examples of Roman rhetoricians, the most famous is Cicero (106 B.C.–43 B.C.).

Cicero

Cicero is recognized both for his theoretical works on persuasion and for his ability to practice the art of rhetoric in speeches that are still studied as examples of excellence in oratory.

Cicero and the Roman rhetoricians were thoroughly pragmatic. They sought to systematize the art of persuasion to make it easier to employ. Roman rhetoricians are credited with having organized the concepts of rhetoric into five "canons" or bodies of principles: invention (*inventio*), organization (*dispositio*), style (*elocutio*), delivery (*pronuntiatio*), and memory (*memoria*). In other words, a persuader must first discover things to say about the issue. The second canon called for structuring the ideas generated. The third canon provided techniques for putting the ideas into effective words. Since Roman society, like Greek society, was primarily an oral culture, emphasis was also placed on effective management of the voice and body in delivering rhetorical speeches. The final canon of memory was a set of principles for recalling the content of the oration. In the days before note cards and TelePrompTers, this was a particularly important skill for persuaders. It is still an important factor in persuasive situations like sales interviews that do not encourage the extensive use of notes.

Quintilian

Another important Roman rhetorician was Quintilian (35–100 A.D.). His *Institutes of Oratory* provided twelve books exploring the proper education of an orator. Quintilian, like other Roman rhetoricians, argued that rhetoric should serve more than just persuasive purposes. He believed that the three aims of rhetoric were to inform, to move, and to charm. This is an important concept because many persuasive situations involve more than argumentation. The most effective persuaders are also effective teachers. In other words, the task of a sales pitch is not just to persuade the client to buy; it is also important to provide information and guidance in the sales process. Finally, the most effective persuaders also charm their receivers. Those persuasive endeavors that leave a lasting impression are those that have a grace and charm that make them particularly memorable.

The art of rhetoric gives both sides an equal chance.

MEDIEVAL RHETORIC

The Middle Ages is a period of Western history that extended from roughly 500 A.D. to about 1500 A.D. During this period, the art of rhetoric flourished in four forms: the continuation of the classical tradition, the art of preaching, the practical art of letter writing, and the art of poetics. These are best exemplified by selecting one individual from each category.

CLASSICAL TRADITION

Rhetoric as an art of persuasive discourse continued throughout the Middle Ages. A prime example of this tradition can be found in the works of Alcuin (735–804), advisor to the Emperor Charlemagne. His most famous work is presented as a dialogue between Alcuin and his student-king Charlemagne. The work is largely an interpretation of Cicero—it closely followed the concepts typically discussed in Roman rhetoric. Rhetoric consists of three genres: deliberative rhetoric aimed

UPI/Bettmann

Rhetoric includes the art of preaching.

at politics, forensic rhetoric concerned with legal pleading, and epideic-tic rhetoric aimed at praise or blame. To accomplish these objectives Al-cuin described the traditional Ciceronian canons of invention, organization, style, delivery and memory.

> The first thing, indeed, is to invent what you may say; the second, to arrange what you may have invented; the third, to express in words what you have arranged; the fourth, to fix in the memory what you have invented and arranged and clothed in words; and the last and highest, to deliver what you have fixed in the memory.[8]

One medieval tradition, then, was a continuation of classical pre-cepts of rhetoric, largely from Cicero. A second tradition introduced what has become known as *ars praedicandi,* or the art of preaching.

PREACHING

As Christianity spread throughout Europe and intertwined with the po-litical processes of emperors and kings, rhetoric took on a new interpre-tation as a means for spreading the word of God and for defending the church against attack from competing ideals. Even though technically he predates the Middle Ages, the most influential figure in this genre of medieval rhetoric was St. Augustine (354–430 A.D.).

Augustine is recognized as extending classical precepts of rhetoric into new areas essential to the church. Invention became a matter of interpreting and expressing sacred works. For rhetoricians like Augustine, *dispositio* concerned structuring sermons for maximum effect. Style or word choice was particularly important for Augustine's concept of Christian rhetoric. He adapted Ciceronian notions of plain, medium, and grand style to apply to style in sermons as represented by both the Bible and by the works of well-known Christians like St. Cypian and St. Ambrose. Delivery, while not a major issue for Augustine, was also important in the art of the preacher to make the sermon intelligible and comprehensible for the listeners. Memory, like delivery, was included in tracts on preaching, even though it received considerably less emphasis than the other canons of rhetoric.

Letter Writing

Letter writing (*ars dictaminis*) was the third genre of rhetoric adapted to the demands of medieval society. To communicate over long distances required extensive use of written communication. To meet this demand the art of rhetoric was expanded from speeches to written forms of communication.

According to James Murphy, a noted scholar of medieval rhetoric, "The very multiplicity of ranks and orders in an emerging feudal society had the effect of increasing the number of relationships—both social and legal—which came to be reflected in writing in one way or another. One ready solution to the problem of writing about such recurring situations was to draft a *formula*—a standardized statement capable of being duplicated in various circumstances."[9] Thus, the origins of the form letter can be traced to the seventh century.

In addition to collections of form letters, rhetoricians of the Middle Ages produced a number of manuals explaining the principles of effective letter writing. Bene of Florence (c. 1220 A.D.), for example, composed a manual for letter writing entitled *Candelabrum*. These manuals consisted of techniques for suitable and elegant writing. They used the traditional canons of rhetoric with a particular emphasis on style. Invention was often treated as of less importance since there were form letters available for imitation. Organization eventually developed into a five-part arrangement of letters: salutation, securing good will, narration (setting forth the circumstances of the letter's purpose), the petition, and the conclusion. Style was divided into the plain, middle, and grand forms as it was in oral preaching. Clear and elegant style used polished language and appropriate figures of speech. While delivery was not a major part of the art of letter writing, there was often some discussion of cadences and a rhythmical prose style, a topic related to both speaking and writing. Memory, of course, was also of lesser importance for letter writers than it was for orators.

POETICS

The final area of rhetoric influential in the Middle Ages was the art of verse writing (*ars poetica*). While we consider the term "grammar" to mean the study of syntax, for medieval rhetoricians the term was much broader and included what we now refer to as the study of literature as well as sentence structures. This "grammatical" genre of medieval rhetoric placed an emphasis on studying both the traditional Latin rules of syntax and the composition of Latin verse. While it may seem that verse writing is no longer related to the art of persuasion as it was for medieval rhetoricians like Geoffrey of Vinsauf's *Poetria Nova* (c. 1210 A.D.) or Alexander of Villedieu's *Doctrinale* (c. 1212 A.D.), the influence of verse in persuasion is still relevant. From the jingles of advertisements that we easily recall (even though we cannot recall material we have concentrated on for a test) to the most memorable and meaningful passages of political speeches (even though we may not remember the less poetic passages of the speeches), there is clearly a close link between poetry and persuasion.

MODERN RHETORIC

The modern period of rhetorical theory extends from the Renaissance to the turn of the twentieth century. Generally this was a period that witnessed new developments in rhetorical theory with an emphasis on the psychology of the receivers.

FRANCIS BACON

Francis Bacon (1561–1626), the English philosopher credited with developing the modern scientific method, is also a pivotal figure in the reemergence of rhetoric and psychology. Francis Bacon advocated a faculty psychology, a belief that the mind is composed of aspects or faculties that operate in different areas. In Bacon's *Advancement of Learning*

(1605) rhetoric was defined as "the application of reason to imagination for the better moving of the will." This emphasis on faculty psychology used to gain, judge, record and transmit knowledge clearly points to a renewed scientific interest in the psychology of human communication.

GEORGE CAMPBELL

George Campbell (1719–1796) was another key figure in modern rhetoric. His *Philosophy of Rhetoric* revised the classical concept of rhetoric as deliberative, forensic, or epideictic in favor of a classification based on psychological effects: "to enlighten the understanding, to please the imagination, to move the passions, or to influence the will."[10] In addition, Campbell placed emphasis on careful audience analysis—persuaders must analyze both general principles of audiences and the particular circumstances of a specific audience.

Even Campbell's discussion of style emphasized audience psychology. He introduced the concept that an effective rhetoric must be lively or "vivid." The vivacity of ideas, making the persuader's words generate an experience nearing that of an experience through the senses, was the central theme of Campbell's consideration of style. In other words, effective language has a near physical effect on receivers.

HUGH BLAIR

Hugh Blair (1718–1800) approached the concept of rhetoric from a slightly different perspective. Blair's primary interest lay in rhetoric's long-standing relationship to poetics. This *belles lettres* tradition emphasized rhetoric as having a lasting impact on people. In other words, if rhetoric were to have a value beyond a short-term or immediate effect, then it must be concerned with truth and beauty as expressed in words. Blair emphasized literary qualities of style with a particular emphasis on "taste" and "beauty."

Rhetorical scholar Douglas Ehninger offered a cogent summary of Blair's unique contribution to the study of rhetoric. According to Ehninger, Blair disregarded "the classical distinctions between rhetoric and poetic, and between spoken and written discourse" and constructed a framework "that cuts across those lines, unifying all four areas into a single science of composition and transmission. Thus his book was entitled *Lectures on Rhetoric and Belles Lettres,* and in addition to advice on public speaking, letter writing and the construction of essays—the usual subject matter of rhetoric—also includes considerations of epic and lyric poetry, tragedy and comedy, and the like."[11]

Richard Whately

Richard Whately (1787–1863) in *Elements of Rhetoric* also reflected a renewed interest in analyzing the psychology of rhetoric. Whately's principal contribution was the introduction of the concepts of presumption and burden of proof. Presumption means that the receivers will initially favor a particular position. For example, in our courts we presume a person to be innocent until proven guilty. Burden of proof means that the responsibility of making a case for change from presumption rests with those who want to change. For example, because a person is presumed innocent, it is the responsibility of the prosecution to make a case that the person is guilty. In other words, Whately introduced the theory that a persuader must undertake the task of proving a case because the receivers will presume that there is no need for change, that a person is innocent until proven guilty, and so on. Once again, we see rhetorical theory in the modern era emphasizing the operation of the minds of the receivers.

CONTEMPORARY RHETORIC

Contemporary rhetoric begins roughly at the turn of the twentieth century. Rhetoric in this century has emerged as a study that draws from a variety of disciplines including English, philosophy, psychology, political science, and many others. Theorists have been primarily concerned with moving beyond the traditional boundaries of classical, medieval, and modern rhetoric that tended to place an emphasis on the interplay of sources with audiences through messages. Contemporary theorists sought to break with the historical traditions of rhetoric.

Kenneth Burke

One of the most influential theorists of the twentieth century was Kenneth Burke (1897–1994). In his seminal article "Rhetoric—Old and New,"[12] Burke claimed that the old rhetoric was based on persuasion, an acting on the audience by the source, but that the new rhetoric was based on identification, an acting with the audience through the symbolic process of communication. This is a clear split from the past focus of rhetoric on argumentation and persuasion in legal, political, and social forums. Burke's new rhetoric was more broadly conceived as the use of symbols (not just speaking or writing) in human interaction (not just speeches and letters).

Burke was a prolific writer and is a difficult person to summarize in this brief space. We will limit our consideration to three key concepts: identification, the dramatic pentad, and the function of the new rhetoric.

Identification, according to Burke, is a matter of closely linking the source with the audience; in identifying with the source, the audience, in a sense, becomes one with rhetor. Close identification is most clearly illustrated by thinking of your best friend; your closest friend is so closely linked that you are often thinking the same things at the same time—at times words are not even necessary—interrupted conversations can be picked up instantly because you are both "on the same wavelength." For Burke, identification is closely associated with persuasive communication: "a speaker persuades an audience by the use of stylistic identifications; his act of persuasion may be for the purpose of causing the audience to identify itself with the speaker's interests; and the speaker draws on identification of interests to establish rapport between himself and his audience."[13] In other words, persuaders should consider how to create identification with the audience rather than try to figure out how to argue them into submission to the source's point of view.

A second key concept in Burke's new rhetoric is the idea of dramatism. Instead of considering language a means for conveying information, Burke suggested that we should see language as a dramatic action. To analyze what happens in rhetoric, Burke suggested using the term *act* to name "what took place in thought or deed," *scene* to characterize "the background of the act, the situation in which it occurred," *agent* to indicate what person or kind of person . . . performed the act," *agency* to specify "what means or instruments" were used, and *purpose* to explain why the act was done.[14] In other words, Burke suggested that people involved in rhetoric engagements should be seen in a full context as goal-directed agents using symbols in a specific situation to accomplish purposes.

As persuaders, we should recognize that our rhetoric is related to all of these interrelated features. For example, when the president delivers a State of the Union address, he is not just giving an informative speech. He is an agent using the speech to place before Congress and the American public an agenda of important issues in the context of the current social scene. He is seeking to get Congress and the American people to identify this agenda as including the most important issues to be dealt with in the coming months.

The third key concept in Burke's rhetorical theory is the function of rhetoric. In the history of rhetoric, we have seen that classical theory focused on instructing, moving, and charming in political, legal, and social settings. For Burke, rhetoric should be seen as functioning logically, emotionally, ethically, and poetically in any form in which people use symbols. As one commentator put it, "for Burke the scope of rhetoric is immense, almost unlimited. . . . for Burke everything has rhetoric in it."[15] In other words, all of our actions are rhetorical, not just our talking or writing. All of our actions have logical, emotional, ethical, and poetic dimensions to them. In persuasion, then, we should consider the full range of human responses, not just the logical and emotional responses of our audiences.

RICHARD M. WEAVER

Another central figure in the contemporary concept of rhetoric is Richard M. Weaver (1910–1963). Like Burke, Weaver took a broad view of rhetoric as having ethical and social consequences. In Weaver's view, "language is sermonic" and "[w]e are all of us preachers in private or public capacities. We have no sooner uttered words than we have given impulse to other people to look at the world, or some small part of it, in our way."[16] For Weaver, rhetoric and the ideas it expresses have consequences and therefore we must consider its broader social and ethical dimensions.

Social dimensions of rhetoric mean that in Weaver's view rhetoric and therefore persuasion have a constructive role to play in advancing cultural values. Cultural ideals are expressed in what Weaver calls "ultimate terms," key words that a group holds in high respect. For example, a word like "progress" or "fact" is held in high esteem in our contemporary culture but words like "Nazi" or "nuclear war" are terms of repulsion. In Weaver's view, such terms reveal the ideals held by the culture and their use demonstrates the values being endorsed by the rhetor. In contemporary times, we often see the use of ultimate terms. Advocates of ecological responsibility are labeled "tree huggers" while their opponents are labeled "polluters." Ultimate terms can be used to determine what values are being endorsed by a society and they can also be used as means for persuaders to advance their views. There is a danger in ultimate terms, however, that Weaver warns us about. In Weaver's words, "the student of rhetoric must realize that in the contemporary world he is confronted not only by evil practitioners, but also and probably to an unprecedented degree, by men who are conditioned by the evil created by others. The machinery of propagation and inculcation is today so immense that no one avoids entirely the assimilation and use of some terms that have a downward tendency. It is especially easy to pick up a tone without realizing its trend."[17] In other words, while rhetoric has a positive power to advance positive values, it can also be misused and abused, sometimes deliberately and sometimes unwittingly. For example, a Caucasian politician using an expression like "you people" to an African-American audience may be unintentionally insulting but his words reflect an attitude and a tone that lacks identification with the audience. It behooves both rhetors and their audiences to analyze carefully the social consequences of their use of language.

Ethical dimensions of rhetoric were a key concern for Weaver. In his view, human beings have four essential abilities. First, there is the capacity for reason which provides us with knowledge. Second, there is the aesthetic faculty that enables us to enjoy beauty. Third, there is a religious impulse which gives us a sense of destiny. Fourth, there is the ethical capacity which enables us "to determine the order of the goods and to judge between right and wrong."[18] In other words, we have more than just the capacity to understand something or to appreciate its beauty, we also have a yearning to see things as a part of the larger order of the universe. Finally, we must be sensitive to the ethics of our actions. We will discuss the relationship between ethics and persuasion in more detail in Chapter Four. For the moment, realize that Weaver urged persuaders to consider not just whether a particular act is effective but also whether it is morally right or wrong. For example, a salesperson may trick a buyer into purchasing an overpriced item but to do so violates the ethical mandates of effective rhetoric.

CHAIM PERELMAN

Another important figure in contemporary rhetoric is Belgian philosopher Chaim Perelman (1912–1984). The concept of argumentation infuses much of Perelman's "new rhetoric." In Perelman's view, rhetoric "aims at gaining the adherence of minds,"[19] and all of the elements of rhetoric are designed to accomplish that end. For example, for Perelman, style is not verbal ornamentation that enlivens discourse but argumentation in that style "brings about a change of perspective" that can bring the receiver to adhere to the source's thesis.[20]

Perelman provided detailed analyses of how rhetors secure the adherence of the audience. His descriptions included five techniques: quasi-logical arguments, arguments based on the structure of reality, relations establishing the structure of reality, the dissociation of concepts, and the interaction of arguments.

Quasi-logical arguments are based on reasoning processes such as frequency. So, for example, a rhetor might seek to convince a receiver that since a foreign country has violated fifty out of its last fifty-two treaties, it is not a trustworthy ally.

The Bettmann Archive

Ethical dimensions of rhetoric were a key concern for Weaver.

Arguments based on the structure of reality derive their force from "their more-or-less close relation with certain logical or mathematical formulae. . . ."[21] This category includes such arguments as cause and effect. For example, a persuader might argue that the use of drugs like marijuana brings about a chemical dependency on harder drugs.

Arguments that establish the structure of reality include arguments by example and reasoning by analogy. We have discussed these forms in some detail earlier in this chapter.

The dissociation of concepts, in Perelman's view, is a third technique of argumentation. This relies on dividing a concept that would otherwise be incompatible with where the arguer wants to go. For example, a lawyer might argue that appearance is different from reality, and that, while circumstantial evidence may appear to show the defendant guilty, the defense evidence will prove the reality of the defendant's innocence.

Finally, Perelman suggested that the interaction of arguments is a powerful technique of rhetoric. Perelman recognized that persuaders do not rely on a single argument in seeking to gain the adherence of the receiver. As a result, arguments interact to influence the audience. Perelman recommended carefully ordering the arguments so as to maximize the acceptance of the thesis. Chapter Six will discuss the ordering of elements in persuasion in more detail. For the moment, remember Perelman's admonition that skillful rhetors think in terms of strategies of sequencing arguments so that the receivers are most likely to accept the overall claim being made.

There are many contemporary rhetoricians, and the field is constantly expanding with new ideas and new interpretations of earlier ideas. In later chapters we shall mention contemporary rhetorical figures like Stephen Toulmin and I. A. Richards. In this short space, we have tried to provide a sense of the development of rhetoric as being concerned, not just with the speaker, the message, and the audience, but with the larger contextual issues of the impact of rhetoric on society at large.

Summary

This chapter undertook the daunting task of condensing 2500 years of Western rhetoric into a few pages. While it is impossible to do justice to the individuals who have contributed to the development of the field of rhetoric, we have witnessed the contribution of key ideas that shape our concept of persuasion.

From the ancient theorists, we discover the origins of Western rhetoric and derive the important principles of rhetoric as a science and an art that deals with practical matters of persuasion. The techniques of *ethos, pathos,* and *logos* are means for informing, moving, and inspiring audiences. Rhetoric was applied to practical matters involved in politics, law, and the society.

From the medieval era we discovered that rhetoric was not limited to the three traditional genres, but was expanded to include the art of preaching. Medieval studies also contributed the recognition that rhetoric employs aspects of both logic and poetics to accomplish these practical ends. Finally, the varieties of medieval rhetoric show that rhetoric is not limited to the spoken word, but that persuaders employ writing and other symbolic means as well as speeches in their efforts to influence others.

Modern rhetoric acknowledges the importance of psychology in creating effective persuasion. A deeper understanding of how audiences think and react gives persuaders better insight into how to make persuasion effective for a particular audience.

Contemporary rhetoricians like Burke, Weaver, and Perelman force us to look beyond the source–message–audience aspects of the model presented in Chapter One. We are urged to recognize and employ the social, cultural, and ethical aspects of persuasion. We should see persuasion as an interaction through symbolization that seeks to link the speaker with the receiver. We should recognize that persuasion is action that involves social and cultural consequences and that therefore must be judged in terms of both the efficacy of the symbols and the ethics of the rhetorical event.

Notes

[1] There are many different definitions of rhetoric This one is based on the work of Donald C. Bryant, "Rhetoric: Its Function and Scope," *The Quarterly Journal of Speech*, 39 (1953), pp. 401–424.

[2] Gorgias, "Encomium on Helen," in *The Older Sophists*, ed. Rosamond Kent Sprague, trans. George Kennedy (Columbia, SC: University of South Carolina Press, 1972), p. 52.

[3] Gorgias, "On the Non-existent," *Ibid.*, p. 46.

[4] Plato, "Phaedrus," in *The Dialogues of Plato*, vol. 1, trans. Benjamin Jowett (New York: Scribner, 1895), 2776.

[5] Aristotle, "Rhetoric," trans. W. Rhys Roberts, *The Works of Aristotle*, vol. II (Oxford: Clarendon Press, 1924), 1356a.

[6] Hillary Rodham Clinton, "Health Care," June 13, 1993. *Vital Speeches of the Day*, 59 (July 15, 1993), p. 583.

[7] Aristotle, op. cit. 1394a15.

[8] Alcuin, *The Rhetoric of Alcuin and Charlemagne*, trans. Wilbur Samuel Howell (New York: Russell & Russell, 1965), p. 71.

[9] James J Murphy, *Rhetoric in the Middle Ages* (Berkeley, CA: University of California Press, 1974), p. 199.

[10] George Campbell, *The Philosophy of Rhetoric* (Carbondale, IL: Southern Illinois University Press, 1963), p. 1.

[11] Douglas Ehninger, "Campbell, Blair, and Whately Revisited" in *Readings in Rhetoric*, eds. Lionel Crocker and Paul A. Carmack (Springfield, IL: Charles C. Thomas, 1965), p. 369. Courtesy of Charles C. Thomas, Publisher.

[12] Kenneth Burke, "Rhetoric—Old and New," *Journal of General Education*, 5 (April 1951), pp. 202–209.

[13] Kenneth Burke, *A Rhetoric of Motives* (Berkeley: University of California Press, 1969), p. 46.

[14] Kenneth Burke, *A Grammar of Motives* (Berkeley, CA: University of California Press, 1969), p. xv.

[15] Joseph Schwartz, "Kenneth Burke, Aristotle, and the Future of Rhetoric," in *Contemporary Rhetoric*, ed. Douglas Ehninger (Glenview, IL: Scott, Foresman and Company, 1972), pp. 256–257. Reprinted with permission of HarperCollins College Publishers.

[16] Richard M. Weaver, "Language Is Sermonic," *Dimensions of Rhetorical Scholarship*, ed. Roger E. Nebergall (Norman, OK: University of Oklahoma Press, 1963), p. 62.

[17] Richard M. Weaver, "Ultimate Terms in Contemporary Rhetoric," *Language Is Sermonic*, eds. Richard L. Johannesen, Renard Strickland, and Ralph T. Eubanks (Baton Rouge, LA: Louisiana State University Press, 1970), pp. 111–112.

[18] Richard M. Weaver, *Visions of Order* (Baton Rouge, LA: Louisiana State University Press, 1964), p. 85.

[19] Chaim Perelman and L. Olbrechts-Tyteca, *The New Rhetoric*, trans. John Wilkinson and Purcell Weaver (Notre Dame, IN: University of Notre Dame Press, 1969), p. 14.

[20] Ibid., p. 169.

[21] Ibid., p. 261.

For Further Thought

1. Examine a contemporary political speech. Cite examples of the speaker using Aristotle's principles of ethos, pathos, and logos.
2. Medieval rhetoric emphasized letter writing. How do direct-mail letters compare to e-mail messages? Are there elements of medieval letter writing that apply to direct-mail that don't apply to e-mail messages? What difference does this make in persuading through electronic channels?
3. Cite an example of something that you read or heard that is so vivid you can recite it from memory. What aspects of the message made the passage vivid? How can those same aspects be incorporated into your persuasive messages aimed at others?
4. Contemporary rhetoric places an emphasis on social responsibility. Cite examples of current trends in persuasion that make ethics and social responsibility important.
5. Using the discussion of aspects of persuasion in the "Introduction" and the coverage of elements of persuasion in Chapter One, consider how the concept of rhetoric has changed over the centuries. For example, in what ways have contemporary rhetoricians shifted their attention from public communication to interpersonal communication and mass communication? Have elements like channels and context affected the development of rhetorical theory?

For Further Reading

Corbett, Edward P. J. *Classical Rhetoric for the Modern Student*. New York: Oxford University Press, 1971.

Crocker, Lionel and Paul A. Carmack. *Readings in Rhetoric*. Springfield, IL: Charles C. Thomas, 1965.

Foss, Sonja K., Karen A. Foss and Robert Trapp. *Contemporary Perspectives on Rhetoric*. Second Edition. Prospect Heights, IL: Waveland Press, 1991.

Golden, James L., Goodwin F. Berquist, and William E. Coleman, *The Rhetoric of Western Thought*. Fourth Edition. Dubuque, IA: Kendall/Hunt Publishing Company, 1989.

Chapter Three

CONTEMPORARY PRINCIPLES
OF PERSUASION

The views of rhetorical theorists described in the last chapter tend to advise sources how to create persuasive messages. In general, the principles of rhetorical theory provide strategies sources can use in creating and delivering persuasive creations. In this chapter we shall explore a different approach to understanding persuasion. Contemporary principles of persuasion are derived largely from psychologists and social scientists, or from communication scholars who take a social science approach. The theorists in this chapter generally take a descriptive rather than a prescriptive approach. Receivers tend to be the focus of these descriptions. In the pages that follow we shall explore the development of theories from this social-scientific perspective.

Competing theories often may seem to be mutually exclusive but the competition is more a matter of pitting a theorist against the unknown rather than one theorist against another. While in a sense the United States was in competition with the Union of Soviet Socialist Republics in space exploration, in reality it was an endeavor of human beings competing with the forces of nature in exploring new celestial territory. In a similar vein, the theories we shall explore in this chapter focus on different perspectives of the persuasive process, but they are not necessarily mutually exclusive.

We can categorize the various theories into two broad groups. The first group we shall refer to as **psychological theories.** These tend to focus on explaining individual motivation. Psychological theories seek to explain how attitudes, beliefs, and values are formed and how they are triggered by given persuasive stimuli. The second broad category can be called **sociological theories.** Here the focus is on the interaction of the individual with others. Just as psychology is the study of emotional and behavioral characteristics of individuals and sociology is the study of the origins, development, and organization of people in groups, so our social theories focus on how people respond, in interaction with each other, in persuasive situations.

PSYCHOLOGICAL THEORIES

We shall examine three types of theories within this broad classification of psychological theories: drive theories, learning theories, and cognitive theories. Drive theories suggest that an individual is motivated by inherent needs. Learning theories share an underlying view: Since attitudes, beliefs, and values are learned, we can apply the psychology of learning to the study of persuasion. Finally, we shall examine the important group of theories called cognitive consistency theories. These theories share the underlying assumption that individuals have a built-in sense of cognitive homeostasis or balance; when persuasive stimuli create imbalance, individuals will seek to reacquire a state of balance.

DRIVE THEORIES

The famous Sigmund Freud is noted for his concept that no behavior is accidental. He emphasized that humans are unconsciously motivated by sex and aggression. Such drives serve as motivational forces in human activity. While Freud did not directly write about persuasion, his views are echoed by many contemporary psychologists.

Abraham Maslow

One such contemporary psychologist is Abraham Maslow, who wrote, "We have, each one of us, an essential inner nature which is instinctoid, intrinsic, given, 'natural,' i.e., with an appreciable hereditary determinant, and which tends strongly to persist. . . . Many aspects of this inner, deeper nature are either (a) actively repressed, as Freud has described, because they are feared or disapproved of or are ego-alien, or (b) 'forgotten' (neglected, unused, overlooked, unverbalized or suppressed), as Schachtel has described. Much of the inner, deeper nature is therefore unconscious."[1]

Persuasion often appeals to basic human drives like food, safety, and social needs.

Box 3.1

MASLOW'S
HIERARCHY OF NEEDS

AESTHETIC   beauty

NEEDS

UNDERSTANDING   frame of
values
philosophy of life

SELF-   fulfillment of potential

ACTUALIZATION

ESTEEM NEEDS   self-esteem, prestige, fame,
glory, recognition

BELONGINGNESS NEEDS   affection, group membership,
family, need for love

SAFETY NEEDS   protection, security, stability, freedom
from fear, need for order, law

PHYSIOLOGICAL NEEDS   bodily needs: food, water, sleep, sex

SOURCE: "Maslow's Hierarchy of Needs" from *Motivation and Personality*, 3rd edition, by Abraham H. Maslow. Revised by Robert Frager, James Fadiman, Cynthia McReynolds, and Ruth Cox. Copyright © 1954, © 1987 by Harper & Row Publishers, Inc. Copyright © 1970 by Abraham Maslow. Reprinted by permission of HarperCollins Publishers, Inc.

Maslow is best known for his description of a "hierarchy of needs." Maslow suggested that our mainsprings of motivation could be considered a hierarchy of needs, a graded rank of motives.[2] His hierarchy is represented in Box 3.1.

In Maslow's view, physiological needs, like the need for food and water, are fundamental. After fulfilling such basic needs, we are motivated by safety needs: the need for shelter, security, protection. Next comes the need for belonging to a community, a family, or even a gang. The fourth level is the need for respect, approval, and dignity. At the fifth level is self-actualization, which Maslow described as "the fullest development of one's talents and capacities."[3] To his original five levels, Maslow later added the idea of a transcendence level that included going beyond needs based on deficiency (physiological, safety, belonging and esteem) to human needs for growth potential that included self-actualization needs, understanding needs, and esthetic needs. In other words, a fully functioning human being is motivated by more than meeting deficiencies; the optimal stage of human development operates to fulfill growth needs that include fulfilling one's potential, seeking knowledge, and appreciating beauty.

The principles of persuasion typically derived from Maslow include the idea that needs serve as grounds for persuasion. For example, ads usually appeal to physiological needs, frequently appeal to safety needs, often appeal to social needs, and occasionally appeal to esteem needs. Only rarely do we find persuasive appeals to self-actualization, and almost never to ultimate knowledge and esthetic needs. Clearly advertisers see in Maslow's hierarchy key ideas in developing persuasive appeals.

A second principle we can derive from Maslow's hierarchy is that an unfulfilled need will be motivating. While persuasive appeals can be made to any of the categories, targeting an unmet need in the life of the receiver will be more motivating but targeting a fulfilled need will be less motivating and thus less persuasive. For example, a person who has just finished a large meal will not be as responsive to an advertisement for pizza as will a person who has not eaten for many hours.

Robert Cialdini

A contemporary perspective on drives as motivations is Robert Cialdini's "weapons of automatic influence." Cialdini wrote, "Although there are thousands of different tactics that compliance practitioners employ to produce yes, the majority fall within six basic categories. Each of these categories is governed by a fundamental psychological principle that directs human behavior and, in so doing, gives the tactics their power."[4] These six "weapons" are reciprocation, commitment and consistency, social proof, liking, authority, and scarcity.

The first weapon that Cialdini described is based on the rule of **reciprocation:** "The rule says that we should try to repay, in kind, what another person has provided us."[5] This is the principle that underlies the influence of a company giving away a free sample, for example. Since the persuader has given the receiver a gift, the receiver will feel a sense of obligation to repay the favor by trying the product.

Commitment and consistency is the principle of "sticking to your guns," of remaining committed to a position and consistent with your previous stands. Cialdini argued that this principle is the basis of the "foot-in-the-door technique," in which a person is asked to comply with a small initial request before being asked to comply with a larger request. For example, many businesses offer "introductory specials," merchandise that is offered at a low price with more and more expensive items following the initial offer.

Social proof, according to Cialdini, "states that one means we use to determine what is correct is to find out what other people think is correct."[6] Notice that children's toys are sold using this "monkey see, monkey do" appeal, but notice also that many adult products and services are sold in a context of social proof rather than inherent worth.

The fourth weapon Cialdini described is **liking.** This is the principle that we are more likely to accept a proposal from someone we like. This has long been recognized in the folklore with the adage that you can catch more flies with honey than you can with vinegar. Attractive celebrities endorsing products, salespeople using compliments and flattery, and politicians campaigning in casual clothes are all examples of this technique at work.

In Cialdini's view, **obedience to authority** is an indisputable principle of human motivation. We shall examine this principle in much greater detain in Chapter Five. For the moment, recognize that we tend to be more willing to accept persuasion from people whom we respect. We are more likely to buy athletic shoes endorsed by Michael Jordan, for example, than we are if the product were endorsed by the proverbial ninety-pound weakling.

The final weapon described by Cialdini is **scarcity:** "[O]pportunities seem more valuable to us when their availability is limited."[7] Artworks and collectibles rely upon the scarcity principle to enhance their value. Notice, for example how some shopping channels use a countdown register to emphasize that the available products are becoming more scarce by the second.

Drive theories assert that we have nearly automatic responses to particular needs. Psychologists like Freud, Maslow, and Cialdini clearly demonstrate the application of these drives in persuasion. An alternative set of theories suggests that while we may have basic drives, our attitudes, beliefs, and values are acquired through our interaction with the environment. In other words, they are learned.

LEARNING THEORIES

We may be born with the ability to develop cognitive skills, but we learn what makes sense. We are born with the capacity to have visceral reactions, but we learn to fear lions rather than kittens and wolves

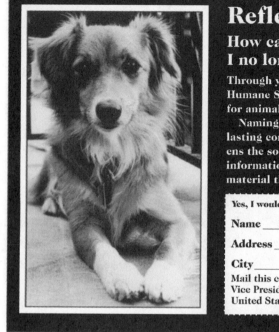

Our beliefs, values, and attitudes are shaped by learning. This ad reflects our learned concern for protecting animals.

rather than dogs. We are not born with an inherent distrust of telemarketers; we learn to distrust their pitches. In short, whether it is logos, pathos, or ethos, we learn to respond to persuasive appeals.

The group of theories discussed in this section share the common theme of applying learning techniques to individual motivation. We shall explore the applications of classical conditioning to persuasion. We shall also examine how operant conditioning operates in a persuasive situation. We shall examine the influence of the reasoned action theory in studies of persuasion. Finally, we shall consider how inoculation theory applies to the study of persuasion.

Classical Conditioning

Does the name Pavlov ring a bell? Ivan Petrovich Pavlov is the famous Russian physiologist whose experiments with dogs formed the basis for the type of learning psychologists call classical conditioning. In his experiments, Pavlov noticed that he could elicit a reflex action of salivating when he put food, an "unconditioned stimulus," in front of a dog. He rang a bell and noted that this "conditioned stimulus" elicited

The Bettmann Archive

Ivan Petrovich Pavlov

only attentive listening at first. By regularly ringing the bell before giving food to the dog, Pavlov noted that he could condition the dog to respond to the bell even when no food was present. In this way, a conditioned stimulus could eventually produce a conditioned response of salivation.

Classical conditioning is the basis for our responses to stereotypes. Notice, for example, that we have an emotional reaction to the sight of our national flag but no such reaction to the flags of other countries. We have an emotional aversion to the sight of a swastika. We are conditioned to respond to flashing red lights and yellow signs marking school zones. In short, many things that we learn come from classical conditioning.

Persuasion finds classical conditioning used extensively in advertising. Sprint telephone learned that hearing a pin drop on TV did not work as effectively as repeatedly pairing a positive stimulus (Candice Bergen) with the company, so as to generate a positive attitudinal response.

Psychologist Arthur Staats argued that all attitudes are formed through classical conditioning.[8] McSweeny and Brierly examined the uses of classical conditioning in consumer affairs.[9] Communication scholars have also sought to apply this theory to persuasion.[10]

Operant Conditioning

More recently, psychologists have extended Pavlov's classical conditioning model to incorporate a view called operant conditioning. The idea underlying operant conditioning is that behaviors that are rewarded will be continued and behaviors that are punished will be terminated. In other words, the intermittent use of rewards and punishments, rather than the repeated pairing of stimulus and response, serves to influence human behavior. We find this type of learning used in "behavior modification" programs that reward people for proper behavior (e.g., getting a gold star in class) or punish people for undesirable behavior (e.g., imposing fines for parking violations).

In persuasion theory, operant conditioning has been shown to be a valuable explanation for why people respond to persuasion. Attitudes that are rewarded are more likely to be developed and maintained, but should the reward be continuous or intermittent? In a study by Kerpelman and Himmelfarb, attitudes were tested under continuous reinforcement situations in which each case of the targeted behavior was reinforced and, under intermittent schedules, some but not all instances of the behavior were rewarded. They found that while attitudes acquired during the continuous reinforcement condition were initially stronger, those acquired during the intermittent schedule were less susceptible to extinction when opposing persuasive messages were encountered.[11] In short, for maximum and long-lasting effect, it is better to provide persuasive rewards on an intermittent, unpredictable schedule.

Reasoned Action Theory

The third psychological theory is based on research conducted by Martin Fishbein and Icek Ajzen. Their concept holds that human behavior is not automatic but intended. They argued that "a person's attitude toward an object is related to his beliefs that the object possesses certain attributes and his evaluations of those attributes. Similarly, attitude is related to the set of a person's behavioral intentions with respect to an object, each intention weighted by its evaluative implications."[12] In other words, the determinant of action is a person's intention. Before you can get a person to buy a can of orange juice, for example, you must get that person to intend to buy orange juice.

According to Fishbein and Ajzen, there are two components of an intention. The first factor is what the individual believes about the act, an **"attitudinal component."** This is a matter of the person's beliefs about the consequences of the behavior and the strength of those beliefs. For example, Jamie believes that it is very likely (belief strength) that eating vegetables provides important vitamins and minerals that the body needs (belief).

The second factor is a "**social normative component.**" This is a matter of the judgments of expectations of other people who are important to the individual and of how motivated the individual is to comply with those expectations. For example, Jamie knows that his mother strongly urged him to eat vegetables (expectation of salient other).

Fishbein and Ajzen suggest that we can create a mathematical model to determine the likelihood of a given behavior. For example, suppose that Jamie believes in vegetarianism. How likely is it that Jamie will actually follow a vegetarian diet? Fishbein and Ajzen's prediction is illustrated in Box 3.2.

Research has indicated that behavioral intentions as described in the theory of reasoned action (attitudinal component and social normative component) predict behavior in many situations, including studies of voting, consumer purchases, seat belt use, and conserving energy in the home. Persuaders can utilize this model in three ways.

First, persuaders can seek to change the attitudinal component. There are at least three tactics a persuader might employ. (1) A persuader might add a new belief about the topic. For example, in trying to persuade someone to adopt an abandoned pet, the persuader might try to introduce a new belief ("Did you know that over 10,000 abandoned pets are put to sleep each day?") (2) A persuader might try to alter the evaluation of an existing belief. ("Pets are really important in keeping us mentally healthy.") (3) A persuader might seek to modify the strength of an existing belief. ("You may remember enjoying having a pet as a kid, but do you remember how much you enjoyed your pet?")

Second, the persuader can seek to change the normative component. Again, persuaders have at least three tactics they can employ. (1) A persuader might try to introduce the views of a new significant other. ("Did you know that the governor has declared this week 'Save a Pet Week'?") (2) The persuader might attempt to alter the perceptions the receiver has about the views of significant others. ("No, your spouse has already indicated a willingness to get a pet.") (3) A persuader might try to influence the motivation to comply with significant others. ("Don't worry about what your neighbors may think. They have pets of their own.")

Third, the persuader can seek to change the relative weights of the two components. In our example, we assumed that both the attitude component and the normative component were of equal importance in the behavioral intention. Actually, the formula for a theory of reasoned

Box 3.2

ILLUSTRATION OF THE THEORY OF REASONED ACTION

Jamie's Attitudinal Component (A_b)

I. Belief Evaluation (e_i)	**II. Belief Strength (b_i)**

Vegetarianism will improve health.

bad –3 –2 –1 0 1 2 **3** good   likely **3** 2 1 0 –1 –2 –3 unlikely

Vegetarianism will make me a wealthier person.

bad –3 –2 –1 0 1 2 **3** good   likely 3 2 1 0 **–1** –2 –3 unlikely

Vegetarianism will make me a better person.

bad –3 –2 –1 0 1 2 **3** good   likely **3** 2 1 0 –1 –2 –3 unlikely

Computation of Attitudinal Component ($A_B = \Sigma\ e_i\ b_i$)

$$A_B = (3 \times 3) + (3 \times -1) + (3 \times 3) = (9) + (-3) + (9) = 15$$

If all of the components are equally important, the average attitudinal component is 5.

Jamie's Social Normative Component (SN)

I. Expectation of Salient Other (NB)	**II. Motivation to Comply (MC)**

Mother believes I should be a vegetarian.

should 3 2 1 0 **–1** –2 –3 should not   low 1 2 **3** 4 5 6 7 high

Spouse believes I should be a vegetarian.

should **3** 2 1 0 –1 –2 –3 should not   low 1 2 3 4 5 **6** 7 high

Religious leader believes I should be a vegetarian.

should 3 2 **1** 0 –1 –2 –3 should not   low 1 2 **3** 4 5 6 7 high

Computation of Attitudinal Component ($SN = \Sigma\ NB_i\ MC_i$)

$$SN = (-1 \times 3) + (3 \times 6) + (1 \times 3) = (-3) + (18) + (3) = 18$$

If all of the people are equally important, the average normative component is 6.

Calculation of Jamie's Behavioral Intentions (BI)

$$BI = (A_B) + (SN) = (5) + (6) = 11$$

Since the maximum number possible in this example is 30 and the lowest possible number is –30, we can say that Jamie clearly intends to become a vegetarian and that it is fairly likely Jamie will become a vegetarian.

action is expressed as $BI = (A_B)w_1 + (SN)w_2$ where BI stands for behavioral intentions, A_B is the attitude toward the behavior, SN refers to the social norm, and w_1 and w_2 are the weights of each factor. Therefore, a persuader might seek to alter the relative weights of the components. For example, suppose the receiver has a positive attitude toward adopting a pet but a negative social norm perception because the receiver's landlord may object to a pet. A persuader might seek to emphasize the attitude component and downplay the normative component. ("It's your decision. You pay the rent each month. The landlord has a security deposit. And anyway, there is nothing in your lease prohibiting a pet, so the landlord's opinion, even if he objects, is irrelevant.")

So far we have considered various learning theories and their relationship to persuasion. There is a related concept that suggests that just as a person may be inoculated against a disease, he or she may be inoculated against persuasion.

Inoculation Theory

William J. McGuire used the analogy of the body fighting a disease in his explanation of the inoculation theory of persuasion. We can fight the flu through action such as getting plenty of rest, avoiding crowds where infection can spread, and so on. We can also take a flu shot that builds our body's resistance by giving us a weakened dose of the flu. By analogy, a person can have a view bolstered by a supportive defense (arguments that favor the intended position) or the person can be "inoculated" against opposing views by being provided with what McGuire called a "refutational defense,"[13] weak forms of counterarguments, weak arguments against the intended position. The receiver can easily construct refutations to these weak counterarguments and thereby build resistance to other arguments posed against the intended position.

Such refutational defense has been shown to be superior to supportive defense in inducing resistance to counterpersuasion efforts. McGuire and Papageorgis also suggested that forewarning a receiver about a counterargument will produce an even stronger resistance to counterpersuasion.[14]

We can derive two ideas from inoculation theory. First, persuaders can help receivers to resist counterarguments if they present a two-sided message. One-sided messages introduce only arguments that support the persuader's position; two-sided messages also include opposing arguments. A persuader may utilize this two-sided approach by merely mentioning opposing arguments, by comparing opposing arguments to the arguments that support the persuader's position, or by directly attacking opposing arguments. For example, if we are trying to convince someone to stop smoking, it is best to acknowledge but refute the pleasure that the smoker gets from the behavior if we want the smoker to stay off cigarettes.

A second principle we can derive from inoculation studies is that forewarning may be used to get receivers to generate their own counterarguments. For example, a politician may be able to ward off an opponent's attack by forewarning the constituents about what those arguments might be and inviting the audience to determine the truth for themselves.

COGNITIVE CONSISTENCY THEORIES

Probably the most widely studied set of theories can be grouped under the heading of cognitive consistency theories. In this section we shall explore the principles of psychological balance, the congruity theory and Leon Festinger's theory of cognitive consistency.

Balance Theory

With the publication of *The Psychology of Interpersonal Relations* Fritz Heider is credited with the earliest contemporary theory of cognitive consistency. Heider explained that people prefer states of balance to states of imbalance or disharmony.[15] In Heider's view, two people interact with respect to a matter of mutual concern. These three elements—the person, the other, and the object of mutual concern—are represented by the letters P for person, O for other, and X for the issue they share an interest in. The relationships are represented in the form of a triangle like the following:

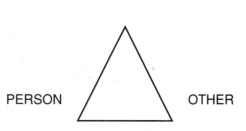

OBJECT

PERSON   OTHER

Now each line in the triangle can represent either a like (positive) or a dislike (negative). Consider, for example, the relationship between Abe and Beth and the issue of opera. In the example, Abe likes opera and likes Beth and both of them enjoy opera. This happy state would be represented as follows:

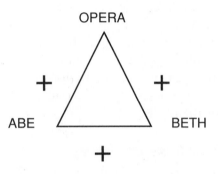

It is also possible, of course, that Abe likes Beth but that they both hate opera. In Heider's terms, this relationship would appear as follows:

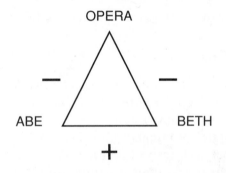

According to balance theory, balanced states consist of three positive relationships or two negative relationships and one positive relationship. Our two examples of Abe and Beth represent balanced states.

Suppose, however, that Abe likes Beth and Beth likes opera but Abe hates opera. Now we have an unbalanced relationship illustrated by the following:

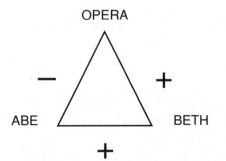

According to balance theory, balanced states are stable but unbalanced states are unstable. As Heider phrased it, "where balance does not exist, the situation will tend to change in the direction of balance."[16] As our unbalanced example illustrates, there will be a stress toward rebalancing in the situation: Abe may convince Beth that opera is a waste of time and money—and they would return to a balanced state of two negatives and a positive—or Beth may convince Abe that opera is an exhilarating and pleasurable experience—and they would return to a balanced state of three positives.

In terms of persuasion, then, balanced states are not very susceptible to persuasion but unbalanced states create a stress to rebalance. Persuaders, then, can take advantage of the unbalanced states where the receiver will be on the verge of change.

Persuaders, however, must take care to close off undesirable states of balance. For example, suppose that Abe is trying to persuade Beth to loathe opera. The goal is to achieve the balanced state described above in which they like each other but both hate opera. However, there is an alternative balanced possibility: Beth may come to dislike Abe while still loving opera:

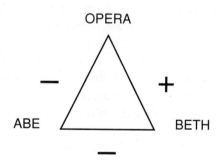

This could be the result of Abe's effort to persuade if he is not careful.

Balance theory provides an important perspective on the psychology of receivers. However, it is limited because it describes only three relationships (person, object, other), but human beings are much more complicated than that. For example, Abe isn't just in a relationship with Beth and opera. He is also related to Beth's parents, to her colleagues and coworkers, her friends, and so on. In addition, Abe and Beth are related on many more issues than opera; they have similarities and dissimilarities on a wide variety of "objects," from food preferences to religious perspectives, from the secular to the sublime. In short, a single person–object–other relationship is insufficient in explaining the total potential for persuasion.

Box 3.3
CONGRUENT STATES

Source	Position on Issue	As Viewed by Receiver
Tobacco Study Institute (positive)	endorses smoking (positive)	viewed positively by Jean (positive)
Tobacco Study Institute (positive)	denounces smoking (negative)	viewed negatively by Jean (negative)
Tobacco Study Institute (negative)	endorses smoking (positive)	viewed positively by Jean (negative)
Tobacco Study Institute (negative)	denounces smoking (negative)	viewed negatively by Jean (negative)

Congruity Theory

Fritz Heider's balance theory was a general theory of interpersonal relationships rather than a specific examination of how persuasion works. Congruity theory, a type of consistency theory, was more specifically aimed at explaining attitudes. According to its developers, Charles Osgood and Percy Tannenbaum, "changes in evaluation are always in the direction of increased congruity with the existing frame of reference."[17] Congruity theory holds that a receiver will have two sets of views, one attitude toward a source and another toward the issue, for example. According to this theory, there are four congruent situations: (1) when a positively evaluated source positively endorses an issue that the receiver views positively, (2) when a positively evaluated source denounces an issue that the receiver also views negatively, (3) when a negatively evaluated source positively endorses an issue that the receiver views negatively, and (4) when a negatively evaluated source denounces an issue that the receiver views negatively. Consider an example involving the receiver, Jean, and the source, the Tobacco Study Institute, on the issue of smoking. The four possible congruent situations appear in Box 3.3.

There are also four incongruent situations: (1) when a positively evaluated source denounces an issue that the receiver views positively, (2) when a positively evaluated source positively endorses an issue that the receiver views negatively, (3) when a negatively evaluated source denounces an issue that the receiver also views negatively, and (4) when a negatively evaluated source endorses an issue that the receiver views positively. Continuing with our example of Jean and the Tobacco Study Institute, the incongruous situations are illustrated in Box 3.4.

Box 3.4
INCONGRUENT STATES

Source	Position on Issue	As Viewed by Receiver
Tobacco Study Institute (positive)	denounces smoking (negative)	viewed positively by Jean (positive)
Tobacco Study Institute (positive)	endorses smoking (positive)	viewed negatively by Jean (negative)
Tobacco Study Institute (negative)	denounces smoking (negative)	viewed negatively by Jean (negative)
Tobacco Study Institute (negative)	endorses smoking (positive)	viewed positively by Jean (positive)

According to the congruity principle, when these incongruous attitudes are associated, there will be a move toward resolving the incongruity. If, for example, Jean, a smoker, respects the Tobacco Study Institute but they report that smoking is a dangerous habit, there will be a move toward resolving this incongruity by reevaluating the view of the Tobacco Study Institute, by reevaluating the view of smoking, or both.

In developing their theory of congruity, Osgood and Tannenbaum sought to bring mathematical precision to determine and predict both the direction and amount of change in attitudes. Their formula and an example appear in Box 3.5.

To apply Osgood and Tannenbaum's formula, a persuader needs specific numerical data. While such data are available in laboratory conditions, they are less likely to be available in field conditions. Furthermore, there is no indication of how to expand the formulation from an individual to groups of receivers. These difficulties limit the practical utility of the mathematical formulation of congruity theory.

Cognitive Dissonance Theory

The most widely known variety of cognitive consistency theories was originated by Leon Festinger. In *A Theory of Cognitive Dissonance* he explained the two central tenets of his theory: "1. The existence of dissonance, being psychologically uncomfortable, will motivate the person to try to reduce the dissonance and achieve consonance. 2. When dissonance is present, in addition to trying to reduce it, the person will actively avoid situations and information which would likely increase the

Box 3.5
FORMULAS FOR CONGRUITY

$$AC_1 = \frac{|a_2|}{|a_1| + |a_2|} \, P_{source}$$

Where AC_1 is the change toward the source, $|a_1|$ represents the absolute value (number excluding a + or – sign) of the view of the source, $|a_2|$ represents the absolute value of the view of the issue, and P_{source} stands for the pressure toward congruity (i.e., the difference in scale units between the position regarding the source and the position of maximum congruence).

$$AC_2 = \frac{|a_1|}{|a_1| + |a_2|} \, P_{issue}$$

Where AC_2 is the change toward the issue, $|a_1|$ represents the absolute value of the view of the source, $|a_2|$ represents the absolute value of the view of the issue, and P_{issue} stands for the pressure toward congruity (i.e., the difference in scale units between the position toward the issue and the position of maximum congruence).

Suppose in our example that our person does not like Rush Limbaugh (–2) but does like Pizza Hut pizza (+1). These values would appear as follows:

Attitude toward source
(Limbaugh)

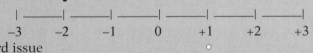

Attitude toward issue
(Pizza Hut pizza)

Putting the values into the equations, we would have the following:

$$AC_1 = \frac{1}{1 + 2} \, (+3) = 1 \quad \text{and} \quad AC_2 = \frac{2}{1 + 2} \, (-3) = -2$$

Therefore, the person's attitude toward the source would have changed up one unit from –2 to –1 and the attitude toward the issue would have changed down two units from +1 to –1. The new placement of congruity would look like the following:

Attitude toward source   **New position**   Attitude toward issue
(Limbaugh)   **(congruity)**   (Pizza Hut pizza)

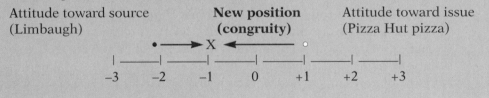

dissonance."[18] In other words, if a person entertains two ideas that are inconsistent (dissonance), he or she will seek to reduce or eliminate the dissonance and will actually avoid situations and messages that may increase dissonance. For example, suppose a person is a Catholic but also has come to favor freedom of choice in the issue of abortion. Since the Catholic church is fiercely opposed to abortion, the individual is likely to experience cognitive dissonance.

In terms of persuasion, Festinger's first tenet has several implications. Festinger suggests that there are three ways to reduce dissonance. First, the person can change the attitude. For example, the person could fall away from the church or could come to accept the right-to-life position. A second way to resolve the dissonance is to bolster or support one or the other of the dissonant positions. For example, the person may seek additional guidance from the officials of the church to support the right-to-life view or the person may seek additional information from the right-to-choose groups to support that position. Finally, the person may seek to reevaluate the importance of the relations in the situation. For example, the person may decide that the matter of abortion is only a small part of the overall Catholic church value system; therefore, it is possible to remain a Catholic but to favor freedom of choice when restricted to the first trimester.

Another important matter to be derived from Festinger's ideas concerns forced compliance. Festinger's theory suggests that as the magnitude of reward or punishment increases, dissonance will be decreased because the person will be more strongly motivated to make a choice and to rationalize that choice. For example, if the person in our example is threatened with excommunication unless he or she renounces his or her position on freedom of choice in abortion, there will be increased pressure to resolve the dissonance rather than merely choose to live with the inconsistency.

Festinger's second principle (that people will tend to avoid situations or information that increases dissonance) also has important ramifications for persuasion. A persuader should recognize that people will actively avoid attempts at persuasion if that persuasion is seen as countering what they already accept. For example, when pro-life protesters march outside abortion clinics, people seeking abortions will not be convinced by the signs but instead will seek to avoid confrontation with the protesters and their messages. In other words, the target audience may not only be hard to reach, they may actively avoid being confronted with counterpersuasive messages.

Cognitive dissonance is frequently operant in persuasive situations. For example, rewards are often offered for people to choose a different product or service. Offering an incentive to switch brands creates dissonance between continuing with a known brand and desiring the reward in return for changing brands; the receiver must choose between the brands. Another example of cognitive dissonance is the self-help concern for quitting smoking. When smokers are presented with persuasive messages from sources they find credible, they experience a conflict between the desire to continue smoking and the knowledge that the behavior is self-destructive. Again, the receiver must choose among alternatives.

SOCIOLOGICAL THEORIES

The psychological theories that we examined in the last unit have a common focus on the individual's reaction to persuasion. Communication factors of persuasion that we considered in Chapter One are ancillary to the primary goal of defining how and why an individual responds to the communication. The theories we explore in this unit, by contrast, fit comfortably into a communication paradigm. This perspective is best represented by Albert Bandura's concept of social learning theory.

SOCIAL LEARNING THEORY

Bandura's theory stands in sharp contrast to psychologists like B. F. Skinner who endorse behavioristic approaches such as operant conditioning. Skinner derogates the value of the so-called "black box" of the human mind that intervenes between the observable stimulus and the observable response. In contrast, Bandura suggests that "[a]lthough cognitive activities are disavowed in the operant conditioning framework, their role in causal sequences simply cannot be eliminated."[19]

Bandura's theory emphasizes human communication. Recall from our introductory chapter that persuasion is a communication process, using symbols in a deliberate way to influence receivers. Compare that perspective to Albert Bandura's view.

> The capacity to use symbols provides humans with a powerful means of dealing with their environment. Through verbal and imagined symbols people process and preserve experiences in representational forms that serve as guides for later behavior. The capability for intentional action is rooted in symbolic activity. . . . Without symbolizing powers, humans would be incapable of reflective thought. A theory of human behavior therefore cannot afford to neglect symbolic activities.[20]

Modeling is a central tenet of Bandura's model. In his theory, people learn by observing the behavior of others rather than through direct

In Bandura's theory of modeling, we learn by observing others. Note how we learn from the behaviors of our parents.

experience. So, for example, we may learn about the usefulness of connecting to the Internet through television ads and conversations with others before we actually log on to experience cyberspace for ourselves.

Bandura's concept has important ramifications for persuaders. It is important for persuaders to be aware that a single persuasive source can provide influential models "simultaneously to vast numbers of people in widely dispersed locations."[21]

FUNCTIONAL THEORIES

Another theorist who has taken a social communication approach to the study of persuasion is Daniel Katz. In his view, attitudes are not merely psychological constructs, they serve important purposes of (1) instrumental, adjustive, or utilitarian function, (2) ego-defense function, (3) value-expressive function, or (4) knowledge function.[22]

Attitudes that serve an adjustment function serve to maximize rewards and to minimize penalties in order to make the most of the world and what it has to offer. For example, our attitude toward our chosen occupation serves a utilitarian function of providing an income for doing meaningful work. Attitudes that serve an ego-defense function help to protect our sense of self-worth. For example, we may displace our displeasure at not making the amateur softball team by losing our temper at a driver going only the speed limit on the trip home. Our view that the other driver is a jerk provides an outlet for our own shortcomings. The value-expressive function projects a positive expression of the type of values we think of ourselves as having. For example, we may project an aura of calm control as we wait in the doctor's office for the test results, our attitude toward waiting expressing the value of strength and self-confidence. Attitudes that serve the knowledge function provide a sense of "meaning to what would otherwise be an unorganized chaotic universe."[23]

Each function, according to Katz, has specific origins, arousal conditions, and change conditions. A summary that Katz provided is reproduced in Box 3.6. The task of a persuader is to determine the function that a given target attitude serves for the receivers. Once that has been determined, the persuader is guided in arousing the attitude to influence behavior or in affecting the conditions necessary to change the attitude.

For example, if an insurance sales agent determines that the client's attitude toward purchasing a policy is serving an adjustment function, the agent would want to press the need to protect the family from the threat of the unexpected death of the family's main wage earner. If the

Box 3.6
KATZ'S FUNCTIONAL THEORY

Determinants of Attitude Formation, Arousal, and Change in Relation to Type of Function

Function	Orgin and Dynamics	Arousal Conditions	Change Conditions
Adjustment	Utility of attitudinal object in need satisfaction. Maximizing external rewards and minimizing punishments	1. Activation of needs 2. Salience of cues associated with need satisfaction	1. Need deprivation 2. Creation of new needs and new levels of aspiration 3. Shifting rewards and punishments 4. Emphasis on new and better paths for need satisfaction
Ego defense	Protecting against internal conflicts and external dangers	1. Posing of threats 2. Appeals to hatred and repressed impulses 3. Rise in frustrations 4. Use of authoritarian suggestion	1. Removal of threats 2. Catharsis 3. Development of self-insight
Value expression	Maintaining self-identity; enhancing favorable self-image; self-expression and self-determination	1. Salience of cues associated with values 2. Appeals to individual to reassert self-image 3. Ambiguities which threaten self-concept	1. Some degreee of dissatisfaction with self 2. Greater appropriateness of new attitude for the self 3. Control of all environmental supports to undermine old values
Knowledge	Need for understanding, for meaningful cognitive organization, for consistency and clarity	1. Reinstatement of cues associated with old problem or of old problem itself	1. Ambiguity created by new information or change in environment 2. More meaningful information about problems

SOURCE: D. Katz, "The Functional Approach to the Study of Attitudes," *Public Opinion Quarterly* 24 (1960), pp. 163–204.

attitude serves an ego-defense function, the agent may want to appeal to the cash value that can be accumulated in a whole life policy to build the client's net worth while providing protection. Should the agent determine that the attitude is serving a value-expression function for the

Functional theories of persuasion suggest we should adapt the message based on whether an attitude serves an adjustment, ego defense, value expression, or knowledge function.

client, the agent will want to stress that having adequate life insurance indicates a well-organized, thoughtful, and well-prepared individual. If the attitude serves a knowledge function, the agent may want to advance the notion that we never know when or how our death may occur and that with all of the random violence, it is a good idea to provide protection in advance.

By considering the arousal and change conditions as outlined in Box 3.6, persuaders can generate the most effective messages. Furthermore, those messages can be adapted more readily to the particular nature of the receiver.

SOCIAL JUDGMENT–INVOLVEMENT THEORY

This theory was developed by researchers Sherif, Sherif, and Nebergall. The basis of the theory holds that attitudes serve as evaluative filters for our perceptions of persuasive messages. As a result, when we encounter persuasive messages, we may determine how similar or different the position is from our existing attitudes. In addition, the theory suggests that the degree of discrepancy between the position advocated and the position already held by the receiver is important. This discrepancy "can be used to predict attitude change, resistance to change, or susceptibility to change."[24]

Rather than conceiving an attitude as a fixed point, Sherif, Sherif, and Nebergall argued that we have latitudes of acceptance, latitudes of rejection, and latitudes of noncommitment. Latitudes of acceptance are the category of positions that we find acceptable. Latitudes of rejection consist of the range of positions that we find unacceptable. Latitudes of noncommitment are the positions that we would neither accept nor reject.

There are two important principles that persuaders should recognize about this theory. First, the degree of ego-involvement determines how the receiver evaluates the persuasive endeavor. Ego involvement means how important the receiver considers the specific issue to be, how close the issue is to being an integral part of the self-concept. For example, for many people *Star Trek* was an innovative television program, but true fans, Trekkies, are very ego-involved in the series and have even invented a Klingon language of extraterrestrials.

The principle of ego involvement has four implications for persuaders:

(1) Highly ego-involved receivers have narrow latitudes of acceptance and noncommitment and wide latitudes of rejection. It will be extremely difficult to change the position because there is a very limited range of ways to present opposing positions. Consider, for example, the

How nuclear energy benefits a typical family of four.

Every year, the ospreys return to their wildlife preserve around the nuclear electric plant near Waterford, Connecticut, where nesting platforms have been built for them by the local utility.

It's one more example of how peacefully nuclear energy coexists with the environment. Because America's 111 operating nuclear plants don't burn anything to generate electricity, they don't pollute the air. They don't produce any greenhouse gases, either.

To help satisfy the nation's growing need for electricity without sacrificing the quality of our environment, we need more nuclear plants. For your family, and others as well.

If you'd like more information, write to the U.S. Council for Energy Awareness, P.O. Box 66080, Dept. OS21, Washington, D.C. 20035.

Nuclear energy means cleaner air.

Social judgment involvement theory suggests that the degree of ego involvement determines how the receiver interprets a message. This ad's special appeal would vary depending on how ego-involved the receiver is with the issue of nuclear energy.

case of a person who grew up in Detroit, the American automobile capital. This person's family has, for generations, worked in the automotive industry. As a result, he or she is highly ego-involved in the issue of American automobiles. It will be extremely difficult to persuade this person to even test drive, let alone purchase, a foreign-made automobile.

(2) Moderately ego-involved people have a small latitude of rejection, a moderate latitude of acceptance, and a moderate latitude of noncommitment. Such people will be relatively easy to persuade. For example, a person who grew up in Minneapolis will not have the same ego involvement in American-made cars as the person who grew up in Detroit. While he or she may feel some compulsion to "buy American," the moderate ego involvement will provide a persuader with a broader range of arguments to use to convince the receiver to purchase a foreign-made automobile.

(3) Low ego-involved receivers have a wider latitude of acceptance, a wider latitude of noncommitment, and a narrow latitude of rejection. These people will be the easiest to persuade. For example, a person who grew up with a significant multicultural background in Hawaii, where every car—American, Asian, or European—has to be "imported" into the islands, will have low ego involvement with American automobiles. As a result, this type of receiver will be much more susceptible to persuasion in purchasing a foreign-made automobile.

(4) People who have high ego involvement are less willing to look at a variety of sides on an issue. The less the ego-involvement, the more likely the person is to be willing to examine all sides of an argument. For example, our person who was born in Detroit may not be willing to consider the fact that even the "foreign" makes are frequently built in the United States. Such a position would be rejected and the person would not see the point as a reasonable consideration.

The second important issue to be derived from the social judgment-involvement theory concerns the concepts of assimilation and contrast. Assimilation means that positions will be perceived as being closer to the receiver's anchor position than they actually are. Contrast means that positions will be perceived as being more discrepant from the receiver's anchor position than they actually are. Sherif, Sherif, and Nebergall suggest that "With high involvement, the range of assimilation is smaller. Conversely, the range of positions subject to contrast effect is greater with higher involvement."[25] Thus, small ranges of assimilation and narrow latitudes of acceptance in highly ego-involved listeners add to the difficulty in discovering arguments that will be acceptable to the receiver.

Elaboration Likelihood Model

The final theory we shall consider in this unit is the elaboration likelihood model of persuasion (ELM). Richard Petty and John Cacioppo developed this model in *Communication and Persuasion: Central and Peripheral Routes to Attitude Change.*[26] They suggested that people desire the correct attitudes and beliefs because those are the elements that will be most useful in dealing with everyday problems. In their view, there are two different but related routes for coming to hold a reasonable attitude. One route is called the central route. This is a largely cognitive approach that requires careful analysis and evaluation of the merits of the case. The second route, termed the peripheral route, is a less rigorous approach that relies on taking one's cue from experts, being attracted to the packaging, or some other easy decision rule. The ELM is reproduced in Figure 3.1.

ELM alerts persuaders to the fact that they must not only know a person's attitude toward an issue or a source, but they must also know whether that attitude was formed through the central route or through the peripheral route if the persuasive message is to be most effective. According to Petty, Cacioppo, Strathman, and Priester, "[c]entral route attitudes will (1) predict behavior better, (2) come to mind more easily, (3) last longer, and (4) be more resistant to counterpersuasion attempts. Thus, it is useful to know not only how positive or negative someone's attitude is but also the extent of message elaboration that formed that attitude."[27]

For example, if a receiver is a vegetarian, it will help to know whether the attitude toward vegetarianism was developed through a central route of reasoning (e.g., concluding that vegetarianism is better for the ecology, reading sufficient legitimate nutritional articles to conclude that vegetarianism is heathier, etc.) or peripherally (e.g., deciding that vegetarianism must be good because Paul and Linda McCartney are vegetarians). If the receiver arrived at the position on vegetarianism through the peripheral route, it is more likely that the person will revert to eating meat occasionally, will be less likely to stick with a vegetarian regime over a long period of time, and will be more amenable to persuasion on converting to omnivorous diets.

Summary

We used two broad classifications to organize our examination of contemporary theories of persuasion. Psychological theories seek to explain

Figure 3.1
ELM Model

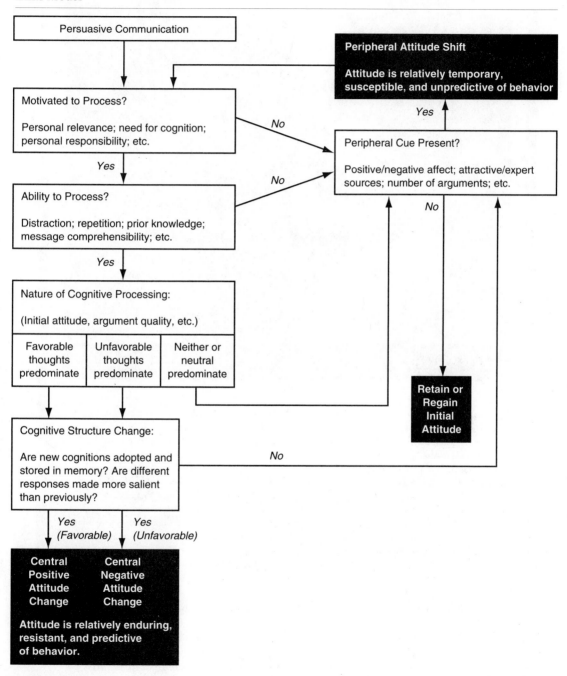

SOURCE: Richard E. Petty and John T. Cacioppo, *Communication and Persuasion: Central and Peripheral Routes to Attitude Change.* New York: Springer Verlag, 1986.

"I Never Thought It Could Happen To Me."

"I thought I had planned for everything." These are the words of a flood victim—they could be yours. Thousands of people every year find out that it CAN happen.

Are you prepared for a flood? Did you know you don't have to live close to water to become a flood victim? Do you have flood insurance?

You need to know the answers to these questions. Because the terrifying truth is that floods can happen anywhere, anytime. Flood insurance is the best way to protect yourself *before* the flood hits. Flood damage often goes way beyond that of house and home. Flood victims not only lose their homes and treasured possessions, but rebuilding costs also eat up life savings, retirement funds and children's college educations.

You can protect yourself—through the National Flood Insurance Program. We have one mission: to restore the quality of life of flood victims as soon as possible. For more information, call your insurance company, agent or 1-800-611-6122, ext. 39.

We can't replace your memories, but we can help you build new ones.

NFIP
National Flood Insurance Program
Administered by FEMA

FEMA

This ad seeks to appeal to the central route (relevance, personal responsibility) but acknowledges the peripheral route (negative affect).

how attitudes, beliefs, and values are formed and how they are triggered by persuasive stimuli. Sociological theories, on the other hand, focus on the interaction of the individual with others in persuasive situations.

Psychological theories include drive theories, learning theories, and cognitive theories. Drive theories are based on the view that people are motivated by inherent need. A prime example is Maslow's hierarchy of needs. A more recent example is Cialdini's weapons of automatic influence. Learning theories share the view that since attitudes are learned, we can apply learning techniques to persuasion. We explored both classical conditioning and operant conditioning to persuasion. We also considered Fishbein and Ajzen's reasoned action theory of persuasion and McGuire's inoculation theory.

Cognitive consistency theories are based on the concept of balance, or homeostasis, in human responses. Fritz Heider's conceptualization held that psychologically balanced relationships are relatively stable but that unbalanced relationships lead to rebalancing. This view found application to persuasion in the congruity theory proposed by Osgood and Tannenbaum. They theorized that when incongruous situations occur, there will be a move to resolve the incongruity. The most widely explored variation on these theories is Leon Festinger's theory of cognitive dissonance. He argued that cognitive dissonance is psychologically uncomfortable and therefore receivers exposed to persuasive messages that do not fit their preexisting views will be placed in a state of dissonance and seek to resolve that dissonance. Festinger also argued that people will avoid situations or information that increases dissonance.

Sociological theories take a communication view of persuasion. These theories included social learning theory, functional theory, social judgment–involvement theory, and the elaboration likelihood model. We began by examining Bandura's social learning theory which emphasized modeling as a way of gaining compliance. Next we considered Katz's functional theory which held that attitudes serve instrumental, ego-defense, value-expressive, and knowledge functions.

Social judgment–involvement theory holds that attitudes are not fixed points but rather there are latitudes of acceptance, rejection, and noncommitment. The degree of ego involvement with the issue determines both the latitude of acceptance or rejection as well as the range of assimilation or contrast a receiver will experience.

Finally, we surveyed the ELM model which suggests that attitudes are formed either through a central route or a peripheral route. We noted the implications for persuasion that are involved in these routes to attitude formation.

Chapters Two and Three provided an overview of the theoretical perspectives on human persuasion. While rhetorical theories and empirical approaches may appear to be incompatible, it is important to acknowledge the value of both the humanistic approach of rhetoric and the scientific approach of the psychological and sociological theories of persuasion. Chapter Four will introduce the important issue of ethics in persuasion.

Notes

[1] Abraham Maslow, *Toward a Psychology of Being,* second edition (New York: Van Nostrand Reinhold, 1968), pp. 190–192.

[2] Abraham Maslow, *Motivation and Personality* (New York: Harper & Row, 1970), pp. 35–58.

[3] Maslow, *Toward a Psychology of Being,* p. 200.

[4] Robert Cialdini, *Influence: The Psychology of Persuasion* (New York: William Morrow, 1993), p. xiii.

[5] Ibid., p. 17.

[6] Ibid., p. 116.

[7] Ibid., p. 238.

[8] Arthur W. Staats, *Learning, Language, and Cognition* (New York: Holt, Rinehart and Winston, 1968), passim.

[9] F. K. McSweeny and C. Brierly, "Recent Developments in Classical Conditioning," *Journal of Consumer Research,* 11 (1984), pp. 619–631.

[10] Judee K. Burgoon, Michael Burgoon, Gerald R. Miller, and Michael Sunnafrank, "Learning Theory Approaches to Persuasion," *Human Communication Research,* 7 (Winter 1981), pp. 161–179.

[11] J. P. Kerpelman and J. Himmelfarb, "Partial Reinforcement Effects in Attitude Acquisition and Counterconditioning," *Journal of Personality and Social Psychology,* 19 (1971), pp. 301–305.

[12] Martin Fishbein and Icek Ajzen, *Belief, Attitude, Intention and Behavior: An Introduction to Theory and Research* (Reading, MA: © Addison-Wesley Publishing Company, 1975), p. 59. Reprinted by permission of Addison-Wesley Publishing Company, Inc.

[13] William J. McGuire, "Inducing Resistance to Persuasion: Some Contemporary Approaches," in L. Berkowitz, ed. *Advances in Experimental Social Psychology,* Volume 1 (New York: Academic Press, 1964), pp. 191–229.

[14] W. J. McGuire and D. Papageorgis, "Effectiveness of Forewarning in Developing Resistance to Persuasion," *Public Opinion Quarterly,* 26 (1962), pp. 24–34.

[15] Fritz Heider, *The Psychology of Interpersonal Relations* (Hillsdale, NJ: Lawrence Erlbaum Associates, 1958), p. 204.

[16] Ibid., p. 207.

[17] Charles Osgood and Percy Tannenbaum, "The Principle of Congruity in Prediction of Attitudes," *Psychological Review,* 62 (1955), p. 43.

[18] Leon Festinger, *A Theory of Cognitive Dissonance* (Stanford, CA: Stanford University Press, 1957), p. 3.

[19] Albert Bandura, *Social Learning Theory* (Englewood Cliffs, NJ: Prentice-Hall, Inc, 1977), p. 10.

[20] Ibid., p. 13.

[21] Ibid., p. 40.

[22] Daniel Katz, "The Functional Approach to the Study of Attitudes," *Public Opinion Quarterly,* 24 (1960), pp. 163–204.

[23] Ibid., p. 167.

[24] Caroline W. Sherif, Muzafer Sherif, and Robert E. Nebergall, "Attitude and Attitude Change: The Social Judgment–Involvement Approach," in *The Process of Social Influence,* eds. Thomas D. Biesecker and Donn W. Parsons (Englewood Cliffs, NJ: Prentice-Hall, 1972), p. 105.

[25] Ibid., p. 117.

[26] Richard Petty and John Cacioppo, *Communication and Persuasion: Central and Peripheral Routes to Attitude Change* (New York: Springer-Verlag, 1986).

[27] Richard Petty, John Cacioppo, Alan Strathman, and Joseph Priester, "To Think or Not to Think: Exploring Two Routes to Persuasion," in *Persuasion: Psychological Insights and Perspectives,* Sharon Shavitt and Timothy C. Brock, eds. (Boston: Allyn & Bacon, 1994), p. 141. Copyright 1994. All rights reserved. Allyn & Bacon.

For Further Thought

1. Find an example of a print ad that seems to apply a psychological theory of persuasion and one that seems to apply a sociological theory of persuasion. Compare and contrast the composition of the two ads. Which type of ad is more likely to be neutral or to agree with the position advocated?

2. Use Cialdini's six "weapons of influence" to generate six arguments you might use to convince a friend to go in with you in buying a used car.

3. Read the opinion/editorial page of your local newpaper. Find appeals that seem based on unbalancing or creating cognitive dissonance in the reader. What did the author do to create this persuasive effect?

4. Use the formula in Box 3.2 to estimate your own behavioral intentions on a controversial topic (like abortion). Interview someone on that controversial topic. Try to get information and data for attitudinal components and social normative components of their views. Using the formula in Box 3.2, estimate that person's behavioral intentions.

5. Compare and contrast one of the rhetorical theories in Chapter Two with one of the theories in Chapter Three. Which is more

useful in advising a politician how to get elected? Which is more useful in describing the impact of Saturday morning television ads on children?

For Further Reading

Arnold, Carroll C. and John Waite Bowers. *Handbook of Rhetorical and Communication Theory.* Boston: Allyn & Bacon, 1984.

Bettinghaus, Erwin, P. and Michael J. Cody. *Persuasive Communication.* Fifth Edition. Fort Worth, TX: Harcourt Brace, 1994.

O'Keefe, Daniel J. *Persuasion: Theory and Research.* Newbury Park, CA: Sage Publications, 1990.

Reardon, Kathleen. *Persuasion in Practice.* Newbury Park, CA: Sage Publications, 1991.

Chapter Four

ETHICS AND PERSUASION

Author M. Hirsh Goldberg related the story of an envelope that looked as if it had come from the U.S. government. It was a regulation-sized, manila envelope with "Buy U.S. Savings Bonds" imprinted on it. "Pay to the order of" and a drawing of the Statue of Liberty were printed on green card stock seen through a cellophane window, just like a check. Eager to get at that government check, people tore open the envelope to discover that it contained a "check" good for $250 worth of gasoline if the recipient bought or leased a car from a dealer.[1] This is a clear example of how people can be persuaded to open "junk mail," but the tactic is ethically questionable.

Unethical persuasion is a problem in our contemporary age of communication, but it is not a new problem. Ethics has been linked to persuasion since the days of ancient Greece. Quintilian, one of the Roman rhetoricians discussed in Chapter Two, was a renowned educator in the first century A.D. He argued that an effective persuader is a good person skilled in speaking. In Quintilian's view, being ethical is essential for persuaders.

> Nature herself will have proved not a mother, but a stepmother with regard to what we deem her greatest gift to man, the gift that distinguishes us from other living things, if she devised the power of speech to be the accomplice of crime, the foe to innocency and the enemy of truth. For it had been better for men to be born dumb and devoid of reason than to turn the gifts of providence to their mutual destruction.[2]

In this chapter we shall explore ethical dimensions of persuasion. We shall begin by examining the relationship of persuasion to propaganda. Then we shall focus attention on specific ethical aspects of sources, messages, channels, and receivers.

PERSUASION AND PROPAGANDA

On October 10, 1990, as the U.S. Congress was preparing to vote on sending troops to the Persian Gulf, a young Kuwaiti woman named "Nayirah" testified before Congress. She said that Iraqi troops had snatched babies from their incubators in a Kuwait City hospital and had left "the babies to die on the cold floor." Americans were shocked and outraged by such atrocities. It turned out, however, that the atrocities did not happen, that the young woman was not a refugee but rather the daughter of the Kuwait ambassador to the United States, and that she had been coached by Hill and Knowlton, an American public relations firm.[3] The problem of using persuasion as propaganda is not new. In 1937, the Institute for Propaganda Analysis published a list of propaganda techniques that they claimed were unscrupulous. The list, reproduced in Box 4.1, was based on the analysis of ideological campaigns employed since the turn of the century.

The problem with the early studies of propaganda was that they focused on tactics while seeking to condemn opposing ideological positions, but the tactics could also be used for desirable ends. Propaganda techniques can be used to support prices for tobacco as well as to oppose smoking. As researchers Garth Jowett and Victoria O'Donnell concluded, "Propaganda is not necessarily an evil thing. It can only be evaluated within its own context according to the players, the played upon, and its purpose."[4]

To understand the relationship of ethics and persuasion we must move beyond identifying propaganda techniques. We must consider ethics in relation to the entire persuasive process. The power to persuade implies the power to mislead. It is not surprising, then, that persuasion is closely linked not just to the persuasive efficacy of the message but also to the moral dimension of moving people in the direction sought by the persuader.

ETHICS AND SOURCES

The source of the message is a particularly important part of ethical consideration. Since persuasion is a deliberate act, it follows that intentionality is a major factor in the ethics of persuasion. There are cases of unintentional misrepresentation. For example, we do not generally hold a people to be liars if they truly believe what they are saying. Note that even in such cases of unintentional misrepresentation, the source of the persuasion is considered a key element in the ethics of persuasion.

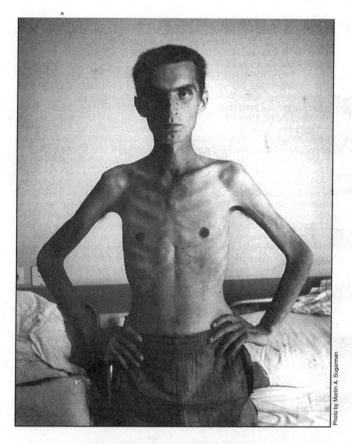

Photo by Martin A. Sugarman

President Clinton, You Have Allowed the Perpetration of Genocide in Bosnia Under the Sponsorship of the United Nations.

Urge the President to unilaterally lift the arms embargo.
Call 202-456-1111.
Or fax 202-456-2461.

MUSLIM PUBLIC AFFAIRS COUNCIL
3010 WILSHIRE BLVD. SUITE 217 • LOS ANGELES, CALIFORNIA 90010 • 213-383-3443

Does this ad use propaganda techniques or ethically sound principles of persuasion?

Box 4.1
PROPAGANDA TECHNIQUES

Name Calling: attaching a negative label to a person, group or idea that the propagandist opposes. (e.g., "This bill is racist.")

Glittering Generality: attaching a positive label to a person, group or idea that the propagandist endorses. (e.g., "That bill is democratic.")

Transfer: associating the topic with something the receiver approves (e.g., "A vote for that bill is a vote for America!") or condemns (e.g., "A vote for that bill is a vote for repression!").

Testimonial: using the reputation of a person to gain endorsement ("The president of the United States supports this idea") or rejection ("Adolf Hitler supported this idea").

Plain Folks: linking the source with the qualities of the receivers (e.g., "I am a middle-class American, just like you, and I would never support an idea that would harm the middle class").

Card Stacking: selecting only the evidence that supports the propagandist's cause, even if that falsifies or distorts that evidence (e.g., "No major magazine has been able to successfully criticize this proposal").

Band Wagon: using the notion that "everyone is doing it" in place of evidence and reasoning (e.g., "Everyone who is anyone has joined this club").

SOURCE: Alfred McClung Lee and Elizabeth Biant Lee, *The Fine Art of Propaganda* (1939). San Francisco: International Society for General Semantics, 1979. (Now located in Concord, CA.)

Over the centuries, ethics theorists have developed many "dos" and "taboos" of ethical intentions for communicators.

Box 4.2 shows Richard L. Johannesen's list of eleven ethical standards. Notice that all of these rules focus on the actions of the source.

These standards can be condensed into four ethical principles represented by the acronym TAGS: *T*ell the truth, *A*cknowledge others, *G*ive sufficient information, *S*how the consequences.

- **T**ell the truth
- **A**cknowledge others
- **G**ive sufficient information
- **S**how the consequences

Box 4.2
ETHICAL RULES

1. Do not use false, fabricated, misrepresented, distorted, or irrelevant evidence to support arguments or claims.

2. Do not intentionally use unsupported, misleading, or illogical reasoning.

3. Do not represent yourself as informed or as an "expert" on a subject when you are not.

4. Do not use irrelevant appeals to divert attention or scrutiny from the issue at hand. Among the appeals that commonly serve such a purpose are: "smear" attacks on an opponent's character; appeals to hatred and bigotry; derogatory insinuations—innuendos; God and Devil terms that cause intense but unreflective positive or negative reactions.

5. Do not ask your audience to link your idea or proposal to emotion-laden values, motives, or goals to which it actually is not related.

6. Do not deceive your audience by concealing your real purpose, by concealing the group you represent, or by concealing your position as an advocate of a viewpoint.

7. Do not distort, hide, or misrepresent the number, scope, intensity, or undesirable features of consequences or effects.

8. Do not use "emotional appeals" that lack a supporting basis of evidence or reasoning, or that would not be accepted if the audience had time and opportunity to examine the subject themselves.

9. Do not oversimplify complex, gradation-laden situations into simplistic two-valued, either–or, polar views or choices.

10. Do not pretend certainty where tentativeness and degrees of probability would be more accurate.

11. Do not advocate something in which you do not believe yourself.

TAGS offers a quick set of rules of integrity for individuals and organizations that are sources of persuasion.

Truthfulness is a vital virtue for persuaders. An honest representation of the facts, an appropriate explanation of the source's expertise and the qualifications of those cited in the message, and a sincere effort to communicate effectively with the receivers are all parts of the process

Box 4.3
SAMPLES OF CODES OF ETHICS
American Society of Newspaper Editors
Statement of Principles

Preamble

The First Amendment, protecting freedom of expression from abridgement by any law, guarantees to the people through their press a constitutional right, and thereby places on newspaper people a particular responsibility.

Thus journalism demands of its practitioners not only industry and knowledge but also the pursuit of a standard of integrity proportionate to the journalist's singular obligation.

To this end the American Society of Newspaper Editors sets forth this Statement of Principles as a standard encouraging the highest ethical and professional performance.

Article I: Responsibility

The primary purpose of gathering and distributing news and opinion is to serve the general welfare by informing the people and enabling them to make judgment on the issues of the time. Newspapermen and women who abuse the power of their professional role for selfish motives or unworthy purposes are faithless to the public trust.

The American press was made free not just to inform or just to serve as a forum for debate but also to bring an independent scrutiny to bear on the forces of power in the society, including the conduct of official power at all levels of government.

Article II: Freedom of the Press

Freedom of the press belongs to the people. It must be defended against encroachment or assault from any quarter, public or private.

Journalists must be constantly alert to see that the public's business is conducted in public. They must be vigilant against all who would exploit the press for selfish purposes.

(continued)

(continued from previous page)

Article III: Independence

Journalists must avoid impropriety and the appearance of impropriety as well as any conflict of interest or the appearance of conflict. They should neither accept anything nor pursue any activity that might compromise or seem to compromise their integrity.

Article IV: Truth and Accuracy

Good faith with the reader is the foundation of good journalism. Every effort must be made to assure that the news content is accurate, free from bias and in context, and that all sides are presented fairly. Editorials, analytical articles and commentary should be held to the same standards of accuracy with respect to facts as news reports.

Significant errors of fact, as well as errors of omission, should be corrected promptly and prominently.

Article V: Impartiality

To be impartial does not require the press to be unquestioning or to refrain from editorial expression. Sound practice, however, demands a clear distinction for the reader between news reports and opinion. Articles that contain opinion or personal interpretation should be clearly identified.

Article VI: Fair Play

Journalists should respect the rights of people involved in the news, observe the common standards of decency and stand accountable to the public for the fairness and accuracy of their news reports.

Persons publicly accused should be given the earliest opportunity to respond.

Pledges of confidentiality to news sources should be honored at all costs, and therefore should not be given lightly. Unless there is clear and pressing need to maintain confidences, sources of information should be identified.

of telling the truth. Persuaders have a covenant with the receivers. Audiences for persuasion have a right to expect the source to have thoroughly researched the topic, to have discovered the truth of a situation, and to present the position honestly.

Acknowledging others means that persuaders give credit where credit is due. Plagiarism is a serious ethical problem. The temptations are great—time is short in preparing a persuasive pitch and there is so much information out there that no one person can be expected to keep up with it all. But the consequences of plagiarism are devastating. The source loses credibility, suffers embarrassment, and may be subject to even more severe disciplinary action.

For example, Senator Joseph Biden dropped out of the presidential race in 1987 because he had plagiarized speeches of other politicians. Here is how *Time* described the events.

> Biden's troubles began with stories in the New York *Times* and Des Moines *Register* three weeks ago pointing out that the Senator's emotional closing statement during an Iowa Democratic debate duplicated a televised speech by Labor Party Leader Neil Kinnock during last spring's British election campaign. . . . [T]he Kinnock tape opened the floodgates. Students of Robert Kennedy's rhetoric began pointing out that some of Kennedy's words—and Hubert Humphrey's too—had been coming out of Biden's mouth, without attribution.[5]

Plagiarism is not limited to the political arena. In 1991, H. Jacob Maitre, a dean at Boston University, was accused of plagiarizing an essay by film critic Michael Medved in a commencement speech.[6]

Plagiarism is also a problem in schools and universities. Most universities have policies condemning such unethical practices. Using another person's intellectual product without proper credit is a violation of honor codes and carries severe punishment. You will also find plagiarism condemned by most codes of ethics of professional organizations.

Giving sufficient information means that persuaders should not commit a sin of omission. In presenting ideas, sources are under an ethical obligation to give as complete a picture as time and energy permit. Leaving out critical information, failing to put quotations in their proper context, or omitting contradictory evidence, deliberately or accidentally, are detrimental to the source's integrity and the integrity of the group the source represents.

Finally, ethical persuaders *show the consequences* of their ideas. In persuasive appeals, the sources should seek to promote positions that benefit the audiences. They are obliged to behave ethically with a clear recognition of the moral consequences of their actions.

Unethical persuaders do serious damage to the rhetorical relationship. Audiences may disregard important information or reject a beneficial proposal just because the source pretended the ideas were original. People also generalize their suspicions to all speakers of the offender's class, casting doubts on the integrity of all politicians, or representatives of the company, or students of the school.

ETHICS AND MESSAGES

While sources are a major component of the ethical dimensions of persuasion, they are not the only element that bears on ethics. The message also has important ethical ramifications.

No one is deceived by Monopoly money. The problem of counterfeit currency is that it appears to be genuine but is not. In a similar vein, no one is persuaded by ridiculous messages. The problem is that there are persuasive messages that appear to be genuine but are not legitimate. Such counterfeit persuasive messages are called fallacies, and they are insidious not because they are defective but because they are defective while appearing to be genuine.

Because fallacies have been studied for centuries, scholars have generated long lists of fallacies and many have acquired some alien-sounding labels, but fallacies are relatively easy to understand even though they may be difficult to spot in persuasive practices.

We can divide the list of fallacies into two major categories: content errors and process errors. If either the content or the process of persuasion is fallacious, the result will be counterfeit.

CONTENT ERRORS

Content errors involve problems with the substance of the persuasion. While these fallacies may seem persuasive, closer examination indicates that the underlying material is defective. Here are six of the most common content errors persuaders use either intentionally or unintentionally.

Faulty Generalizations

Sometimes people derive generalized ideas from specific instances. For example, our neighbor might generalize that domestic automobiles are poorly constructed, based upon his experience with his last two automobile purchases. While some generalizations are legitimate, some are not and are considered fallacious. Faulty generalizations occur when persuaders jump to conclusions without carefully considering a sufficient number of cases or when they ignore counterexamples. To illustrate, if a politician argues that privatizing schools produces improved graduation rates, it is possible that other factors that influence graduation rates were ignored. It is possible that the private school's student population excluded many students at risk of dropping out and included parents better motivated to stress the importance of remaining in school.

Sometimes generalizations are faulty because counterexamples are ignored. A student once argued, for example, that South Vietnam could never win the Vietnam War because no war was ever won fighting from the south to the north. When another student pointed out that Rome conquered what is now France, Germany, and Britain, the counterexample was dismissed as "the exception that proves the rule."

Faulty Cause

Persuaders very often look for causes in arguing a case. Financial analysts, for example, will look for leading indicators of inflation because certain conditions such as commodities futures prices, production capacity, unemployment rates, and the rate of increase in wages are all factors that create inflationary pressure. But causal reasoning can also be fallacious. Astrology, for example, claims that one's birth date and time are factors that influence one's personality and fortune. The location of the planets at the time of one's birth has nothing to do with one's current life circumstances, yet many people are true believers and seriously advocate living one's life according to the advice of "psychic friends."

Faulty Analogy

Persuaders often make legitimate comparisons in their arguments. Decisions in court cases, for example, often turn on whether the matter under consideration is similar to an established legal precedent. Such reasoning rests upon the idea that what is true of a known case will also be true of a similar case under consideration.

Analogies, too, can be fallacious and lead to questionable conclusions. For example, many small businesses will make decisions based upon the actions of major corporations without realizing that the circumstances for a publicly traded, multinational company are vastly different from circumstances for a small, private business. A computer system that is appropriate for a major drug company like Merck would be inappro-

Public Service

1   **Dan Bachmann/Terry Taylor**, art directors
    Ted Nelson, writer/creative director
    Earle Palmer Brown (St. Petersburg, FL), agency
    Friends of Animals, client

2   (poster)
    Tom Lichtenheld, art director
    Sally Hogshead, writer
    Bill Westbrook, creative director
    Buck Holzmer, photographer
    Fallon McElligott (Minneapolis), agency
    Children's Defense Fund and Friends, client

3   **Robert Prins**, art director
    Jeff Spiegel, writer
    Humans for Humans, agency
    Los Angeles Mission, client

Emotional appeals can be effective, as this ad illustrates. But emotional appeals can also be misused.

priate for a small drugstore; the businesses are just not analogous. While we all recognize that "you cannot compare apples and oranges," the real trick is to recognize that we actually have an apple and an orange.

Appeal to Emotion

As we indicated in Chapter One, emotions are powerful persuasive forces, so why should an appeal to emotion be considered a fallacy? The ethical problem is not that persuaders use emotional appeals but that they may misuse emotional appeals. Prosecutors, for example, are restricted in displaying gruesome pictures of a crime scene because the value of the exhibit as proof must outweigh its emotional impact that may "inflame the passions" of the jury. In other words, decisions must not be based on emotion alone.

Another misuse of emotional appeal is the use of overly emotional appeals that can incite mob behavior. For example, while the U.S. Constitution protects freedom of speech, there are restrictions on the use of "fighting words" or on creating a clear and present danger through the use of words. Freedom of speech does not extend to inciting riots or making threats against others.[7]

Appeal to Authority

While endorsements are common forms of appeal in sales, this type of persuasion can also be abused. In this type of fallacy, the persuader argues that we should accept the claim on the basis of authority rather than for any cogent reason. For example, a politician who opposes a constitutional amendment on the grounds that the Founding Fathers did not include the issue in the Constitution, rather than articulating a case against the suggested amendment, is misusing the appeal to authority. Parents often use this fallacious appeal to authority when they claim the child should do something "because I said so."

Faulty Statistics

There is an old saying that "figures don't lie but liars can figure." Statistics can be every bit as misleading as any other form of persuasion. Unfortunately, most people place too much faith in quantification, and this can lead to disastrous results.

Among the many instances of the abuse of statistics in advertising cited by Cynthia Crossen in *Tainted Truth* is the case of a hundred drivers who tested Chrysler cars against the Toyota Tercel Deluxe and preferred Chrysler's car 91 to 9. As Crossen explained, "It is true that among the 100 people tested—a tiny group—Chrysler came out on top. But whether any other group of 100 people would find the same thing is doubtful. That is because Chrysler's group was not representative of America—not even of California, where all the respondents lived. All were so-called import intenders, defined by Chrysler as domestic brand car owners 'who are thinking about buying an imported car.' Not a single one of them owned a foreign car."[8]

PROCESS ERRORS

Just as a product can be defective because of the manufacturing process rather than the raw materials, persuasion can be fallacious because of the process of reasoning employed. Four of the most common types of fallacious reasoning are outlined below.

Question Begging

This type of fallacy usually employs a circular definition, so that the point at issue is defined within the claim or the issue is evaded otherwise. For example, the argument that claims "If guns are outlawed, only outlaws will have guns" makes no reasonable point about Fourth Amendment rights, about the use of guns in sport, or in any other reasonable situation. Instead, it reasons in a circular manner and *appears* to be making a legitimate point because it is couched in "if . . . then" language which we associate with logic.

Non Sequitur

This is a Latin term for "it does not follow." In other words, a common fallacy is to pose reasons that upon close inspection are actually irrelevant. The argument that we should retain a wasteful government agency because eliminating it would not make a perceptible dent in the deficit is a clear example of a *non sequitur*. Saving only a fractional percentage of the deficit may not show significant impact but that does not justify continuing a wasteful program.

Ad Hominem

Again a Latin phrase (lit., "to the person"), here the argument is not based on issues but rather on the personalities of the advocate. To argue that only racists call for abolishing Affirmative Action is to focus on the personalities of the advocates rather than the reasonableness of the argument. In a like manner, to claim that only bleeding heart liberals support Affirmative Action is to commit the *ad hominem* fallacy on the opposing side of the issue.

Slippery Slope

This is one of the most common forms of fallacies. The argument is that taking one step inevitably leads one down a slippery slope to an undesirable situation. This was used in the "domino theory" that if Vietnam fell, Cambodia would be next, and then the Philippines, and then Australia, and then the United States; therefore, we must fight in Vietnam. The slippery slope fallacy is also used in more contemporary arguments. For example, someone might argue that, if we allow prayer in schools, we shall be opening the door to state-based religion; next we shall have school boards constructing acceptable prayers, and then the government controlling religion.

ETHICS AND CHANNELS

Throughout this chapter you will find codes of ethics from a variety of professional organizations. An examination of these codes indicates that while most issues of ethics and persuasion deal with the intentions of the persuader and the quality of the persuasive message, there are also ethical aspects of the media used in the persuasive effort. For example, Article 6 of the Code of Professional Standards for the Practice of Public Relations states: "A member shall not engage in any practice which tends to corrupt the integrity of channels of communication or the process of government."[9]

How does ethics apply to the channels of communication? Philosopher Jacques Ellul claimed that "no propaganda can exist unless a mass can be reached and set into motion. Yet, the peculiar and remarkable fact is that the mass media really create their own public. . . ."[10] In other words, because the media have the effect of an agent, they take on the ethical responsibilities of a persuasive agent. For example, if a newspaper presents an unbalanced picture in a political race by providing more positive stories, more pictures, and better placement for one candidate and more negative stories, fewer flattering pictures, and coverage only on the inside pages for the opposing candidate, the newspaper has committed an unethical act even though the newspaper is not a single person but rather a collection of people serving as a conduit of political information.

The media are frequently subjected to criticism on moral grounds. When a male talk show guest was surprised on television by a male admirer and later killed that person, the persuasive impact of the media came under attack. As Senator Bob Dole argued, the entertainment industry has crossed over from portraying violence to inciting it. "A line has been crossed—not just of taste but of human dignity and decency. It is crossed every time sexual violence is given a catchy tune. When teen suicide is set to an appealing beat. When Hollywood's dream factories turn out nightmares of depravity."[11] Dole's polemic, like Dan Quayle's attack on the influence of the television character, Murphy Brown, and Spiro Agnew's assault on the impact of newscasters share a common theme of objecting to the persuasive power of mass media and its impact on people.

In a very real sense, the media must acknowledge their ethical responsiblity for the content of their channels and its potentially destructive effect on receivers. As E. S. Strafford wrote,

> If this new technology offers tools for shaping attitudes and opinions in remarkably more controllable ways, are we really obligated to see that such tools are not misused? As these new technologies permit compelling persuasion, provide seemingly incontestable evidence, and

rationalize so convincingly almost any philophy or action, they will certainly be used, for good or ill. Should we assume that this emerging new capability, the capability to influence and eventually to control human behavior, must find its level of application by trial and error in the whole scheme of things? In other words, shall this civilization, like certain inept managements, merely react, and through a period of violent oscillations of censorship and gross permissiveness eventually develop an acceptable norm for mass communications? Or should we try to anticipate, try to employ these enormous new information and knowledge powers toward agreed upon cultural goals which, hopefully, will contribute to a happier, more stable, progresssively better world?[12]

As technology changes and develops, the issue of ethics takes on new forms. Should information providers, like America On Line or CompuServe, be responsible for the content of the messages generated by their subscribers? Is it ethical for people to provide recipes for homemade bombs to potential terrorists over computer networks? To what extent should the government intercede in the public access programs on cable network channels? These and many more issues of ethics must be addressed by the participants in the electronic world of the twenty-first century.

ETHICS AND RECEIVERS

So far, we have focused on the ethical dimensions of creating persuasive messages, but ethics extends to receivers as well. In cases of fraud there are two ethical aspects: The source is under an ethical obligation to present a fair message and the receiver is under an ethical obligation to avoid being deceived. While some would argue that the seller must be honest, there are those who argue *caveat emptor*—let the buyer beware. Where does the ethical obligation lie—with the source or with the receiver? Communication expert Kenneth Anderson has resolved this dilemma with the 200% theory of responsibility. According to Anderson,

> In evaluating our activity, typically we accept responsibility for the impact of our communication efforts both on ourselves and on other people. We thus are (or should be) willing to assume 100% responsibility for the action and impact of our communication effort. . . .
>
> As we think of ourselves in the role of receiver we certainly wish to exercise our own judgment. We want and need to assure ourselves that actions urged, means employed, and effects eventuated will meet our ethical requirements. Thus, in our role as receiver we will surely wish to assume responsibility, 100% responsibility, for our decisions/actions.
>
> The result of all this is that we now have the 200% theory in which both the speaker/writer and listener/reader attempt to exercise the fullest of their ability responsibility for the communicative interaction and its result.[13]

Box 4.4

PUBLIC RELATIONS SOCIETY OF AMERICA CODE OF PROFESSIONAL STANDARDS FOR THE PRACTICE OF PUBLIC RELATIONS

Members of the Public Relations Society of America base their professional principles on the fundamental value and dignity of the individual, holding that the free exercise of human rights, especially freedom of speech, freedom of assembly and freedom of the press, is essential to the practice of public relations.

In serving the interests of clients and employers, we dedicate ourselves to the goals of better communication, understanding and cooperation among the diverse individuals, groups and institutions of society, and of equal opportunity of employment in the public relations profession.

We pledge:

To conduct ourselves professionally, with truth, accuracy, fairness and responsibility to the public;

To improve our individual competence and advance the knowledge and proficiency of the profession through continuing research and education;

And to adhere to the articles of the Code of Professional Standards for the Practice of Public Relations as adopted by the governing Assembly of the Society.

Articles of the Code

These articles have been adopted by the Public Relations Society of America to promote and maintain high standards of public service and ethical conduct among its members.

1. A member shall deal fairly with clients or employers, past and present, or potential, with fellow practitioners and the general public.
2. A member shall conduct his or her professional life in accord with the public interest.
3. A member shall adhere to truth and accuracy and to generally accepted standards of good taste.
4. A member shall not represent conflicting or competing interests without the express consent of those involved, given after a full disclosure of the facts; nor place himself or herself in a position where the member's interest is or may be in conflict with a duty to a client, or others, without a full disclosure of such interests to all involved.

(continued)

(continued from previous page)

5. A member shall safeguard the confidences of present and former clients, as well as those of persons or entities who have disclosed confidences to a member in the context of communications relating to an anticipated professional relationship with such member, and shall not accept retainers or employment that may involve disclosing using or offering to use such confidences to the disadvantage or prejudice of such present, former or potential clients or employers.

6. A member shall not engage in any practice which tends to corrupt the integrity of channels of communication or the processes of government.

7. A member shall not intentionally communicate false or misleading information and is obliged to use care to avoid communication of false or misleading information.

8. A member shall be prepared to identify publicly the name of the client or employer on whose behalf any public communication is made.

9. A member shall not make use of any individual or organization purporting to serve or represent an announced cause, or purporting to be independent or unbiased, but actually serving an undisclosed special or private interest of a member, client, or employer.

10. A member shall not intentionally injure the professional reputation or practice of another practitioner. Howver, if a member has evidence that another member has been guilty of unethical, illegal or unfair practices, including those in violation of this Code, the member shall present the information promptly to the proper authorities of the Society for action in accordance with the procedure set forth in Article XIII of the By-laws.

11. A member called as a witness in a proceeding for the enforcement of this Code shall be bound to appear, unless excused for sufficient reason by the Judicial Panel.

12. A member, in performing services for a client or employer, shall not accept fees, commissions or any other valuable consideration from anyone other than the client or employer in connection with those services without the express consent of the client or employer, given after a full disclosure of the facts.

13. A member shall not guarantee the achievement of specified results beyond the member's direct control.

14. A member shall, as soon as possible, sever relations with any organization or individual if such relationship requires conduct contrary to the articles of this Code.

Adopted 1954; Revised 1959, 1963, 1977, 1983

Box 4.5
THE ADVERTISING CODE OF AMERICAN BUSINESS

1. *Truth.* Advertising shall tell the truth, and reveal significant facts, the concealment of which would mislead the public.
2. *Responsibility.* Advertising agencies and advertisers shall be willing to provide substantiation of claims made.
3. *Taste and Decency.* Advertising shall be free of statements, illustrations or implications which are offensive to good taste or public decency.
4. *Disparagement.* Advertising shall offer merchandise or service on its merits and refrain from attacking competitors unfairly or disparaging their products, services or methods of doing business.
5. *Bait Advertising.* Advertising shall offer only merchandise or services which are readily available for purchase at the advertised price.
6. *Guarantees and Warranties.* Advertising of guarantees and warranties shall be explicit. Advertising of any guarantee or warranty shall clearly and conspicuously disclose its nature and extent, the manner in which the guarantor or warrantor will perform and the identitiy of the guarantor or warrantor.
7. *Price Claims.* Advertising shall avoid price or savings claims which are false or misleading, or which do not offer provable bargains or savings.
8. *Unprovable Claims.* Advertising shall avoid the use of exaggerated or unprovable claims.
9. *Testimonials.* Advertising containing testimonials shall be limited to those of competent witnesses who are reflecting a real and honest choice.

This code was developed by the American Advertising Federation and Association of Better Business Bureaus International. It has been endorsed by International Newspaper Advertising and Marketing Executives, Association of Newspaper Classified Advertising Managers, National Newspaper Association, Magazine Publishers Association, American Association of Advertising Agencies, National Association of Broadcasters and many other trade groups.

Clearly there is a moral obligation for receivers to apply their understanding of persuasive communication to analyzing and assessing the persuasive messages that bombard them. On the political front, citizens are obliged to be aware of the campaign strategies used to convince them. As Wendell Phillips said, "Eternal vigilance is the price of liberty."[14] In the commercial arena, consumers must be savvy clients.

Consumer advocate Ralph D. Davis reminds us of the myriad of competing messages that bombard each of us every day and cautions us to remember that we, the consumers, are ultimately the decision makers.[15] In short, we must all be aware of the ethical obligation we undertake as recipients of persuasive messages—the responsibility to think clearly and critically but not cynically about those persuasive messages.

Summary

Historically, persuasion has been linked to ethics, the moral dimension of human activity. This chapter has explored some of those relationships.

Persuasion was first examined in relationship to propaganda, the dissemination of ideological material for the purpose of advancing a cause. Studies of propaganda tended to focus on identifying techniques like card stacking and glittering generalities. But card stacking, a propaganda technique, is much like setting an agenda through persuasion, something *all* persuaders, not just propagandists, do. Glittering generalities are used by both heroes and villains, so there appears to be little inherently ethical or unethical about the techniques. Some people consider propaganda to be unethical, but the persuasive tactics do not define something as propaganda. Propaganda, then, seems to be a judgment about persuasive communication rather than an identifiable set of unethical techniques.

Since persuasion is an act done by an agent, it follows that there are clear links between ethics and sources of persuasion. The rules of ethical behavior for sources can be summarized by the acronym TAGS: Tell the truth, Acknowledge others, Give sufficient information, and Show the consequences of your ideas.

We also considered the relationship of ethics and messages, and here we focused specifically on fallacies and counterfeit persuasive messages. From the myriad of fallacies identified over the centuries, we selected some of the most common forms and divided those into the two categories of content and process fallacies. Content fallacies included faulty generalizations, faulty causes, faulty analogy, inappropriate appeals to emotion, misuse of appeal to authority, and faulty statistics. Process errors included question begging, *non sequitur* fallacies, *ad hominem* arguments, and the slippery slope flaws.

We also examined the relationship of ethics and channels. The development of electronic media has raised additional ethical matters. Instead of just the issues of sources and receivers, we are asking whether the media have ethical responsibility for the content they carry.

Finally, we touched on the ethical role of receivers in the persuasive process. If sources are 100 percent responsible for creating ethically sound messages, receivers are 100 percent responsible for applying critical thinking to attempts at persuasion.

Notes

1 M. Hirsh Goldberg, *The Book of Lies* (New York: Quill Books, 1990), pp. 101–102.

2 Quintilian, *The Institutes of Oratory*, trans. H. E. Butler, in 4 vols. (Cambridge, MA: Harvard University Press, 1968), XII.i.2–4.

3 John R. MacArthur, *Second Front: Censorship and Propaganda in the Gulf War* (New York: Hill and Wang, 1992), pp. 57–77.

4 Garth S. Jowett and Victoria O'Donnell, *Propaganda and Persuasion*, second edition (Newbury Park, PA: Sage Publications, 1992), p. 271.

5 Jacob V. Lamar, Jr. with David Beckwith and Hays Gorey, "And Then There Were Six," *Time* (October 5, 1987), p. 24.

6 George Easterbrook, "The Sincerest Flattery," *Newsweek* (July 29, 1991), p. 45.

7 See Oliver Wendell Holmes' famous decision in *Schenck v. United States*. Congressional Quarterly, *Guide to The U.S. Supreme Court* (Washington, DC: Congressional Quarterly, Inc., 1979), p. 397.

8 Cynthia Crossen, *Tainted Truth: The Manipulation of Fact in America* (New York: Simon and Schuster, 1994), p. 76.

9 Public Relations Society of America, "Code of Professional Standards for the Practice of Public Relations" in Conrad Fink, *Media Ethics* (New York: McGraw-Hill Book Company, 1988), p. 306.

10 Jacques Ellul, *Propaganda: The Formation of Men's Attitudes* (New York: Vintage Books, 1973), p. 104.

11 Robert Dole, "Remarks at GOP Fund Raiser May 31, 1995."

12 E. S. Safford, "The Need for a Public Ethic in Mass Communication," ed. Lee Thayer, *Ethics, Morality and the Media* (New York: Hastings House, Publishers, 1979), p. 147.

13 Kenneth E. Anderson, "Communication Ethics: The Nonparticipant's Role," *Southern Speech Communication Journal*, 49 (Spring 1984), p. 220.

14 Wendell Phillips, "Speech in Boston, Massachusetts, January 28, 1852," *Speeches Before the Massachusetts Anti-Slavery Society* (1853), p. 13.

15 Ralph D. Davis, *False Teeth to a Chicken* (Chicago: International Publishing Corporation, 1991), p. 9.

For Further Thought

1. Are there any situations (e.g., a physician talking to a terminally ill patient) in which the ethical rules of persuasion might not apply? If so, how do we distinguish those situations from ordinary persuasive situations?

2. Explore cases of plagiarism in speaking and writing. How do these compare to cases of forgery in the fine arts? What are the consequences of plagiarism at your college or university?
3. Are there any situations in which it is ethically permissible to lie? For example, would it be permissible to lie to save an innocent person's life?
4. Should the use of propaganda techniques described in this chapter invalidate the point being argued? What can persuaders do to avoid giving the impression of propaganda? What can receivers do to combat propaganda?
5. Read the "letters to the editor" column in your local paper. Do the writers use any of the fallacies described in this chapter?

For Further Reading

Crossen, Cynthia. *Tainted Truth*. New York: Simon and Schuster, 1994.

Denton, Robert E. Editor. *Ethical Dimensions of Political Communication*. New York: Praeger, 1991.

Johannesen, Richard L. *Ethics in Human Communication*. Third Edition. Prospect Heights, IL: Waveland Press, 1990.

Jowett, Garth S. and Victoria O'Donnell. *Propaganda and Persuasion*. Newbury Park, CA: Sage Publications, 1992.

Kahane, Howard. *Logic and Contemporary Rhetoric*. Sixth Edition. Belmont, CA: Wadsworth Publishing Company, 1992.

PART TWO

ELEMENTS OF PERSUASION

Chapter Five

SOURCES

Roger Ailes is a political consultant who served as an advisor to Ronald Reagan and George Bush. He summarized his principles of successful communication this way. *"You are the message.* What does that mean, exactly? It means that when you communicate with someone, it is not just the words you choose to send to the other person that make up the message. You are also sending signals about what kind of a person *you* are—by your eyes, your facial expression, your body movement, your vocal pitch, tone, volume, and intensity, your commitment to your message, your sense of humor, and many other factors."[1]

So far we have explored principles of persuasion in rhetorical theory, psychological and sociological theory, and the field of ethics. In this chapter we shall narrow the focus to examine the key element in the persuasive process that Ailes identified, the source.

ETHOS

As we noted in Chapter Two, Aristotle is credited with identifying ethos as a form of persuasive proof. "An orator," he wrote, "must not only try to make the argument of his speech demonstrative and worthy of belief; he must make his own character look right. . . . There are three things which inspire confidence in the orator's own character—the three, namely, that induce us to believe a thing apart from any proof of it: good sense, good moral character, and good will."[2] In other words, Aristotle advocated that persuaders must be perceived by their receivers as being people who are competent, trustworthy, and speaking in the best interests of the receivers.

Table 5.1

Factors of Ethos

Aristotle[a]	Falcione[b]	McCroskey and Young[c]	Berlo, Lemert, and Mertz[d]	Norman[e]
Good Sense	Competence	Competence	Qualification	Culture
Good Character	Safety	Character	Safety	Conscientiousness
	Emotional Stability			Emotional Stability
Goodwill				Agreeableness
			Dynamism	Extroversion

[a] Aristotle, *The Rhetoric*, Book 2, Chapter 1.

[b] Raymond L. Falcione, "The Factor Structure of Source Credibility Scales for Immediate Supervisors in the Organizational Context," *Central States Speech Journal*, 25 (Spring, 1974), pp. 63–66.

[c] James C. McCroskey and Thomas J. Young, "Ethos and Credibility: The Construct and Its Measurement After Three Decades," *Central States Speech Journal*, 32 (Spring, 1981), pp. 24–34.

[d] David Berlo, James Lemert, and Robert Mertz, "Dimensions for Evaluating the Acceptability of Message Sources," *Public Opinion Quarterly*, 33 (1969), pp. 563–576.

[e] Warren T. Norman, "Toward an Adequate Taxonomy of Personality Attributes," *Journal of Abnormal and Social Psychology*, 66 (June 1963), 574–583.

Contemporary scholars, too, have demonstrated the important role of ethos in persuasive communication. As James McCroskey and Thomas Young acknowledged, "Throughout most of the twenty-four-hundred-year history of the study of rhetoric, ethos has held a central position. Aristotle's view that ethos is the most potent means of persuasion has been supported by many contemporary rhetorical scholars."[3]

Using a measurement technique known as semantic differential scales, in which bipolar terms like "trained . . . untrained," "dishonest . . . honest" are used to rate sources, scholars have identified over sixty elements that constitute receivers' perceptions of ethos. These elements appear to be related to a few broad categories as summarized in Table 5.1.

It is clear that while there is not complete agreement about the factors influencing an audience's perception of the source's credibility, there are at least three overall dimensions that receive general agreement: competence, trustworthiness, and dynamism. In other words, a source must be perceived as competent, informed about the topic, intelligent, and trained in the area under discussion. In addition to being

Box 5.1
ENHANCING ETHOS

In *The Communication Handbook*, Joseph DeVito suggested several ways a speaker can enhance ethos.

To increase one's competence he suggested that sources should "(1) Tell the audience of your special experience or training that qualify you to speak on your specific topic. . . . (2) Cite a variety of research sources. . . . (3) Stress the particular competencies of your sources if your audience is not aware of them. . . . (4) Demonstrate confidence with your materials and with the speech situation generally. . . . (5) Demonstrate your command of the language. . . . (6) Do not needlessly call attention to your inadequacies as a spokesperson."

To demonstrate one's trustworthiness or character DeVito recommended: "(7) Stress your fairness. . . . (8) Stress your concern for enduring values. . . . (9) Stress your similarity with the audience, particularly your beliefs, attitudes, values, and goals. . . . (10) Demonstrate your long-term consistency. . . . (11) Demonstrate a respect and courtesy for the audience members. . . . (12) Make it clear to the audience that you are interested in their welfare rather than simply seeking self-gain."

Finally, DeVito provided four suggestions to improve dynamism or, as he termed it, charisma: "(13) Demonstrate a positive orientation to the public speaking situation and to the entire speaker–audience encounter. . . . (14) Demonstrate assertiveness. . . . (15) Be enthusiastic. . . . (16) Be emphatic."

SOURCE: Joseph DeVito, *The Communication Handbook* (New York: Harper & Row, 1986), pp. 84–86.

perceived as competent, a source must be perceived as trustworthy, that is, as being fair, objective, unselfish, sincere. Finally, sources must be perceived as dynamic: frank, decisive, and energetic. In a study of 153 students at the University of New Mexico, Lawrence Rosenfeld and Timothy Plax concluded that the dynamism feature may well be the most important factor of a communicator's credibility.[4]

Box 5.1 illustrates how speakers should operate to enhance each of the three principal areas of ethos. DeVito has provided a number of ways sources can encourage positive perceptions in the minds of their receivers.

DeVito, like Aristotle, emphasized the importance of source credibility in speaking situations. Contemporary studies of business speakers reflect that the Aristotelian concept of ethos remains influential in gaining an audience's acceptance.[5] But not all persuasive situations involve speechmaking. To fully understand the role of the source, we must broaden the concept of ethos to include features and situations beyond the traditional concept of ethos.

SOURCE CREDIBILITY

Contemporary scholars prefer to use the concept of source credibility rather than ethos because it incorporates a broader range of persuasive situations.[6] As we noted in the previous section, whether the term is ethos or source credibility, the constituent elements appear to be features of competence, trustworthiness, and goodwill.

The research on source credibility is extensive and occasionally contradictory. For example, Charles Gruner's research indicated that the use of humor can enhance perceptions of character, but Pat Taylor found that using humor may actually decrease credibility.[7] Despite such contradictory findings, there appears to be consensus on at least five principles of source credibility.

1. *Highly credible sources will produce more persuasive effect than low credibility sources.*

    Carl Hovland and Walter Weiss conducted a classic study in the 1950s that confirmed Aristotle's emphasis on the importance of credibility.[8] Identical persuasive messages on topics like antihistamine drugs and the future of movies were provided to two groups of college students. For one group the messages were identified as coming from highly credible sources but for the other group the identical messages were attributed to a low credibility source. The results confirmed that opinion change was greater for the messages identified as coming from a highly credible source.

    While many studies have confirmed the principle of the strong influence of highly credible sources, there is a definitional problem that should be mentioned. The problem lies in defining a low credibility source.

    In real-life situations, we rarely encounter the full force of persuasion from low credibility sources. For example, if we find a particular talk show host to have low credibility, we are more likely to change the channel than to listen to the story.

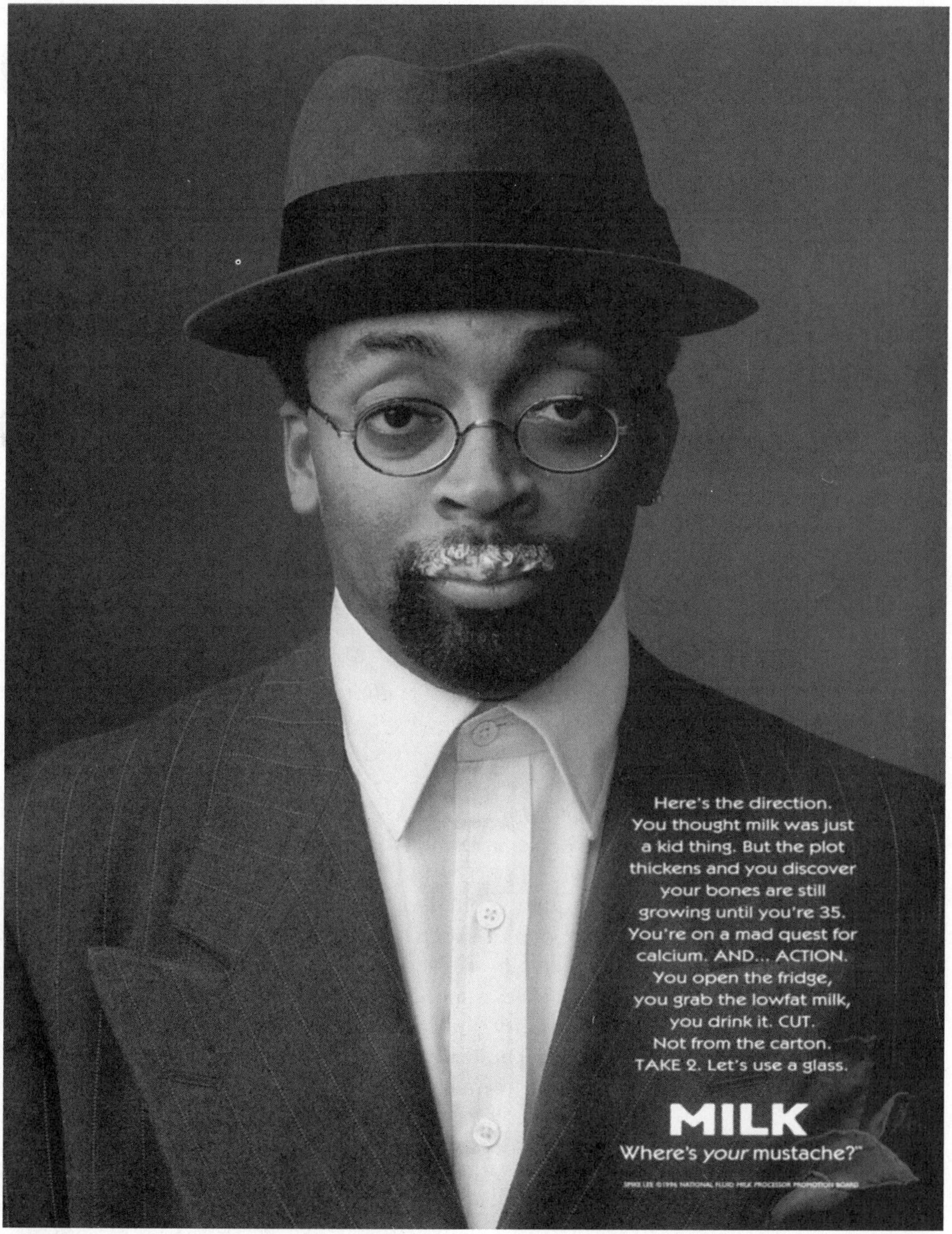

Credible sources generate persuasive effect.

In real-life situations, people are more likely to rate a source as neutral rather than as having low credibility. In a study of the characteristics of low levels of credibility, Ruth Ann Clark, Roy Stewart, and Alan Marston reported that in "the low credibility condition, mean ratings were closer to neutral than to the low end of the scale on every dimension."[9] In other words, persuaders are much more likely to engender neutral perceptions than low ratings in receivers.

Even though people may tend to be favorably disposed or, at worst, neutral about others, the influence of *high* credibility is undeniable. As executive communication consultant Myles Martel wrote, "Credibility is the major pillar to any persuasive strategy."[10]

2. *Credibility is not something a source has; it the receiver's perceptions of the source.*

This generalization is an important principle for us to remember. In persuasion, we are what we are perceived as being. Bruce VandenBergh, Lawrence Solely, and Leonard Reid studied the perceptions of credibility in advertisers. Their conclusion highlights the principle of perception. "This study found the highly credible advertiser to be perceived as: Attractive or likeable, trustworthy, prestigious, competent, competitive, and familiar. . . . Knowledge of the dimensions which make advertisers credible sources *in the eyes of the consumer* is of obvious value to advertisers who are concerned with the believability of their advertising messages."[11]

Consider, for example, the impact of oral delivery factors on persuasive appeals. David Addington studied the impact of vocal cues on credibility. The four specific vocal cues he studied were rate, vocal quality, pitch variety, and articulation. He concluded that perceptions of competence, trustworthiness and dynamism were all affected by delivery and that articulation cues, the actual production of clear speech sounds, had the most significant effect on credibility.[12] Clearly the *perceptions of the receivers* are what counts in persuasion, and therefore their perceptions of the source are what counts in credibility.

Because source credibility is actually a perception by the receivers, Robert Burns' adage about "the gift to see ourselves as others see us" is particularly relevant. In persuasion the gift to see ourselves as others see us is translated into what rhetorical critics Rod Hart and Don Burks called "rhetorical sensitivity."[13]

According to Hart and Burks, rhetorically sensitive sources neither pander to the interests of the audience nor do they rigidly hold to their views, unwilling to adapt to their receivers. Rhetorically sensitive sources, in this view, are flexible and are willing to strategically adjust their communication to their audience to attain their persuasive goal.

Our second principle of source credibility also means that since source credibility is a perception, the source cannot really gain or lose it. But the source can alter the receivers' perceptions by manipulating persuasive variables. Some of those variables are discussed later in the text. For the moment, let us turn to our third principle of credibility.

3. *Credibility is not a fixed entity.*

Some of the earliest studies of source credibility confirmed that the effects of credibility tend to wash out over time. Kelman and Hovland, for example, tested audience responses to recorded messages on lenient treatment for juvenile delinquents. The same message was introduced to three different groups. For one group the message was identified as coming from a judge (high credibility), for a second group the source was identified as a member of a studio audience (neutral credibility), and for the third group the source was identified as an ex-criminal who had been a juvenile delinquent (low credibility). As expected, the "judge" version showed more opinion change than the "ex-criminal." When Kelman and Hovland readministered questionnaires about juvenile delinquency to the same people they had tested three and four weeks earlier, they found that the group exposed to the high credibility source showed less opinion change than they had immediately after exposure to the message.[14]

More contemporary studies confirm that credibility changes even within the persuasive process. Robert Brooks and Thomas Schiedel tape-recorded a speech and spliced seven 30-second silences into a 25-minute recording. The receivers evaluated the credibility of the speaker during the pauses as well as at the end of the speech. A control group heard an uninterrupted version and filled out the evaluion form only after the speech. The results indicated that the source's credibility rose and fell during the speech.[15]

In summary, research supports that credibility is not a stable perception. It is a variable that can change even during the message itself as well as after the message is completed.

4. *Credibility is linked to external factors.*

One of the key differences between ethos and source credibility is that source credibility includes factors extrinsic to the rhetorical message, whereas ethos is limited to the elements of the art of rhetoric. Some of the extrinsic factors that are most closely related to credibility are power, physical attractiveness, and similarity.

In terms of human relationships, **power** is the ability of one person to control or direct another. In persuasion this often manifests itself in terms of authority. The most famous example of the study of authority was a series of experiments conducted by Stanley Milgram. In these studies, Milgram asked people to participate in a "learning experience" by administering electric shocks to people who got the answer wrong. In reality the "learners" were not harmed but the "teachers" were told to continue administering the "shocks" even though the learners begged them to stop. Despite their belief that they were administering painful, even potentially lethal, shocks, 62 percent obeyed the dictates of the experimenter to continue administering the shocks.[16] The experiments demonstrated, among other things, that people will ordinarily follow the instructions of an authority figure. Clearly, if a persuader stands in a power relationship with the receiver, compliance is easier to achieve.

Lawrence Wheeless, Robert Barraclough, and Robert Stewart argued that "investigation of power and compliance-gaining belongs within the domain of persuasion studies."[17] They identified three mechanisms of power tactics: (1) previewing expectancies and/or consequences, (2) invoking relationships and/or identification, and (3) summoning values and/or obligations. The first tactic involves the kind of power that teachers have with students in motivating them to study. Teachers typically have the power to reward or punish with grades and usually make their expectations for behavior clear on the syllabus. The second kind of tactic (invoking relationships and/or identification) is the type of power relationship that most politicians have with their constituents. This type of power attempts to establish identification between the source and the receiver and may involve such appeals as flattery, liking, and esteem. Finally, there are power relationships that invoke common values and/or obligations. For example, our parents have a legitimate power that oblige us to comply with their requests. This type of persuasion may use appeals like guilt, debt, and moral appeal.

Another element of persuasion frequently studied is the matter of **physical attractiveness.** Several studies have confirmed that when a source is attractive, there will be more compliance than when the source is unattractive.[18]

Advertisers, of course, have recognized the impact of endorsements by attractive people. Your campus brochures, for example, are likely to show beautiful people in front of attractive buildings on lovely days. The more appealing the source, the more likely it is that the receiver will be persuaded. In other words, physical attractiveness is a definite advantage for the credibility of sources.

Finally, an important extrinsic feature of source credibility is **similarity** of source and receiver. A review of literature on source credibility led Winston Brembeck and William Howell to conclude "[s]imilarity between the persuader and persuadee in terms of culture, race, tradition, customs, and values apparently can be a helpful source of influence. Similarity of attitude toward the topic is likely to be the most important influence."[19] Reviewing much of the same literature, Ronald Applbaum and Karl Anatol concluded that "[w]hile we can link source–receiver similarity to source attraction, there is little evidence that source–receiver similarity affects the receiver's image of the source's honesty, integrity, objectivity, or intelligence."[20] Apparently the evidence for the influence of similarity is not entirely clear.

A classic study confirming the importance of similarity was conducted by Timothy Brock.[21] Unlike many studies of credibility, Brock conducted his study in an actual paint store with real customers. He found that customers buying paint were more likely to follow the recommendations of a salesperson they perceived as having painting experiences similar to their own, even if the recommendation was for a more expensive product.

In contrast, Michael Sunnafrank found that similarities between source and receiver do not always influence the persuasive process;[22] other credibility factors may be more important than similarity. Other studies have also found that persuasive effectiveness can actually be *reduced* by similarity.[23] There appears to be some empirical support for the maxim that familiarity breeds contempt.

It appears that similarity between the source and the receiver may be important in some circumstances but it is not a determining factor in the persuasive process. Daniel J. O'Keefe phrased it well when he wrote, "Perhaps it is now clear just how inadequate is a generalization such as 'Greater similarity leads to greater persuasive effectiveness.' The effects of similarity on persuasive outcomes are complex and indirect, and no single easy generalization will encompass those varied effects."[24]

A study of advertising by C. Akin and M. Block compared ads using celebrity endorsements with advertisements using noncelebrity endorsements. Their findings indicated that while both celebrity and noncelebrity endorsements influenced the audience's intent to purchase, the celebrity endorsers were perceived as more trustworthy and competent.[25] Celebrities have the power of their celebrity status, their physical attractiveness or "stage presence," and our identification with them to enhance their persuasive persona.

5. *Credibility is linked to internal factors.*

There is a much stronger connection between credibility and internal factors than there is between credibility and external factors. Research clearly supports the nexus between the receivers' perceptions of source credibility and intrinsic factors like the content of the message, the language employed, and the delivery.

The use of sound and novel **evidence** enhances credibility. Fleshler, Ilardo, and Demoretcky, for example, found that the use of specific evidence enhances credibility more than the use of vague documentation.[26] A review by Michael Burgoon and Judee Burgoon indicated that sound reasoning also enhances credibility.[27]

The use of specific **linguistic cues** has also been shown to affect source credibility significantly. For example, the use of intense language (e.g., metaphors and adjectives) will reduce credibility if the audience is not favorably predisposed toward the speaker and the topic.[28]

Finally, **delivery factors** play a significant role in credibility. Some studies have found that delivery does not appear to affect the expertness dimension of credibility.[29] However, a recent study of twenty-two vocalic, kinesic, and proxemic cues came to the following conclusions: "Greater perceived competence and composure were associated with greater vocal and facial pleasantness, with greater facial expressiveness contributing to competence perceptions. Greater sociability was associated with more kinesic/proxemic immediacy, dominance, and relaxation, and with vocal pleasantness. Most of these same cues also enhanced character judgment."[30]

FACTORS THAT INFLUENCE CREDIBILITY

The research on ethos and source credibility is somewhat confusing. It is clear the one of the problems is that factors tend to affect each other, that credibility is a multidimensional concept. For example, credibility is influenced by the introduction of evidence, but evidence is a message factor; credibility is influenced by similarities between the source and the receiver, but similarity is both a source and a receiver variable. Furthermore, credibility appears to vary across contexts. Jo Liska, for example, tested credibility scales in four different situations and concluded: "The study was designed to explore the general hypothesis that listeners' conceptions of believability are dependent upon the topic-situation. The results clearly support the hypothesis."[31]

Despite the complexity of the feature and the sometimes contradictory findings of the research, we can offer a few generalizations about ethos and source credibility.

1. To increase credibility, sources should pay attention to situational variables. Such "extrinsic factors" as prior reputation, what is said in an introduction of the source, and status are influential. Summarizing research published to that date, Wayne Thompson advised, "To use extrinsic ethos advantageously, therefore, the speaker should arrange for a favorable introduction, provide cues of high status, and groom and conduct himself in accord with the listeners' values and expectations."[32] Sources can also enhance credibility by assuring that the receivers have information about the source's occupation, experience with the topic, and background.

2. To enhance credibility, sources must construct well-supported, organized messages with clear and vivid language presented in a professional manner. According to Marvin Karlins and Herbert Abelson, the audience's perceptions of the message directly affects its perceptions of the source.[33] Research has indicated that intrinsic factors of message construction are particularly important when receivers are involved in the issue.[34] Therefore, appropriate use of evidence and reasoning[35] as well as emotional appeals[36] enhance the perception of the source's credibility. Message organization has been shown to have an effect on credibility. A disorganized message is difficult for an audience to comprehend and reduces the perceived credibility of the source.[37] As we have already discussed, linguistic cues and presentational variables also influence the audience's perceptions of credibility.

3. To enhance credibility, sources should give careful consideration to the effects of the channel. In a study of the interaction of channels and source credibility on processing arguments, Steve Booth-Butterfield and Christine Gutkowski found that source factors in a printed message with simple content had no persuasive effect but that source-credibility factors become much more important in the more complicated auditory and visual media.[38] The adage that seeing is believing found some support in an interesting study by William Seiler. He found that low credibility sources who used visual aids enhanced their credibility, particularly the trustworthiness and authoritativeness factors.[39] A study by Alice Eagly and Shelly Chaiken found that receivers focused more on the source than the message when the communication was videotaped. A similar emphasis on the source was found when the message was audiotaped, but when the message was presented in written form, receivers focused on the message content rather than the source of the message.[40] In short, persuaders should carefully consider the most appropriate channel to use if source credibility is expected to be a significant factor in the persuasive process.

Summary

Since persuasion is a deliberate attempt to influence receivers, the source is the first key element to consider in examining the persuasive process. Sources are not only the originators of persuasive messages, they are also influential factors in their own right.

Ethos is the term Aristotle used to describe the use of the speaker's personality as proof in the rhetorical process. Traits of ethos that appear to be the most influential are competence, trustworthiness, and dynamism. Competence means that the source of the persuasive message should be perceived as being informed about the topic, intelligent, trained in the topic being advocated for maximum persuasive effect. Trustworthiness means that the source is seen as fair, objective, unselfish, and sincere. Finally, dynamic means that for maximum persuasive impact sources should come across as frank, decisive, and energetic.

Source credibility is a term that is closely related to Aristotle's concept of ethos. In that section we noted five principles of source credibility: (1) Highly credible sources will produce more persuasive effect than low credibility sources. (2) Credibility is not something a source has; it is the receiver's perceptions of the source. (3) Credibility is not a fixed entity. (4) Credibility is linked to external factors. (5) Credibility is linked to internal factors.

Finally, we examined three major factors that influence credibility. First, to increase credibility, sources should pay attention to situational variables such as prior reputation, what is said in an introduction of the source, and the receiver's perceptions of the source's status. Secondly, sources should construct well-supported, organized messages with clear and vivid language presented in a professional manner in order to enhance credibility. Third, to enhance credibility, sources should give careful consideration to the effects of the channel. More information about channels will be found in Chapter Seven.

Having examined the source as a key element in persuasion, we can turn our attention to the important factor of messages. In Chapter Six we shall explore studies from communication, psychology, and linguistics that explain how the message functions to influence receivers in the persuasive process.

Notes

[1] Roger Ailes and Jon Krausher, *You Are the Message* (New York: Doubleday, 1989), p. 25.

[2] Aristotle, "Rhetoric," trans. W. Rhys Roberts, *The Works of Aristotle*, vol. II (Oxford: Clarendon Press, 1924), Book II, Chapter 1.

[3] James C. McCroskey and Thomas J. Young, "Ethos and Credibility: The Construct and Its Measurement After Three Decades," *Central States Speech Journal,* 32 (Spring, 1981), p. 24. Used with permission of Central States Speech Association.

[4] Lawrence B. Rosenfeld and Timothy Plax, "The Relationship of Listener Personality to Perceptions of Three Dimensions of Credibility," *Central States Speech Journal,* 26 (Winter, 1975), p. 278.

[5] Larry Beason, "Strategies for Establishing an Effective Persona: An Analysis of Appeals to Ethos in Business Speeches," *Journal of Business Communication,* 28 (Fall, 1991), pp. 326–346; S. B. Kenton, "Speaker Credibility in Persuasive Business Communication: A Model Which Explains Gender Differences," *The Journal of Business Communication,* 26 (1989), pp. 143–157.

[6] Edward P. Bettinghaus and Michael J. Cody, *Persuasive Communication,* (New York: Holt, Rinehart and Winston, Inc., 1987), p. 84.

[7] Compare Charles R. Grunner, "The Effects of Humor in Dull and Interesting Informative Speeches," *Central States Speech Journal* 21 (1970), pp. 160–166, with Pat M. Taylor, "An Experimental Study of Humor and Ethos," *The Southern Speech Communication Journal,* 39 (Summer, 1974), pp. 359–366.

[8] Carl I. Hovland and Walter Weiss, "The Influence of Source Credibility on Communication Effectiveness," *Public Opinion Quarterly,* 15 (1951), pp. 635–650.

[9] Ruth Ann Clark, Roy Stewart, and Alan Marston, "Some Values of Highest and Lowest Levels of Credibility," *Central States Speech Journal*, 23 (Fall, 1972), p. 195. Used by permission of the Central States Communication Association.

[10] Myles Martel, *The Persuasive Edge* (New York: Fawcett Columbine, 1989), p. 25.

[11] Bruce VandenBergh, Lawrence Solely, and Leonard Reid, "Factor Study of Dimensions of Advertiser Credibility," *Journalism Quarterly*, 58 (Winter, 1981), p. 632. Emphasis added.

[12] David W. Addington, "The Effect of Vocal Variations on Ratings of Source Credibility," *Speech Monographs*, 38 (1971), pp. 242–247.

[13] Rod Hart and Don M. Burks, "Rhetorical Sensitivity and Social Interaction," *Speech Monographs*, 39 (June 1972), pp. 75–91.

[14] H. Kelman and C. Hovland, "'Reinstatement' of the Communicator in Delayed Measurement of Opinion Change," *Journal of Abnormal and Social Psychology*, 48 (1953), pp. 327–335.

[15] Robert D. Brooks and Thomas M. Schiedel, "Speech as a Process: A Case Study," *Speech Monographs*, 35 (March, 1968), pp. 1–7.

[16] Stanley Milgram, *Obedience to Authority*. New York: Harper & Row, 1974.

[17] Lawrence Wheeless, Robert Barraclough, and Robert Stewart, "Compliance-Gaining and Power in Persuasion," in Robert Bostrom, ed. *Communication Yearbook 7* (Beverly Hills, CA: Sage Publications, 1983), p. 139. Reprinted by permission of Sage Publications, Inc.

[18] Shelly Chaiken, "Communicator Physical Attractiveness and Persuasion," *Journal of Personality and Social Psychology*, 37 (1979), pp. 1387–1397; J. Mills and E. Aronson, "Opinion Change as a Function of Communicator's Attractiveness and Desire to Influence," *Journal of Personality and Social Psychology*, 1 (1965), pp. 73–77.

[19] Winston Brembeck and William Howell, *Persuasion: A Means of Social Influence* (Englewood Cliffs, NJ: Prentice-Hall, 1976), p. 266.

[20] Ronald Applbaum and Karl Anatol, *Strategies for Persuasive Communication* (Columbus, OH: 1974), p. 77.

[21] Timothy Brock, "Communicator–Recipient Similarity and Decision Change," *Journal of Personality and Social Psychology*, 1 (1965), pp. 650–654.

[22] Michael Sunnafrank, "Attitude Similarity and Interpersonal Attraction in Communication Processes: In Pursuit of an Ephemeral Influence," *Communication Monographs*, 50 (December 1983), pp. 273–284.

[23] Dominic Infante, "Similarity Between Advocate and Receiver: The Role of Instrumentality," *Central States Speech Journal*, 29 (1978), pp. 187–193; S. W. King and K. K. Soreno, "Attitude Change as a Function of Degree and Type of Interpersonal Similarity and Message Type," *Western Speech*, (1973), pp. 218–232; C. Leavitt and K. Kaigler-Evans, "Mere Similarity versus Information Processing: An Exploration of Source and Message Interaction," *Communication Research*, 2 (1975), pp. 300–306.

[24] Daniel J. O'Keefe, *Persuasion: Theory and Research* (Newbury Park, CA: Sage Publications, 1990), p. 151. Copyright © 1990 by Sage Publications. Reprinted by permission of Sage Publications, Inc.

[25] C. Akin and M. Block, "Effectiveness of Celebrity Endorsements," *Journal of Advertising Research*, 23 (1983), pp. 57–62.

[26] H. Fleshler, J. Ilardo, and J. Demoretcky, "The Influence of Field Dependence, Speaker Credibility Set, and Message Documentation on Evaluation of Speaker and Message Credibility," *Southern Speech Communication Journal,* 39 (1974), pp. 389–402.

[27] M. Burgoon and J. Burgoon, "Message Strategies in Influence Attempts," in G. Hanneman and W. McEwen, eds. *Communication and Behavior* (Reading, MA: Addison-Wesley, 1975), p. 153.

[28] J. J. Bradac, J. W. Bowers, and J. A. Courtright, "Three Language Variables in Communication Research: Intensity, Immediacy, and Diversity," *Human Communication Research,* 5 (1979), pp. 257–269.

[29] W. B. Pearce and F. Conklin, "Nonverbal Vocalic Communication and Perceptions of Speakers," *Speech Monographs,* 38 (1971), pp. 235–237; W. B. Pearce and B. J. Brommel, "Vocalic Communication in Persuasion," *Quarterly Journal of Speech,* 58 (1972), pp. 298–306.

[30] Judee K. Burgoon, Thomas Birk, and Michael Pfau, "Nonverbal Behaviors, Persuasion, and Credibility," *Human Communication Research,* 17 (Fall 1990), p. 140. Reprinted by permission of Sage Publications, Inc.

[31] Jo Liska, "Situational and Topic Variables in Credibility Criteria," *Communication Monographs,* 45 (March, 1978), p. 90.

[32] Wayne Thompson, *The Process of Persuasion* (New York: Harper & Row, 1975), p. 74.

[33] Marvin Karlins and Herbert Abelson, *Persuasion* (New York: Springer Publishing Company, 1970), p. 122.

[34] Richard E. Petty and John T. Cacioppo, "Issue Involvement Can Increase or Decrease Persuasion by Enhancing Message-Relevant Information," *Journal of Personality and Social Psychology,* 37 (1979), pp. 1915–1926.

[35] See, for example, J. Cantor, H. Alfonso, and D. Zillman, "The Persuasive Effectiveness of the Peer Appeal and a Communicator's First-Hand Experience," *Communication Research* 3 (1976), pp. 293–310.

[36] See, for example, M. A. Hewgill and G. R. Miller, "Source Credibility and Response to Fear-Arousing Communications," *Speech Monographs,* 32 (1965), pp. 95–101.

[37] H. Sharp and T. McClung, "Effects of Organization on the Speaker's Ethos," *Speech Monographs,* 33 (1966), pp. 182–183.

[38] Steve Booth-Butterfield and Catherine Gutowski, "Message Modality and Source Credibility Can Interact to Affect Argument Processing," *Communication Quarterly,* 41 (Winter, 1993), p. 88.

[39] William Seiler, "The Effects of Visual Materials on Attitudes, Credibility and Retention," *Speech Monographs,* 38 (1971), pp. 331–334.

[40] Alice Eagly and Shelly Chaiken, "Communication Modality as a Determinant of Persuasion: The Role of Communicator Salience," *Journal of Personality and Social Psychology,* 45 (1983), pp. 241–256.

For Further Thought

1. What is the difference between *ethos* and source credibility? Does the difference matter in creating persuasive messages?

Does the difference matter in analyzing and evaluating persuasive messages?

2. Monitor your reactions during an extended persuasive presentation like a political speech. Does your estimation of the source change during the presentation? What factors caused the change, if any occurred?

3. Find an example of an ad that appears to use "ordinary"-looking people rather than "attractive" people. Would the ad have more impact if it used an attractive person? Why or why not? Find an ad that uses attractive people. Would the ad have less impact if it used "ordinary"-looking people? Why or why not?

4. Consider a sales situation. What external factors can be manipulated to enhance the sales agent's credibility? Consider such situational features as conducting the interview in the agent's office versus conducting it in the client's home.

5. Channels as well as sources may have credibility. Are you more likely to believe an ad you see on television, one you hear on the radio, or one you read in your favorite magazine? What channel features influence credibility? Do different channels have different appeals to different audiences? What channels seem more credible to your grandparents' generation? to your parents' generation? to your generation?

For Further Reading

Ailes, Roger and John Kraushar, *You Are the Message.* New York: Doubleday, 1989.

Cialdini, Robert B. *Influence: The Psychology of Persuasion.* New York: Quill, 1994.

Davidson, Jeffrey P. *Blow Your Own Horn.* New York: Berkeley Books, 1991.

Dilenschnider, Robert L. *Power and Influence: Mastering the Art of Persuasion.* New York: Prentice-Hall Press, 1990.

Kouzes, James M. and Barry Posner. *Credibility.* San Francisco, CA: Jossey-Bass Publishers, 1993.

Tedeschi, J. T. *Impression Management Theory and Social Psychological Research.* New York: Academic Press, 1981.

Chapter Six

MESSAGES

In the last chapter we discussed sources of persuasion. You may have noticed that aspects of credibility are manifested in the source's behavior and words. In Chapter Eight we will examine aspects of receivers of persuasion. Again, observable behavior is our only measure of the attitudes, beliefs, or values held by respondents. In other words, we depend upon observable aspects of the persuasive process in discussing the principles, elements, and techniques of persuasion. In that regard, we are fortunate in this chapter because messages, generated by sources and received by respondents, are the most observable aspect of the persuasive process. To understand how messages generate a persuasive effect, we will begin by exploring the emerging field of semiotics.

PERSUASION AND SEMIOTICS

According to linguist David Crystal, semiotics is a broad term for the linguistic field that studies "the structure of all possible sign systems, and the role these play in the way we create and perceive patterns (or 'meanings') in sociocultural behaviour. The subject is all-inclusive, therefore, dealing with patterned human communication in all its modes (sound, sight, touch, smell, and taste)."[1] In other words, semiotics is a study of the total realm of human signs and symbols. Each of the three areas comprising semiotics—semantics, syntactical structure, and pragmatics—is directly related to persuasion.

SEMANTICS

Semantics is the study of the relationship of signs or symbols and their meanings. While linguists sometimes use the terms interchangeably, we will find it useful to distinguish between signs and symbols.

Semiotics is a study of the total realm of human signs and symbols.

Signs are perceivable indications of events. Signs, in other words, bear a direct correspondence to what they stand for. A fever, for example, is a sign of an infection. When threatened, a dog will signal its displeasure by raising its hackles, growling and baring its teeth, signs of the affective state of the animal. A symbol, like a sign, is also a representation of what it stands for, but in symbolism, the relationship between the symbol and its referent is an *indirect* relationship, a relationship created by the human mind. For example, the word "dog" does not bear a direct, one-to-one correspondence to the furry four-legged creature it represents. The relationship between the verbal or written symbol "dog" and its real world referent is imputed by our minds. That is why some linguistic communities use the symbol "dog," others use *"chien,"* others *"perro,"* and still others *"Hunde."*

The field of semiotics examines both the use of signs and the use of symbols in human communication. Much of what we say in this section about the human use of symbols also applies to signs since both are used in human persuasion. Since humans have attached meaning to symbols, and since there is a wide range of symbols to embed the most accurate meaning, symbols are often more complex than signs. For instance, selecting "cur" or "man's best friend" provides an indication of emotional as well as informational meaning in discussing the creatures we call "dogs."

Kenneth Burke, one of the contemporary rhetoricians mentioned in Chapter Two, once defined human beings as "symbol using" animals.[2] We are creatures that use—and some would add misuse—symbols. We use verbal and nonverbal symbols in sales presentations to convince clients to trade money symbols for an insurance policy constructed of symbols. We use verbal and nonverbal symbols in our personal lives to establish, to build relationships, and even to destroy interpersonal relationships with others. We use symbols to attract audiences to entertainments where we use various types of symbols for enjoyment in movies, sports events, and parties. In short, our lives are filled with symbols that serve to inform, persuade, and entertain.

Symbols are representations. Words or images represent the thoughts going on inside the symbol user, and perceiving those symbolic words or images influences the thoughts going on inside receivers. This relationship is illustrated in Figure 6.1.

Note that the word symbol "Chip" can represent different thoughts for different people. In a computer context, it might refer to a component; in a food context, it means a snack; in poker it means a token. Symbols can be accurate or inaccurate, adequate or inadequate, in representing thoughts and they can be effective or ineffective in influencing the thoughts of their intended recipients.

Generally, semantic meaning takes two related forms: denotative and connotative. Denotative meaning is the public, largely cognitive association of the term and its referent. For example, the denotation of Richard Nixon is the thirty-seventh president of the United States. Connotative meaning is the often individualistic, emotional loading we attach to terms. Thus, the connotation of Richard Nixon is either political saint or political sinner, depending on one's political orientation to his presidency.

Persuaders must be sensitive to both the denotative and the connotative association that receivers attach to the signs and symbols used in the persuasive message. For example, a persuader attempting to pitch a new country-western song to a record producer might say it is a strong ballad like Jeannie C. Riley's "Harper Valley P.T.A." It is vital to know whether the receiver, the record producer, knows (denotatively) the 1967 hit and has positive connotations for singer and the song.

SYNTACTICS AND STRUCTURE

The study of the relationship between symbols and their meanings is called semantics, but symbols also have relationships to each other. The structural relationships of symbols to each other is called syntactics. Syntax is the set of rules that makes symbolic sequences meaningful.

Figure 6.1
"Chip"

For example, "The warden carried the cat in his hand" is a meaningful sequence in English, but "Warden the in his the carried cat hand" is not a meaningful sequence in English. Even when the sequence follows the rules of the language, it makes a considerable difference in meaning. For example, both "The batter hit the ball" and "The ball hit the batter" are well-formed English sentences but the sequence makes a significant difference in meaning.

Syntactics also applies to the structure of signs and images. Consider, for example, Roy Paul Nelson's advice on designing advertisements: "The principles of design are to the layout artist what rules of

Figure 6.2
Sign

grammar are to the writer. . . . [T]he following list, from an advertising standpoint, can be considered reasonably universal and inclusive:

1. The design must be in balance.
2. The space within the ad should be broken up into pleasing proportions.
3. A directional pattern should be evident.
4. A unifying force should hold the ad together.
5. One element, or one part of the ad, should dominate all others.

"Reduced to single words, the list might read: balance, proportion, sequence, unity, and emphasis."[3]

To see Nelson's principles of visual syntax in action, look carefully at the sign in Figure 6.2.

Notice the way that factors like emphasis and balance convey a nearly universal visual message that has a persuasive impact on our activities.

Persuaders must link symbols in meaningful and compelling sequences to be successful. This is obvious at the sentence level of verbal communication: "Do not touch that hot stove" is clearly more persuasive than "Touch not that hot stove" even though the semantic content of the two sentences is largely the same.

Syntactics also has important ramifications in the larger sense of message construction. The elements of the message must be linked in a **compelling sequence.** Consider, for instance, Thomas Bivens' advice to public relations practitioners. "A sentence contains a single idea. A paragraph contains a number of sentences related by a single theme. So too, a complete piece of writing, whether it's a press release, a backgrounder, or an article for the company newsletter, contains a series of paragraphs unified by a single theme and related by logical transitions."[4] Bivens clearly understands that the whole message must be structured for maximum impact.

One sequencing issue that has been extensively studied is the matter of whether an advocate should present only one side of an issue or both sides in a persuasive presentation.[5] This is a matter of **one-sided versus two-sided messages.** One-sided messages present only the materials that support the persuader's point of view. Two-sided messages acknowledge and often offer development of alternative views. For example, in advocating freezing immigration into the United States for two years, a proponent must decide whether to present only the arguments that support the position or to introduce opposing arguments also.

Generally, studies support the conclusion that one-sided presentations should be selected when the audience will be favorably disposed to the advocate's position. For example, a political candidate addressing his or her own party need only present ideas that support the party's platform.

Studies also support the view that when change rather than reinforcement is the goal, one-sided messages seem to be more effective. As a result, a sales agent pitching a new client should choose a one-sided message but, in seeking to renew an existing client's contract, should use a two-sided message.

Two-sided messages are preferred when the advocates need to enhance their credibility to persuade their skeptical receivers. A young person trying to convince an older receiver, for example, may need to use a two-sided message to acknowledge that there are competing views and thereby enhance credibility.

Two-sided messages are also more effective with intelligent audiences. It is likely that more intelligent audiences will have heard of competing points of view. A persuader should take care to acknowledge those views with this sort of receiver.

Another major issue of message structure is the controversy over **primacy** and **recency.** In the 1950s, Carl I. Hovland and his associates published their studies on the impact of organization in persuasive messages.[6] One focus of those studies was whether arguments placed first (primacy) or last (recency) in a message had a greater persuasive effect. The primacy–recency debate proved to be enormously complicated because there was evidence to support either primacy or recency, depending on a plethora of variables. Researchers Ronald Applbaum and Karl Anatol summarized the results of empirical studies of primacy and recency. Their summary is reproduced in Box 6.1.

Box 6.1
SUMMARY OF PRIMACY–RECENCY RESEARCH

No universal rule of primacy or recency exists in persuasive situations.

a. There is no advantage in being the first communicator when two sides of an issue are presented by two different speakers.

b. When a receiver makes a public response about his position after hearing one side of an argument, the second side is less effective in changing attitudes.

c. When one speaker presents two sides of an issue in one presentation, we are usually more influenced by the side presented first.

d. When a receiver's needs are aroused before a communication satisfies these needs, the communication is more readily acceptable than if the need arousal follows the communication.

e. Attitudes change more when desirable ideas precede undesirable ideas.

f. The pro–con order is more effective than the con–pro order when an authoritative communicator presents both sides.

g. If a time lag exists between the presentation of two sides of an issue, the side presented last has an advantage.

h. When no time lag exists between the presentation of two sides of an issue, the first side has an advantage.

i. When a receiver hears a series of communications about a variety of subjects, primacy operates at first but diminishes as the series of communications progresses.

j. Salient topics, uninteresting subjects, and moderately unfamiliar issues tend to yield to recency effects.

k. Nonsalient, controversial topics, uninteresting subject matter, and highly familiar issues tend toward primacy effects.

l. The placement of reward or punishment in a message will affect primacy–recency effects.

SOURCE: Ronald L. Applbaum and Karl W. E. Anatol, *Strategies for Persuasive Communication* (Columbus, OH: Charles E. Merrill Publishing Company, 1974), p. 108.

The question of where to place the stongest arguments, then, depends upon many variables in the persuasive situation.

Structure applies at all levels of message composition. From the syntax of words linking together to form meaningful sentences forming meaningful and persuasive messages, structure is a powerful aspect of

We place great faith in numbers.

language that can build persuasive effect. At a still larger level, even messages must be linked together in a persuasive series. For example, the order of witnesses in a court trial can make the difference between success or failure in convincing a jury. The interactions that take place in a sales interview (e.g., the conversation in the opening, the exchanges in the demonstration, and the colloquy in the closing) follow an agreed-upon sequence for maximum effectiveness.

Syntactics can also be said to apply to the even larger level of sequencing persuasive communication events into a campaign. As we shall see in Chapter Twelve, sequencing and timing of messages in a campaign are critical to the success of the persuasion.

PRAGMATICS

Pragmatics, the third area of semiotics, is concerned with the relationship of signs and symbols to their users. Pragmatics examines how human communicative behavior interacts with the people who are engaged in the communication. For example, when a couple sign over a down payment on a house, their signs and symbolic activities are a result of a whole persuasive sales campaign seeking to influence them: advertisements, impressions of the available homes, conversations with the real estate agent, discussions between the buyers, and so on.

Each of these signs and symbols has a semantic meaning. "For sale" means something different from "Lease with an option to buy." The signs and symbols also bear syntactic relationships to each other. The ad in the newspaper leads to contacting the real estate agent; the discussion with the real estate agent leads to conversations between the buyers. In addition to those semantic and syntactic relationships, there is a pragmatic relationship. The ad describes a large kitchen that is important to one person and a location close to a school that is important to another party. The earnest behavior of the buyers is an important pragmatic aspect for the real estate agent to select and introduce various home choices. Bear in mind that the semantic and syntactic components of our messages interact with each other to determine the pragmatic outcome of the communication.

Pragmatics has several important contributions to make to the study of persuasion. Consider the following principles.

Pragmatics can assist us in understanding the ethics of persuasion. As we noticed in Chapter Four, ethical evaluations of persuasion often turn on the intention of the persuader. The study of pragmatics is directly concerned with the intentions of the participants in the discourse. For example, whether a speaker intended an utterance as a sincere argument or as an ironic commentary is a pragmatic matter of the speaker's intention.

Another important lesson to derive from the study of pragmatics is that there is a difference between the pragmatic effect of informing and the pragmatic effect of persuading. While the goals and procedures of the two intentions are related, they are also quite different. When we are conversing with a friend, for example, we may simply relate what we did when our civic group sponsored a chili cook-off to raise money for the needy; that is a matter of informing. On the other hand, if we are describing the fun we had in working at the cook-off and the good that the results will do for the community, our intentions may be to persuade our friend to join the group; that is a matter of persuading.

Finally, pragmatics points us to a study of the impact of the communication. For example, pragmatics is concerned with issues like the implication embedded in sentences. Whether people will fall for advertising "tricks" like the nonspecific comparison ploy is a pragmatic issue: "Our product contains 1/3 less salt" does not specify what is being compared. Does the product contain 1/3 less salt than seawater, than competing products, than previous formulations of the same product?

Semiotics provides us with a useful paradigm for considering persuasive messages. We must be concerned with the semantic content of persuasive messages, to be sure. But we must also consider the impact of syntactics in the persuasive process. Finally, we must give appropriate consideration to the pragmatic effects of persuasion. To examine how persuasive messages achieve their pragmatic effects, we should look at the components of an argument.

PERSUASION AND INFORMAL LOGIC

Aristotle is credited with systematizing the area of philosophy we call logic. As we discussed in Chapter Two, he adapted the formal rules of arguing logically to fit the kind of everyday reasoning found in rhetorical endeavors. In contemporary terms, logic applied in naturally occurring persuasive situations such as politics, commerce, and everyday communication is called informal logic to distinguish it from the more formal and abstract philosophical field of formal logic, "the study of proofs and rules of inference in axiomatized formal systems."[7]

Informal logic offers us a clear perspective for examining what happens when people create persuasive messages. While lengthy messages or persuasive campaigns stretching over a long period of time may become quite complicated, the essence of persuasive messages is relatively easy to describe.

A clear contemporary description of persuasive arguments was originated by Stephen Toulmin in his book called *The Uses of Argument*.[8] The Toulmin model of an argument is illustrated in Figure 6.3.

Toulmin's theory suggests that arguments can be diagrammed as consisting of **claims** (the point or thesis) supported by **data** (evidence) and established by **warrants** (reasons connecting the data to the claim).

CLAIMS

We argue about many different kinds of claims. Usually we are seeking to get our receiver to accept a policy proposal that we ought to take a particular course of action, such as that the government should regulate pornography on the Internet. Sometimes, however, we argue values; "Joe Namath is the greatest quarterback ever to take the field," for example. At still other times, we may argue about definitions, that a particular act is excusable because the person was legally insane. We even argue about facts; we didn't know for certain whether O. J. Simpson

Figure 6.3
A Toulmin Model of Arguments

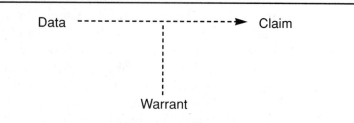

killed Nicole Brown Simpson and Ron Goldman, so we conducted a trial that introduced evidence and testimony supporting and refuting the factual claim of whether or not he committed the murders.

The determination of the claim is important for three reasons. First, claims are the whole point of the message. Second, claims must be related to the other parts of the argument. Third, claims must be considered in light of the goals of the interaction. Consider each of these in more detail.

First, the claim is important because it is the point that is being made and therefore the claim indicates the direction in which the whole argument is leading. As creators of persuasive messages, we need to have a clear concept of what we want the receivers to accept in the final analysis; as receivers of persuasive messages, we need to have a clear concept of what is being asked of us in our decision-making process.

Second, the claim is important because evidence and reasoning must be *relevant* to the claim. If the claim is not clear, all sorts of distracting, irrelevant matters may confuse the point of the argument. For both sources and receivers, it is critical to keep a clear sense of the claim under consideration in the persuasive process.

Finally, clear claims are necessary because we need to distinguish whether there is a hidden agenda in the arguments we are involved in. Sometimes persuaders are seeking to use a current argument to further other hidden agendas. For example, the broker who is advocating investment in a microwave telecommunications company may tell a client that the emerging market is a sure-fire, high-return venture that is consistent with the client's financial objectives. However, there may be significant financial incentives for the broker to advocate this particular company or the broker may have a particular sales quota that must be met, regardless of the client's needs and interests. It is important to understand what is really being advocated in persuasive situations to keep from victimizing or being victimized by arguments.

Sometimes different types of claims are interrelated to establish an end point claim. The Senate Judiciary Committee's hearings on Justice Clarence Thomas, for example, sought to determine matters of fact (whether particular events alleged by Anita Hill actually took place), matters of definition (whether specific events should be deemed sexual harassment), and matters of value (whether the allegations of sexual harassment were important enough to warrant rejection of his candidacy). All of the foregoing issues were related to the ultimate policy issue—whether Clarence Thomas should be recommended to the full Senate for confirmation as a Supreme Court Justice.

DATA

In the Toulmin model of arguments, data are pieces of evidence that form the grounds for supporting a conclusion. For example, to support the claim that there should be government controls on drug prices, an advocate might cite statistics that indicate wholesale drug prices rose 128 percent between 1980 and 1992—more than six times the rate of inflation for that period.

In other words, data provide persuaders with information to be used in proving their claims and provide decision makers with the grounds for accepting or rejecting the claim.

Over fifty years of experimental research on the use of evidence supports several important conclusions.[9] It is clear that receivers expect to be presented with credible evidence, especially in situations they see as persuasive. The use of evidence is linked to the source's credibility. Fresh evidence is more important than evidence with which the audience is already familiar. Persuaders, then, must be concerned with what the receivers will accept as data.

Overall, there are three general criteria for acceptability of data: relevancy, materiality, and competency. In other words, for evidence to be acceptable in an argument, it should be related to the claim (relevant), significant in establishing a connection to the claim (material), and adequate and sufficient to establish the claim (competence).

For example, if we are considering whether there should be mandatory drug testing for employees in a factory, some evidence will be irrelevant (whether married people or single people are more likely to be drug users), whereas other evidence will be relevant (drug testing will reduce the insurance premiums the company must pay). Some evidence will be more material to the claim than other evidence. "If substance abusers realize they cannot get employment, they may be motivated to stop taking drugs" may not be as significant as the fact that the absenteeism rate is four times greater among drug users. Finally, the evidence must be competent. The money saved by drug testing and the increased productivity must be deemed sufficient grounds to outweigh counterarguments like "Drug testing harms employee morale and will make the company legally liable for false-positive test results."

Now that we have examined the general criteria for acceptable data, we can turn our attention to different types of data. Data, or evidence, used in persuasive messages can be divided into two major categories: physical and verbal.

Physical Data

Physical data are pieces of evidence that are not created by language. In legal trials physical evidence may consist of fingerprints, blood, or any object or substance that has a bearing on the issue under consideration.

In more ordinary persuasive situations, there are also numerous examples of physical evidence. The test drive of the automobile, the product free sample, and the stereo system demonstration in a showroom are all examples of the use of physical data in commercial persuasion.

Among the tests of physical evidence are reality, purity, and indicativeness. To be acceptable to receivers, physical evidence should be able to pass each of these tests.

Reality   The first test of physical evidence holds that it must be perceived as real rather than fanciful. History is filled with examples of fraudulent physical evidence. A prime example is the Piltdown man. In 1908, an amateur paleontologist in Piltdown, England, claimed to have discovered the "missing link" between apes and humans. For many years, the remains were thought to be between 200,000 to 1 million years old and were solid evidence of the evolution of human beings. It was not until the 1950s that fluorine analysis and X-ray examination proved that the Piltdown man was a fake constructed of a human skull with an ape's jawbone.[10]

Receivers exposed to physical evidence will apply their experience to determine whether they consider the physical evidence to be realistic. For most people "seeing is believing," but they also recognize that physical evidence can be faked and are therefore skeptical about the evidence presented to them by persuaders.

Purity   Physical evidence must be perceived as real, but it must also be perceived as untainted. People are skeptical when physical evidence might be contaminated. In the O. J. Simpson trial, for example, the jury was asked to accept the argument that the blood evidence presented by the prosecution was tainted by sloppy collection and therefore was not reliable.

Purity of physical evidence is also important in less notorious persuasive situations. For example, in product tests of soft drinks, receivers are asked to compare the tastes of competing refreshments. The expectation in such tests is that the samples are pure samples of the various items. If the samples are tainted, by allowing one carbonated sample to go flat, for example, the test is not fair. Such tainted evidence, if discovered, will boomerang on the persuader attempting to use it.

Indicativeness   When presented with physical evidence, receivers are asked to interpret the evidence in a particular way. Assuming that physical evidence is real and untainted, there is still the matter of determining what the evidence means. This is the test of indicativeness. Does the existence of a fingerprint at the scene of the crime mean that the defendant committed the act? How indicative of the deed is the existence of the fingerprint?

Consider, for example, the graphs in Figure 6.4.

Note that the simple geometric operations line selection, simplification, as well as other factors can distort the indications of maps and graphs. As geographer Mark Monmonier explained, "Reality is three-dimensional, rich in detail, and far too factual to allow a complete yet uncluttered two-dimensional scale model. Indeed, a map that did not generalize would be useless. But the value of a map depends on how well its generalized geometry and generalized content reflect a chosen aspect of reality."[11] In a similar vein, even photographs may offer different indications. Does a photograph of the surface of Mars indicate a face that was constructed by some alien race or is it a naturally occurring topographical feature? In such cases, the physical evidence may be real and untainted, but may not pass the test of indicativeness.

Indicativeness is an important part of brand recognition. Trademarks are protected because manufacturers know that their reputation for providing quality will indicate that their product is desirable. Consider, for example, why you purchase a specific brand rather than a generic version of that product. It is a matter of your expectation that the brand-name product will be better than the competing alternatives that are of unknown quality.

Figure 6.4

Generalizing from Geometry

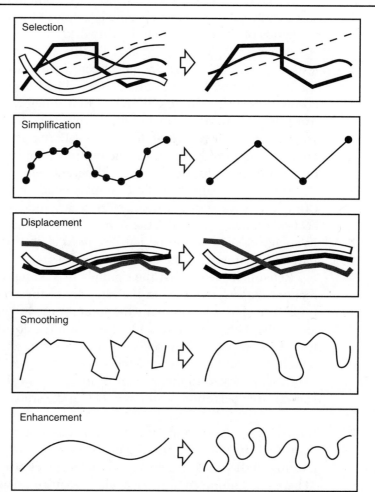

SOURCE: Mark Monmonier, *How to Lie with Maps* (Chicago, IL: The University of Chicago Press, 1991), p. 26.

Physical data, then, are bits of evidence frequently used in persuasive situations. To be effective, physical evidence must pass the receiver's tests of reality, purity, and indicativeness.

Verbal Data

There are many forms of verbal evidence, and each form has its own tests of acceptability. We will examine three of the most common forms of data used in persuasion: examples, statistics, and testimony.

Examples   Examples are specific instances that point to a claim. To prove that government should control the content of the Internet, for instance, advocates will cite specific examples of pornography falling into the hands of minors through the network.

When examples are used as data, they must pass certain evidentiary tests. Typically these tests include recency, accuracy, and reliability.

Recency means that examples should be chosen from contemporary events if possible. We are all aware that times change and an example from the distant past may bear little relevancy to contemporary events. To cite the repair record of Toyotas and Fords in 1970 as an example of quality would not be a reasonable use of examples because a more current example might provide a very different comparison.

Accuracy means that the examples cited should be representative. Citing one essay written by one first-year student is not necessarily an accurate representation of the writing skills of the entire first-year class. In such a case, it would be inaccurate to claim that the single example indicates that writing tutorials are unnecessary.

Reliability means that the example used should be free from contradiction, that we can rely on the integrity of the example. As an illustration, consider the argument that watching violent television leads to aggressive behavior among children. Studies do indicate that children will emulate what they see on television, but there are also cases in which *some* children react aggressively after seeing nonviolent shows like *Sesame Street*. In this case, it is important to show that those few instances are aberrations and not a flaw in the study.

Statistics   We live in an age that places great faith in numbers, but statistical data should pass special tests if we are to rely on them. According to theorists George Ziegelmueller, Jack Kay, and Charles Dause, "The tests unique to statistical data require answers to four specific questions: (1) Are the statistics based on adequate sampling techniques? (2) Is the statistical unit an appropriate one? (3) Do the statistics cover an appropriate time period? (4) Are comparisons between comparable units?"[12]

The first test refers to adequate sampling techniques. This means that the statistics should be drawn from an appropriate base. For example, to draw a statistic on family income from applications for financial aid at a university would give a misleading presentation of the population as a whole. None of the families who chose not to apply for financial aid would be represented in the data, and all families who did not have children applying for admission to that university, or any university, would also be excluded from the sample. We should expect that statistics cited by persuaders would be based on a fair and representative sample.

The test of an appropriate statistical unit indicates that the appropriate statistical procedure was followed in determining the data. For example, if we wanted to discuss the number of Americans below the poverty level in 1990, we might cite the actual number (33.6 million), a percentage of the population (13%), a ratio (more than one out of seven), or as a change from a previous date (a 6 percent increase from 1989). Which statistical unit is most appropriate depends upon how we are using the statistics.

The question of whether the statistics cover an appropriate time period means that statistics should be drawn from a reasonable base period. For example, the inflation rate during the 1970s is not a good time frame for basing generalizations about the American economy. In a similar vein, it would be inappropriate to compare retail sales in November and December with sales in January and February because purchasing patterns are quite different immediately before Christmas as compared to immediately after Christmas.

Finally, the test of comparable units means that the quantification used should make legitimate comparisons. For example, to compare the average income of Canadians with that of U.S. citizens without recognizing variations in curency valuations would be to use noncomparable units. In statistics, as in most types of evidence, it is important to make comparisons of similar entities, or as the old adage goes, "Don't compare apples to oranges."

Testimony   Very often persuaders will use the testimony of someone else as evidence to support a claim. Letters from satisfied customers are used to convince a reluctant buyer. Products are endorsed by celebrities in commercials. Experts are interviewed for their views on important issues. In short, any time the source is using the words of another party, he or she is employing testimony.

Like the other forms of data, there are special tests of tesimonial evidence. One of the most important tests is whether the person cited has appropriate credentials. For example, Dr. James Benjamin has a Ph.D. in communication and would therefore not be a good source to cite about the effects of smoking on one's health, but George Petterson, M.D., probably would not be a good reference to cite about rhetorical theory.

Another important test of testimonial data is whether the party has direct experience in the area being cited. If we were seeking the best athletic shoe, would we be better off taking the word of a Hollywood

Persuaders can use testimony to support their claims.

star or a professional athlete? Is testimony of an eyewitness more credible than that of someone who saw the same event on television?

Finally, there is the matter of source bias. The best testimony comes from objective sources. People may be swayed by their involvement in the issue under consideration, and therefore, may possess a slanted perspective. An engineer employed by an airline manufacturer, for example, may have a conflict of interest in testifying about aircraft safety.

In summary, the data represent what we have to go on in making an argument. To be effective, evidence must be able to pass general tests of relevance, materiality, and competence. In addition, reasonable receivers will also apply specific tests based upon the type of data presented.

WARRANTS

In the Toulmin model, warrants are reasons that link the data to the claim. In other words, warrants are the connections between what we have to go on (evidence) and where we are going (claim). For example, to argue that we should install a stoplight at a busy school intersection because it will save children's lives rests on the generalized experience that stoplights reduce accidents and have been effective in controlling traffic in other school districts. Therefore, what is true of the general experience will also be true of the particular intersection in question.

Warrants are particularly important to persuasion because they provide the links between the evidence and the claim. They reflect the reasoning process we go through in arriving at conclusions and in evaluating arguments made by others. According to researchers Rodney Reynolds and Michael Burgoon, reasoning is intimately linked to our deepest belief structures.[13] In short, warrants express the reasons why a claim should be accepted.

In real-life arguments, warrants are often implicit rather than explicit. The classic deductive syllogism of "All men are mortal; Socrates is a man; therefore Socrates is mortal" would most likely be expressed in a real argument as "All men are mortal, and so is Socrates."

Warrants, whether explicit or implicit, are crucial links in the argumentative process. We cannot expect people simply to take our word for a persuasive claim. The case must make sense to the receivers. People must be provided with both evidence and good reasons if they are to adopt our claims.

While logicians have developed dozens of different forms of reasoning, we will consider four of the most common types of material reasoning: induction, deduction, cause, and analogy.

Induction

As mentioned in Chapter Four, we often reason from specific instances to generalized conclusions. This is a process of taking examples or instances and drawing a conclusion about the examples as a group. We might, for example, cite specific examples of corruption in charitable operations to draw the conclusion that we need to reform the laws governing financing in charitable organizations.

To reason inductively always involves an "inductive leap." This means that since we cannot examine *every* example, at some point we have to be willing to "leap" to the conclusion. To return to our charitable organization illustration, we do not have the time, energy, or resources to audit every single one of the charitable organizations in the United States for corruption. Therefore, we must rely on a sample of the whole to justify our claim. There is no specific number of examples that make an inferential leap safe, but persuaders should be ready to provide more than a single instance to warrant a generalization.

Deduction

Logicians explain that the second major form of reasoning is deductive. Here we begin with generalizations and follow specific rules to reason to specific conclusions in a process of logical entailment. In other words, if deductive reasoning follows the rules of logic, it is said to be *valid*. For example, we may begin with the general premise that the Constitution protects freedom of the press. From this we may deduce that the supermarket tabloid is entitled to the protection afforded the rest of the press.

Edward Corbett described six rules of the form of valid deductive arguments.[14]

1. *There must be three terms and only three terms.* We cannot argue validly, for example, that the Constitution protects freedom of the press, the Constitution guarantees the right to bear arms, the tabloid is a newspaper and therefore the tabloid has the right to bear arms.
2. *The middle term must be distributed at least once.* For example, "All newspapers are protected under the Constitution, All religions are protected under the Constitution, therefore all newspapers are religions" fails the test of a distributed middle term.

3. *No term may be distributed in the conclusion if it was not distributed in the premise.* For example, to argue that most forms of speech are protected by the Constitution, that pornography is a form of speech, and therefore pornography is protected by the Constitution is invalid because the conclusion does not follow from the limitation of distribution made by the premises.

4. *No conclusion may be drawn from two* particular (*as opposed to* universal) *premises.* This means that deductive reasoning must involve some generalization or universal quality. We cannot validly argue, for example, that the New York *Times* is protected by the Constitution, that the Chicago *Tribune* is protected by the Constitution, and therefore the Austin *American Statesman* is protected by the Constitution. Remember that formal validity has to do with following the rules rather than the truth of any given element; the Austin *American Statesman* is protected by the Constitution, it just does not follow deductively, from the chain of reasoning described in the example that a particular newspaper is protected just because the New York *Times* and the Chicago *Tribune* are protected.

5. *No conclusion may be drawn from two negative premises.* This means that at least one of the premises must be affirmative. For example, no pornography is protected by the Constitution, no libel is protected by the Constitution, therefore newspapers are not protected by the Constitution is an invalid syllogism.

6. *If one of the premises is negative, the conclusion must be negative.* The final rule is self-explanatory. You cannot validly argue that newspapers are protected by the Constitution, that no pornography is protected by the Constitution, and that therefore a pornographic newspaper is protected under the Constitution.

Cause

Another important form of reasoning is connecting causes and effects. We argue, for example, that cutting funding for Public Television will harm the education of children because educational programs like *Sesame Street* will be forced off the air.

There are also rules concerning the validity of causal reasoning. These rules include the following.

1. *The cause and the effect must occur together.* For example, we cannot argue that cutting the defense budget accounts for the drop

in standardized test scores among American schoolchildren. While it may be true that the test scores drop at the same time that we close military bases, that may be coincidence rather than causality.

2. *The cause must be capable of bringing about the effect.* While it may be true that money will reduce some of the conditions (like poor nutrition) associated with low test scores, we cannot legitimately argue that funding alone will improve test scores.

3. *Intervening causes must be accounted for.* If we cut the funding of Public Television and children's test scores drop, we must still account for other causal factors that could account for the decline. It is possible, for example, that the tests were revised to be more challenging, that there was a greater number of lengthy teachers' strikes, or that there were errors in calculating the results of the tests.

4. *Unspecified effects must be accounted for.* In causal reasoning, we must pay particular attention to consequences that could occur that are outside the scope of the causal link. For example, cutting federal spending on public television may force public television stations to drop funding for services like carrying reading services for the blind on their second audio channels.

Analogy

The last form of reasoning we will discuss is reasoning by analogy. In this form of reasoning we draw conclusions based on comparisons. For example, we may use the analogy that computers and human brains function similarly. From this analogy, we may then argue that the well-known principle of GIGO (Garbage In, Garbage Out) forces us to oppose the garbage of sex and violence on television if we don't want our children to imitate the "garbage" they see on TV.

There are two main tests of reasoning by analogy. Arguments by comparison must (1) compare similar items, and (2) avoid overextending the comparisons.

A valid comparison will equate similar items. A valid argument by analogy will compare items that are similar in all important respects. To compare, for example, militia groups in the United States today with the army of the American Revolution would be a faulty comparison. While both groups are armed forces, George Washington's army was a military wing of the Continental Congress seeking independence from a foreign colonial power. Militia groups do not answer to any governing body nor are they political groups seeking separate independence from the existing government.

Comparisons must not be overextended. For example, someone might argue that there were many similarities between Kennedy and Lincoln (Lincoln was elected in 1860 and Kennedy was elected in 1960, both had vice presidents named Johnson, both were proponents of civil rights) and that, therefore, there was a historical imperative for Oswald to assassinate Kennedy. Such an argument obviously strains credibility, but many arguments by analogy become overextended, as the examples of faulty analogies in Chapter Four indicated.

EMOTIONAL PROOF AND BRAIN STUDIES

So far we have been examining the features of persuasive messages that appeal to the cognitive processes of the receivers. As we noted in Chapter One, however, people are not just thinking machines. We are also feeling creatures. As such, emotional appeals make up an important part of informal logic. "Argumentation that takes place in the conversational marketplace of everyday, persuasive appeals," wrote philosopher Douglas Walton, "is heavily interlaced with emotional overtones and suggestions. As an example, successful advertising seems for the most part to consist of well-orchestrated appeals to emotions. And it is quite plausible to suggest that many political debates and controversies are decided as much on the basis of emotional appeals and loyalties as on purely dispassionate reasoning."[15]

We can turn to the recent studies of the human brain for assistance in examining how emotions are aroused through persuasive messages. As psychologist Nico Frijda wrote, "Certain parts of the brain are indispensable for the manifestations of emotion, and certain hormones are necessary or facilitative for the readiness with which emotions, or certain emotions, are evoked; these brain structures and hormones can thus be regarded as conditions for the occurrence of emotions."[16]

We are inspired by emotional descriptions like Ronald Reagan's addressing the nation after the space shuttle *Challenger* disaster: "The crew of the space shuttle *Challenger* honored us by the manner in which they lived their lives. We will never forget them, nor the last time we saw them, this morning, as they prepared for their journey and waved goodbye and 'slipped the surly bonds of earth' to 'touch the face of God.'"[17] The emotional stimuli pass through four major sequences in the brain: the brainstem, the hypothalamus, the limbic system, and the neocortex.

UPI/Corbis-Bettmann

The space shuttle Challenger *disaster.*

These segments and their attendant emotional connections are pictured in Figure 6.5.

A very primitive part of the brain called the reticular activating system in the brainstem is stimulated by sensory signals. This activating system is the part of the brain "responsible for the 'energizing' aspects of motivation and emotion."[18] Above the reticular formation, the hypothalamus is a collection of cells that gather and integrate information relevant to the subjective aspects of emotional states. In other words, the hypothalamus regulates the emotional reaction by stimulating and inhibiting physiological responses to emotion. The third structure of the brain involved in emotional response is the limbic system. While the function of this system is not completely understood, neurologists believe that it is composed of two subsystems: the septal system, associ-

Figure 6.5
The Brain and Emotions

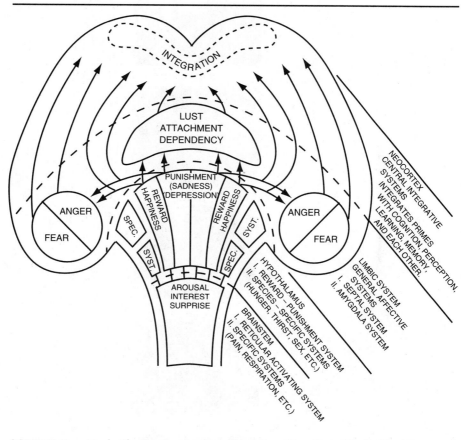

SOURCE: Ross Buck, *The Communication of Emotions* (New York: The Guilford Press, 1984), p. 86.

ated with sex and sociability and the amygdala system associated with aggression and fear. The final section of the brain, the neocortex, is the highest-functioning portion. The neocortex "is responsible for foresight, finer discriminations, and analysis of linguistically mediated information."[19] In other words, the neocortex integrates and associates lower-level operations with the higher-level brain processes such as those associated with the interpretation of symbols.

These systems in our brains are interconnected so that emotions that are generated in the deep structures such as the limbic system are

SOURCE: Timex

Humor is a widely used emotional appeal.

In 1929,

George Myers was ruined because he had his money on Wall Street. 67 years later, the same could happen to his granddaughter if she doesn't.

In a time in which the only thing we can depend on is ourselves, investing is more than a luxury. It is a virtual necessity. And our best hope for financial independence.

For over 130 years, John Hancock has forged an investment strategy that has helped millions of individuals, institutions, and pension funds to realize their financial potential. A savvy, disciplined approach that seeks out opportunities for growth while shunning reckless speculation and excessive volatility.

To that end, we offer <u>mutual funds</u>, with a wide range of investments from stocks to bonds. The tax-deferred, long-term growth potential of <u>fixed and variable annuities</u>. And, as you would expect, the protection and growth potential of <u>variable life insurance</u>.

To learn more, contact your John Hancock representative or your personal financial advisor.

**INSURANCE FOR THE UNEXPECTED.
INVESTMENTS FOR THE OPPORTUNITIES.**

John Hancock

WORLDWIDE SPONSOR

Fear appeals are among the most extensively studied emotional appeals.

interpreted by the higher functioning neocortex. We can think about our emotional reactions and formulate responses to what we feel, see, and hear. Our higher-level problem-solving cortex allows us to mediate and control our initial emotional responses. Conversely, our deeper cortical structures provide our intellectual processes with the passion necessary for conviction.

For example, when we see a swastika, we may have immediate negative emotional reactions generated through our limbic systems, due to past associations with that symbol. However, our cortex may inhibit the emotional reaction by cognitively recognizing that what we took for a Nazi swastika was actually an older religious symbol called the Greek cross.

There are many types of emotional appeal used in persuasive messages. Commercials offer examples of the wide variety of emotions used to sell products: patriotism, joy, fear, greed, sorrow, reverence, hope, pride, and so on. Two of the most studied emotional appeals, fear and humor, will be the focus of our attention on the relationship of persuasion to these two emotions.

Fear appeals are closely related to persuasive effect.[20] While mild fear appeals are generally considered to be superior in generating a persuasive effect, there are conditions in which stronger fear appeals are more effective than mild fear appeals.[21] Strong fear appeals have been found to be more effective when there was a low interest or relevance felt by the listeners. Strong fear appeals also appeared to be more effective in generating immediate attitude change. Highly credible sources were found to be more effective when they used strong fear appeals than when the same source used a milder fear appeal.

Humor is another widely used emotional appeal.[22] Most studies indicate that humor does not function as a strong persuasive force in changing attitudes. However, it can be used as a reinforcer of previously existing attitudes. In addition, humor may help to disarm an antagonistic audience. Humor may also enhance the trustworthiness of the source.

In summary, it is clear that people are motivated by their emotional responses as well as by their intellectual reasoning processes. It is best to think of logical and emotional appeals in combination. A good blend of appealing to the minds and the hearts of the receivers is the best approach to take in most persuasive situations. We take pleasure in making logical connections and we feel because we have reason to feel. For maximum effectiveness, persuasive messages should neither rely entirely on cold logic nor entirely on the heat of passion.

Summary

In this chapter we have seen that semiotics, a general term for the linguistic study of signs and symbols, offers a convenient set of categories for discussing the relationship of message factors and persuasion. Semiotics consists of the study of semantics (the relationship of signs and their meanings), syntactics (the study of the relationship of signs to other signs), and pragmatics (the relationship of signs to their users).

Semantics is relevant to persuasion because it examines the substance of signs and symbols used in the messages that constitute the content of persuasive messages. Aspects of semantics like connotation and denotation are important meanings in persuasive messages.

Syntactics is vital because it is the study of structure. We looked at persuasive messages at the sentence level and the impact of structure at the message level. Specifically we looked at the issues of one-sided versus two-sided messages and at primacy and recency. We also noted that syntactics will influence persuasion at the message-series level.

Pragmatics, the relationship of signs and symbols to their users, is also closely related to persuasion. We noted that pragmatics helps us to understand the relationship of ethics and persuasion. It also serves as a reference point for understanding the difference between information and persuasion. Finally, pragmatics provides a paradigm for understanding the implications embedded in persuasive sentences.

Having covered semiotics, we turned next to the area of informal logic. We looked at the form of arguments as described by Stephen Toulmin. The claim, the point of the argument, forms the thesis that the persuader is seeking to get the receiver to accept. Data constitute the evidence, or what the persuader has to go on in establishing the claim. We examined two typical types of data in persuasion: physical data and verbal data. We also noted specific tests for the use of these types of data. Finally, we looked at warrants, the reasoning process that links data to claims. We looked at induction, deduction, cause, and analogy as common forms of reasoning in persuasion.

Finally, we explored emotional proof in persuasion. We noted how emotions are generated by persuasive stimuli. We also considered the use of specific emotional appeals like humor and fear.

Notes

1 David Crystal, *The Cambridge Encyclopedia of Language* (New York: Cambridge University Press, 1987), p. 399. Reprinted with the permission of Cambridge University Press.

2 Kenneth Burke, *Language as Symbolic Action* (Berkeley, CA: University of California Press, 1968), p. 3.

3 Roy Paul Nelson, *The Design of Advertising* (Dubuque, IA: William C Brown and Company, 1977), p. 104.

4 Thomas Bivens, *Handbook for Public Relations Writing* (Lincolnwood, IL: NTC Business Books, 1991), p. 298.

5 J. W. Kohler, "Effects on Audience Opinion of One-Sided and Two-Sided Speeches Supporting and Opposing a Proposition," in *The Process of Social Influence*, ed. Thomas Biesecker and Donn Parson (Englewood Cliffs, NJ: Prentice-Hall, 1972), pp. 351–369; R. A. Jones and J. W. Brehm, "Persuasiveness of One- and Two-Sided Communications as a Function of Awareness: There Are Two Sides," *Journal of Experimental Social Psychology*, 6 (1970), pp. 47–56; R. Rosnow, "One-sided versus Two-sided Communication under Indirect Awareness of Persuasive Intent," *Public Opinion Quarterly*, 32 (1968), pp. 95–101; C. I. Hovland, A. A. Lumsdaine, and F. D. Sheffield, "The Effects of Presenting One Side versus Both Sides in Changing Opinions on a Controversial Subject," in *Experiments on Mass Communication* (Princeton: Princeton University Press, 1949), pp. 201–227.

6 Carl I. Hovland, ed. *The Order of Presentation in Persuasion* (New Haven, CT: Yale University Press, 1957).

7 Trudy Govier, *Problems in Argument Analysis and Evaluation* (Providence, RI: Foris Publications, 1987), p. 203. Permission granted by Mouton de Gruyter.

8 Stephen Toulmin, *The Uses of Argument* (Cambridge, MA: Cambridge University Press, 1958), passim.

9 J. C. Reinard, "The Empirical Study of Evidence," *Human Communication Research*, 15 (Fall 1988), pp. 3–59.

10 Frank Spencer *Piltdown: A Scientific Forgery*. New York: Oxford University Press, 1990.

11 Mark Monmonier, *How to Lie with Maps* (Chicago, IL: The University of Chicago Press, 1991), p. 25.

12 George Ziegelmueller, Jack Kay, and Charles Dause, *Argumentation: Inquiry and Advocacy* (Englewood Cliffs, NJ: Prentice-Hall, 1990), p. 103.

13 Rodney A. Reynolds and Michael Burgoon, "Belief Processing, Reasoning and Evidence," in *Communication Yearbook 7*, ed. Robert Bostrom (Beverly Hills, CA: Sage Publications, 1983), pp. 83–104.

14 Edward P. J. Corbett, *Classical Rhetoric for the Modern Student* (New York: Oxford University Press, 1971), p. 65.

15 Douglas Walton, *Informal Logic* (New York: Cambridge University Press, 1989), p. 82. Reprinted with the permission of Cambridge University Press.

16 Nicolo H. Frijda, *The Emotions* (Paris: Cambridge University Press, 1993), p. 124. Reprinted with the permission of Cambridge University Press.

17 Ronald Reagan, "Address to the Nation," February 3, 1986, *Weekly Compilation of Presidential Documents* (Washington, DC: Government Printing Office, 1986), p. 105.

18 Ross Buck, *The Communication of Emotion* (New York: The Guilford Press, 1984), p. 79.

[19] Frijda, *The Emotions*, p. 381. Reprinted with the permission of Cambridge University Press.

[20] J. Dabbs and H. Leventhal, "Effects of Varying the Recommendations in a Fear-Arousing Communication," *Journal of Personality and Social Psychology*, 1 (1965), pp. 525–531.

[21] L. Berkowitz and D. Cottingham, "The Interest Value and Relevance of Fear-arousing Communications," *Journal of Abnormal and Social Psychology*, 60 (1960), pp. 37–43; F. J. Boster and P. Mongeau, "Fear-arousing Persuasive Messages" in *Communication Yearbook 8*, R. N. Bostrom and B. H. Weastly, eds. (Beverly Hills, CA: Sage Publications, 1984), pp. 330–375; S. Kraus, E. El-Assal, and M. DeFleur, "Fear-threat Appeals in Mass Communication: An Apparent Contradiction," *Speech Monographs*, 33 (1966), pp. 23–29; H. Leventhal and P. Niles, "A Field Experiment on Fear-Arousal with Data on the Validity of Questionnaire Measures," *Journal of Personality*, 32 (1964), pp. 459–479; H. Leventhal and J. C. Watts, "Sources of Resistance to Fear-Arousing Communication on Smoking and Lung Cancer," *Journal of Personality and Social Psychology*, 4 (1966), pp. 137–146.

[22] Charles Gruner, "An Experimental Study of Satire as Persuasion," *Speech Monographs*, 32 (1965), pp. 149–153; Charles Gruner, "A Further Study of the Use of Satire as Persuasion," *Communication Monographs*, 33 (1966), pp. 184–185; Charles Gruner, "Effect of Humor on Speaker Ethos and Audience Information Gain," *Journal of Communication*, 17 (1967), pp. 228–233; B. Sternhal and C. S. Craig, "Humor in Advertising," *Journal of Marketing*, 37 (1973), pp. 12–18; D. Markiewicz, "The Effects of Humor on Persuasion," unpublished doctoral dissertation, Ohio State University, 1972.

For Further Thought

1. Analyze a persuasive message such as a television ad using the semiotic systems of semantics, syntactics, and pragmatics. Do the different systems produce different ideas about the advertisement?

2. Use the Toulmin model to analyze a persuasive message such as a political speech. Was the claim clearly stated in the message? Were appropriate and sufficient data provided? Were the warrants reasonable and cogent? If not, what could the source have said to make the message more acceptable?

3. Find an example of an ad that uses physical data to support the claim. Use the standards of reality, purity, and indicativeness to assess the appeal used in the ad.

4. Analyze the appeal of different types of verbal data. For what types of receivers are examples more persuasive than statistics? For what types of receivers are statistics more persuasive than testimony? How can a persuader deduce which type of verbal data to emphasize in a persuasive presentation?

5. Use your understanding of emotional proof to explore and elaborate on the peripheral route of the Elaboration Likelihood Model in Figure 3.1 of Chapter Three.

For Further Reading

Jensen, Vernon. *Argumentation.* New York: Van Nostrand Reinhold, 1981.

Kahane, Howard. *Logic and Philosophy.* sixth edition. Belmont, CA: Wadsworth, 1990.

Minsky, Marvin. *Society of Mind.* New York: Touchstone Books, 1986.

Restak, Richard M. *The Brain.* New York: Bantam Books, 1984.

Spence, Gerry. *How to Argue and Win Every Time.* New York: St. Martin's Press, 1995.

Walton, Douglas. *Informal Logic.* New York: Cambridge University Press, 1989.

Chapter Seven

CHANNELS

In a speech at the University of South Carolina in 1987, social activist Abbie Hoffman said, "The idea that the media is there to educate us, or to inform us, is ridiculous because that's about tenth or eleventh on their list. The first purpose of the media is to sell us . . . things we don't need. One moment it'll be 'Don't do drugs' and ten minutes later it's Miller time."[1]

Hoffman, like most of us, acknowledges the persuasive impact of the media, the channels that connect the sources with the receivers. Surprisingly, little research has specifically explored the impact of the channel in the persuasive process. Perhaps it is the difficulty of isolating the specific influence of channels rather than the content,[2] or perhaps it is that all of the elements of persuasion interact in producing persuasive effects and to tease out one factor would be to destroy the whole. Whatever the reason, while we do know that the media are pervasive as well as persuasive, only limited evidence is available.

We can begin this chapter by dividing channels into two broad categories: personal channels and mass channels. Personal channels are live, face-to-face links between sources and receivers. Mass channels are connections that are mediated through some mechanical means such as print, radio, or television.

PERSONAL CHANNELS AND NONVERBAL COMMUNICATION

Nonverbal communication can be defined as "actions and artifactual cues that are not linguistic but that may have meaningful effects."[3] This means that nonverbal communication consists of actions that we

Using positive kinesic behaviors significantly improves a source's credibility.

© Michael Newman/PhotoEdit

employ with our voices and bodies and artifacts that are objects in the environment as well as adornments like hairstyles and jewelry.

The definition also indicates that nonverbal communication offers cues, fallible indicators that are subject to interpretation, cultural variation, and misunderstanding. They serve as suggestions rather than signals.

Our explanation of nonverbal communication also indicates that it is not the language itself. Nonverbal messages are not the words themselves, but all the accompanying features of communication.

Finally, our definition indicates that while nonverbal communication cues are not the words themselves, they do have meaningful effects. Communication researchers Hickson and Stacks suggest six such meaningful effects.[4] These effects are identified in Box 7.1.

Box 7.1
MEANINGFUL EFFECTS IN NONVERBAL COMMUNICATION

Effect	Example
REPETITION	Waving while saying, "Goodbye!"
CONTRADICTION	Saying, "I love you" sarcastically.
SUBSTITUTION	Waving an arm rather than saying, "Over here!"
ACCENTUATION	"*I* am firm on this" versus "I am firm on *this*."
COMPLEMENT	Saying, "This fast" while snapping the fingers.
REGULATION	Pointedly looking at one's watch while listening.

1. *Repetition.* Nonverbal communication can reinforce a message to assure understanding. For example, crowds may hold up four fingers while chanting "four more years" or a forefinger while shouting "We're number 1" to reinforce their verbal messages.
2. *Contradiction.* Sometimes nonverbal communication has the effect of countering the verbal message. For example, a physician may seek to persuade a patient by expressing nonverbal disapproval of the patient's diet while sarcastically saying, "Uh-huh. That's really good for you."
3. *Substitution.* A third effect of nonverbal communication is serving as an emblem, as a replacement for verbal communication. Congress, for example, may indicate their approval of an idea in a president's message by applauding with a standing ovation rather than through any verbal feedback.
4. *Accentuation.* Nonverbal communication may emphasize particular parts of the verbal message. Consider, for example, the difference in meaning created by stressing different words in the slogan "You deserve a break today."
5. *Complement.* Nonverbal communication may also achieve the effect of supplementing the verbal message. For example, salespersons may snap their fingers to indicate how easy the product is to use.
6. *Regulation.* The sixth effect of nonverbal communication is to serve as a communication traffic signal. Nonverbal communication may have the effect of controlling the flow of communication. For example, a client may signal a readiness to close the interview by glancing at a clock and fidgeting.

Clearly nonverbal communication is an important part of persuasion through personal channels. We will explore four such channels: auditory channels that transmit messages though sound, visual channels that communicate through sight, olfactory channels that appeal to the sense of smell, and tactile channels that link sources and receivers through touch.

AUDITORY CHANNEL

The auditory channel carries sound signals. The field of nonverbal communication concerned with vocal features like rate, volume, and pitch is called **paralinguistics.**

In an early study of paralinguistics, Mehrabian and Williams studied the persuasiveness of vocal cues. They found that increased intonation, more volume, faster rate, and less faltering speech were all paralinguistic cues linked to "enhancing the persuasiveness of a communication."[5] Later studies have supported the concept that such vocal cues affect the impact of persuasive messages.[6]

As we noticed in Chapter Five, nonverbal characteristics of the voice are also linked to source credibility. Addington, for example, studied the impact of the paralinguistic cues of rate, pitch variety, voice quality, and articulation on source credibility. He determined that all of the cues influence judgments of competence, trustworthiness, and dynamism. He also claimed that a receiver's perception of competence is most influenced by the source's changes in vocal cues.[7] In a later study, Pearce and Conklin[8] demonstrated that vocal cues not only influence receivers' judgments about the source's trustworthiness and dynamism but also the source's likableness.

In a more recent study, Burgoon, Birk, and Pfau confirmed that several vocal and other nonverbal cues interact to influence perceptions of credibility.[9]

In personal channels, vocal channels are influential in persuading others but most persuasive encounters involve the visual channel as well as the auditory channel. Since we process more information visually than we do aurally, it is appropriate to examine the impact of the visual channel in persuasion.

VISUAL CHANNEL

In the field of nonverbal communication, there are three areas that are processed through vision. These three areas are kinesics, proxemics, and artifacts. Kinesics is the study of the movements of bodies, includ-

People become uncomfortable when someone invades their personal space.

ing posture, gestures, eye behavior, and facial expression. Proxemics examines the influence of space and spatial relationships. Artifacts are objects that serve a purpose in nonverbal communication.

Kinesics

Kinesics is a field of nonverbal communication pioneered by Ray Birdwhistle in his book *Kinesics and Context.* Kinesics incorporates visual elements including motion and appearance. As we have noted in Chapter Five, physical appearance is an important factor in persuasion. Shelly Chaiken, for example, conducted a field study of the impact of attractiveness[10] on people's willingness to fill out a questionnaire and sign a petition. Chaiken's study indicated that attractive people influenced attitudes (answers on the questionnaire) and behavior (willingness to sign a petition) to a significantly greater degree than did less attractive sources. In addition, the study demonstrated that more attractive sources were perceived as friendlier and more fluent.

With a few exceptions,[11] sources who are liked are more persuasive than sources who are disliked.[12] Since attitudes of liking and disliking are indicated by kinesics, a source may significantly influence persuasion by using body posture that indicates liking. For example, McGinley,

LeFevre, and McGinley studied the impact of kinesics on opinion change. They studied the response of women to female sources who used open positions (e.g., leaning backward, hands held outward, elbows away from body, legs stretched out) and female sources who used closed positions (e.g., knees pressed together, hands folded in the lap, elbows close to body). Receivers who were exposed to sources using the open positions showed more opinion change toward the source's position than did women exposed to sources using the closed position.[13]

Dale Leathers divided kinesic cues into positive and negative categories that affect a source's credibility. He suggested, for example, that sources should use positive gestures that appear spontaneous and relaxed, elbows out and away from the body. He also recommended that sources should avoid negative gestures like hand-to-face gestures, tugging at clothing, finger-tapping. Actively engaging in controlling negative behaviors and using positive kinesic behaviors significantly improves a source's credibility.[14]

Eye behavior is another kinesic cue that has been shown to be significantly related to persuasiveness. For example, a study by Sommers, Greeno, and Boag examined the kinesic behavior of salespeople. Those who used both high levels of eye gaze and body movements were more effective than salespeople using low levels of such kinesic cues.[15]

Proxemics

Proxemics is the study of space and spatial relationships in nonverbal communication. The term was coined by Edward T. Hall[16] and has come to represent a complex set of spatial dimensions that influence human communication. We will select for consideration two important dimensions from the multiple features of proxemics: distances and relationships.

Distances involve zones or territories that human beings create and use for a variety of communication purposes. Hall identified four such zones: intimate distance, personal distance, social distance, and public distance.[17] Intimate distance ranges out approximately 18 inches from the person. Personal space ranges from 18 inches to approximately 4 feet. Social distance ranges from 4 feet to 12 feet. Public distance ranges from 12 feet out to 25 or more feet. These distances are charted in Figure 7.1.

People become uncomfortable when someone invades their personal space, unless there is a good reason, such as being crowded into an elevator. As a result, persuaders are often advised to take care not to

Figure 7.1

Edward T. Hall's Proxemic Zones

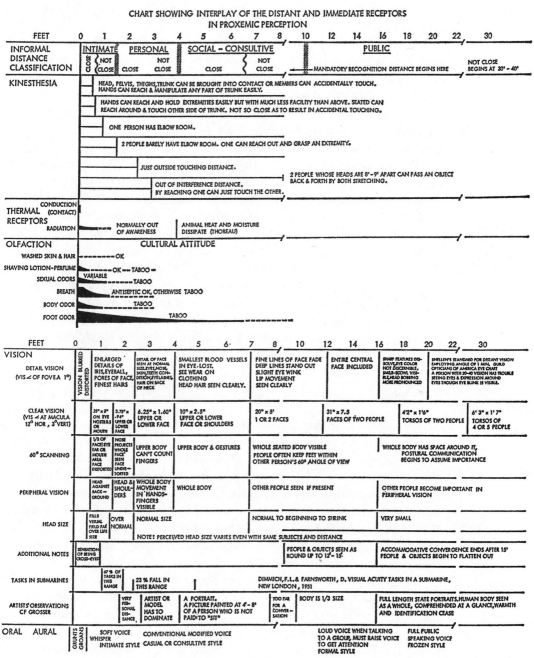

invade the personal space of the receivers. In a study of proxemics in sales contexts, McElroy and Loudenback found an adverse effect only in cases where a male sales agent invaded the personal space of a male client.[18]

The second dimension of proxemics to consider is the impact of spatial relationships in persuasion. Persuasion is clearly linked to the concept of power. As Herbert Simons wrote, "[p]ersuasion, broadly defined, is not so much an alternative to the power of constraints and inducements as it is an instrument of that power, an accompaniment to that power, or a consequence of that power."[19] And power is partially a product of proxemic placement.

We all have heard that King Arthur designed his Round Table so that all of his knights would be seated equally. The Arthurian legend underscores the perception that the head of a rectangular table is a power position. There is some validity to this common understanding. In a study of seating positions, Pellegrini found that people sitting at the head of the table were perceived as more persuasive, more talkative, dominant, self-confident, and intelligent.[20] However, King Arthur probably did not know that people consider the most powerful position at a round table to be at the twelve o'clock position and that power appears to diminish as one moves the table at the three, six, and nine o'clock positions with the least powerful position at the eleven o'clock place at the table.[21]

Artifacts

Artifacts like clothing play a significant role in persuasion. Clothing cues are directly related to attractiveness and status, which, as we have seen, are related to persuasion. Thomas Hoult, for example, found that attractiveness was increased by "appropriate" attire, and Mills and Aronson found that an attractively dressed woman was more persuasive than the same woman when she was dressed unattractively.[22] Leonard Bickman conducted a study of the impact of clothing on compliance and found that when the source was dressed in high status clothing, the receivers were much more willing to comply with requests.[23]

Artifacts also include objects in the communication environment. A study of nonverbal communication in medical settings indicated that the office equipment, such as the examination table and medical instruments, contribute to the physician's authority.[24] A study of faculty offices indicated that an office equipped with professional furnishings such as plaques and books increased the perceptions of the occupant's authoritativeness and trustworthiness.[25]

Artifacts like clothing and objects play a significant role in persuasion.

OLFACTORY CHANNEL

Robert Lucky is the executive director of research at AT&T's Bell Labs. In an interview with Bill Moyers, Lucky explained the important role of personal channels in human communication with this anecdote:

> I was talking with a Minister of Commerce in England about this— Lord somebody or other—and he said, "Teleconferencing will never work." And all of a sudden he reached out, and he embraced me. And he said, "I need to smell the person I'm dealing with." And I was just frozen. You know what I mean? I thought, "My deodorant has failed!"
>
> And when these things happen, you can't think of a single thing to say. My mind was a blank. And I never thought of a reply. But I finally understand what he meant. He meant smell as a metaphor for something that was human, that wasn't conveyed by the electronics.[26]

Note the impact of attire and other artifacts in the photographs here and on p. 175.

Smell is one of the most important but least studied areas of persuasive communication. We all intuitively recognize the importance of the "new car smell" in selling automobiles. We intuitively recognize that the olfactory channel has a significant impact on people. We know, for example, that perfumes can increase the attractiveness of the wearers, although smell appears to interact with other nonverbal channels.[27]

How, exactly, smells affect us is not clear. W. B. Key suggested that odors evoke memories that are linked to strong emotions and that those emotions are used to sell products.[28] For example, the smell of shoe polish, glue, and leather may put me in mind of my grandfather's shoe repair store. That particular combination of odors evokes pleasant memories and makes me more receptive to buying products in a store. Realtors know the value of smell in setting up memories or even stereotypical expectations. They advise homeowners to bake bread while showing their houses to prospective buyers because the smell adds a comfortable homey atmosphere to the walk through.

The spirit of the west. The power of a woman. The fragrance that captures it all.

LADY STETSON
It's how the west was won.

Smell is one of the most important, but least studied, areas of persuasion.

TACTILE CHANNEL

Finally, we should recognize the impact of touch in personal channels of persuasion. Nonverbal communication researchers refer to the field of tactile communication as *haptics*. Research in this area demonstrates the importance of the role of touch in human affairs.[29] Tactile connections are important for emotional adjustment. Touch can provide comfort and encouragement. Touch is even important in social settings; a firm handshake, for example, is an important initiation in American business transactions.

Research tends to confirm that persuaders who touch their receivers are more effective. For example, Willis and Hamm found that if interviewers touched respondents lightly on the upper arm, the interviewee was much more likely to complete a rating scale or to sign a petition.[30]

Persuaders should be warned, however, that there is such a thing as too much nonverbal communication. Overuse of touch, or any other channel of nonverbal communication, can have deleterious effects. As Peter DePaulo explained, "a nonverbal ingratiation attempt can backfire if it comes across as too strong."[31]

MASS CHANNELS

As we discussed earlier in this chapter, mass channels are impersonal. They use a mechanical means to link the persuader with the receiver. Usually mass channels reach a large number of receivers with a single message. In this section we shall examine persuasive aspects of mass media. We shall look at print media including paper and electronic print forms. We shall then explore radio which focuses on the auditory channel. Finally, we shall consider the persuasive impact of television which combines visual with auditory channels.

Media researchers summarized several decades of mass media studies with ten principles. We can adapt these principles of mass communication channels for use by persuaders.

1. *There is no "magic bullet" in media.* According to Lowery and DeFleur, the magic bullet theory of the early twentieth century "portrayed media audiences as composed of irrational creatures guided more or less by their instincts. . . . It was this vision of the personal and social conditions that led people early in the century to believe that those who controlled the media could effectively control the public. For this reason, propaganda was thought to be extremely effective; there was little doubt that

People use the media as models.

people could not resist mass advertising; and the use of media by demagogues to control the political process was a matter of deep concern."[32] Contemporary researchers reject this view of the power of mass media over human beings.

2. *Receivers actively use media to accomplish their goals.* Receivers are not just passive recipients. In fact, people turn to particular parts of the newspaper or select some media and reject others because they are actively involved in using the media to satisfy their needs.

3. *News media set agendas.* While there is a popular notion that news media objectively report just the facts, in reality, the news media highlight the importance of selected issues and downplay the importance of other issues. In other words, the decision to cover a given issue emphasizes its importance while the issues that are not covered are deemphasized.

4. *The media are instrumental in the diffusion of innovation.* New ideas, new products, new services are brought to the attention of receivers through the mass media. Therefore, the mass channels are critical for quickly and efficiently spreading innovations through the society.

5. *Media appear to use a "two-step flow" of communication.* While it may seem that media have a direct influence on receivers, the two-step flow theory suggests that media influence opinion leaders who, in turn, use more personal channels to reach receivers. There is disagreement about this theory. Steven Chaffee, for example, argued forcefully that media as a rule have a very direct impact on receivers.[33] Others suggest that the mass and the personal channels work together to produce persuasive effects.

6. *Media have a selected and limited impact on receivers.* Lowery and DeFleur cited numerous studies that show the media to have limited impact on receivers.[34] It appears that mass media serve most effectively to reinforce rather than to change opinions. It is also evident that receivers select which media they will attend to, choose which channels are most interesting or most compatible with previously held beliefs, and subject the media's content to their own interpretations.

7. *People use the media as models.* The depiction of behavior in the media serves as a model for the behavior of the receiver. This appears to be particularly true of television and movies because behavior is actually shown rather than verbally depicted, as in print or radio. When a favorite character changes hairstyle, millions of viewers, gradually or immediately, alter their hairstyle to be more like the new trend.

8. *Media establish social expectations.* We learn the expected rules and norms of social behavior from a number of sources. Our parents, for example, set out very clear expectations of what is appropriate and what is inappropriate behavior at home. But the media provide "an almost endless parade of groups and social activities, with their behavioral rules, specialized roles, levels of power and prestige, and ways of controlling their members. . . ."[35]

9. *The media define reality.* Lowery and DeFleur suggested that Plato was correct when he argued that our reality is defined by our perceptions rather than by actual events themselves; therefore, shadows on the wall of a cave are reality for people who have never known anything else.[36] The representations of the

media provide definitions of reality that we later apply when similar events occur in our own lives.

10. *More intense uses of media cultivate more intense views of reality.* This variation on the previous principle is based on research conducted by George Gerbner and others on the impact of television violence. Gerbner found that people who were heavier viewers of the violence portrayed on television were more fearful of the world than viewers who watched less television. The "cultivation theory" suggested that the content of the media may generate views more in line with the media's messages than with reality.

These principles and theories provide a useful overview of the relationship of persuasion to mass media. With this overview in mind, we can examine the mass channels more specifically.

PRINT

Print media include newspapers, magazines, direct mail, and books. Since we shall specifically examine advertising and political campaigning in later chapters, we shall focus here more specifically on the persuasive impact of the print channel.

Despite the focus of the public on television, the print media are still highly influential. Surveys indicate that 63 percent of all adults in the United States spend an average of twenty-eight minutes a day reading a daily newspaper.[37] It is also known that print media tends to reach higher income and higher educational levels of the public.[38]

Most of the research on print media focuses on issues like readership (who reads what), circulation variables, and typography and readability research rather than a specific examination of the persuasive impact of the print channel.[39]

We do know that the print media require more active participation than radio or television.[40] Even though Marshall McLuhan defined books as a "hot medium" with high definition requiring low participation by perceivers, print media generally require more intellectual, as distinct from McLuhan's perceptual, participation. The receiver must actively participate with imagination to make the words and pictures come to life.

While it is difficult to determine the persuasive impact of the print channel on readers, we can conclude that the print media do present an influential view of reality. One scholar examined how interpersonal

UPI/Bettmann

Radio has been a powerful medium for persuasion.

relations were depicted in popular magazines over a period of twenty-two years. She concluded that popular magazines "can be presumed to reflect and to inspire attitudes in their readers. . . ."[41]

Radio

Since its inception in the early twentieth century, radio has been a powerful media for persuasion. Just how influential radio can be is illustrated by the events of October 30, 1938. That evening Orson Welles broadcast a dramatization of H. G. Wells' *War of the Worlds*. Millions of listeners were convinced that "Mercury Theater on the Air" was being interrupted by genuine news reports detailing an invasion from Mars.[42]

While radio's popularity declined with the growing influence after World War II, the medium is currently witnessing a revival. Current figures indicate that 80 percent of Americans listen to the radio daily and that the average listening time totals three hours per day.[43]

The innovation of radio call-in programming has added to radio's contemporary influence. Unlike previous radio programming, call-in programs encourage greater interactivity with the listening audience. The commercial aspects of persuasion cannot be overlooked.

Radio is also influential because it is readily available in emergency situations. When a natural disaster threatens or electricity is cut off, most people will turn to a portable battery-powered radio.

Finally, radio has an influence in an important location where television and print cannot: the automobile. In fact, radio is the only mass medium that can reasonably be expected to reach receivers in that locale.

Our mobile society is exposed to persuasive commercials while listening to their favorite radio station—country and western, rap, classical, or rock—on the drive to work or school. Radio allows access to the newest musical releases while subjecting the listeners to commercial advertisements designed to persuade that audience to buy the targeted product.

TELEVISION

The final mass channel we shall explore is television. It is a vital part of American lives. As rhetorical scholars Medhurst and Benson wrote,

> [E]ven in its formative years it [television] presented artistic and propagandistic possibilities far beyond those of any previous medium. Like film, television could capture the dynamics of sight, sound and motion, alter space/time relationships and employ narrative conventions to create 'reality.' Like radio, it could transcend geographical boundaries, deliver the same message to millions of listeners or viewers simultaneously, and create a sense of personal involvement. Most important, unlike its predecessors, television was, from the outset, a medium of intimacy. It entered the home, became part of the environment, and soon began to fulfill roles ranging from babysitter to entertainer to vehicle for social indoctrination and education.[44]

It is obvious that television is the most pervasive mass medium. Ninety-eight percent of the homes in the United States have at least one television set and Americans now spend nearly seven hours a day watching television.[45]

Because it is so pervasive and so much a part of the American lifestyle, more attention has been paid to the impact of television than to any other mass channel. As a result, there is a mass of evidence. However, some of the evidence is conflicting and much of the research is faulty. Media researchers Lowery and DeFleur explained,

A major flaw evident in many of the research projects included in the report [NIMH's review of research entitled *Television and Behavior*] is that they present data from descriptive content analyses without documenting the effects of that content. A very real problem with content analyses based on samples of TV characters is that researchers show what they have found and then go on to draw inferences about behavior of the members of the audience. This is a flagrant non sequitur. Proof of influences on audiences is obviously much more tedious, qualified, and time-consuming than describing media content. Perhaps this is the reason why such documentation has not been pursued with vigor.[46]

Much of the research focuses on the content of the media rather than the persuasive effect of the channel.

Despite the problems in synthesizing the research, there are a few observations on television as a persuasive channel that seem warranted.

First, television appears to be less effective than print channels at delivering complex messages but it appears more effective at engendering emotions. For example, Chaiken and Eagly found that receivers exposed to a complex message in written form were more influenced than receivers exposed to a videotaped version of the same message.[47] The linear flow of the televised message dooms the receiver who missed a vital part. The receiver then must attempt to understand the remainder of the message by making assumptions about what was missed.

Second, television allows greater use of source credibility. Studies have confirmed that source characteristics become more important and influential in television than in print media.[48] In fact, among the media, television is the most credible channel. The Roper Organization, a polling company, asked a random sample of people, "If you got conflicting or different reports of the same news from radio, television, the magazines and the newspapers, which of the four versions would you be most inclined to believe—the one on radio or television or magazines or newspapers?" Forty-nine percent of the respondents said television, while 26 percent said newspapers, only 7 percent responded radio, 5 percent chose magazines, and 13 percent responded "don't know."[49] Thus, the television version of an advertisement, with its simultaneous visual and auditory channels, is more believable than other media that must rely solely on one channel.

We will have more to say about the role of television in political campaigns and in product advertising in later chapters. For the moment, consider the words of Orson Welles, the actor, director and producer mentioned earlier, "I hate television. I hate it as much as peanuts. But I can't stop eating peanuts."[50]

Summary

We began this chapter by examining the field of nonverbal communication as a significant part of personal channels. We noted that nonverbal cues have at least six meaningful effects in persuasive communication: repetition, contradiction, substitution, accentuation, complement, and regulation.

Next we considered the persuasive dimension of each of the nonverbal channels. We noted that paralinguistics is closely tied to source credibility, especially competence, trustworthiness, dynamism, and likeableness. We saw that kinesics, proxemics, and artifactual cues all play important parts in the total persuasive process. To a lesser degree, the olfactory channel of smells and the tactile channel of touch can also be used in making persuasion more effective.

Research in mass channels indicated ten important principles for persuaders to bear in mind in planning media strategy. (1) There is no "magic bullet" in media. (2) Receivers actively use media to accomplish their goals. (3) News media set agendas. (4) The media are instrumental in the diffusion of innovation. (5) Media appear to use a "two-step flow" of communication. (6) Media have a selected and limited impact on receivers. (7) People use the media as models. (8) Media establish social expectations. (9) The media define reality. (10) More intense uses of media cultivate more intense views of reality.

Finally, we looked at the specific persuasive implications of the various media. Print appears to be a more persuasive media for higher income groups and for higher educational levels. Despite the influence of television, radio is still influential, especially in a mobile society that spends considerable time in automobiles where neither print nor television channels can effectively reach receivers. While television has been studied extensively, we noted that it is less effective than print in delivering complex persuasive messages. However, television allows the greatest use of source credibility.

So far we have examined the critical elements of sources, messages, and channels in persuasive communication. There is one additional element that we must consider. The key element—receivers—is the topic of the next chapter.

Notes

[1] Abbie Hoffman, "Speech at the University of South Carolina," September 16, 1987, quoted in *The New York Public Library Book of 20th Century*

American Quotations, eds. Stephen Donadio, Joan Smith, Susan Mesner, and Rebecca Davison (New York: Warner Books, 1992), p. 280.

2 Daniel J. O'Keefe, *Persuasion: Theory and Research* (Newbury Park, CA: Sage Publications, 1990), p. 184.

3 James Benjamin, *Communication: Concept and Contexts* (New York: Harper & Row, 1986), p. 45.

4 Mark L. Hickson and Don W. Stacks, *NVC: Nonverbal Communication* (Dubuque, IA: William C. Brown Publishers, 1985), pp. 16–17.

5 A. Mehrabian and M. Williams, "Nonverbal Concomitants of Perceived and Intended Persuasiveness," *Journal of Personality and Social Psychology,* 13 (1969), pp. 37–58.

6 See, for example, W. B. Pearce and B. J. Brommel, "Vocalic Communication in Persuasion," *Quarterly Journal of Speech,* 58 (1972), pp. 298–306; N. Miller, G. Maruyama, R. J. Beaber, and K. Valone, "Speed of Speech and Persuasion," *Journal of Personality and Social Psychology,* 34 (1976), pp. 615–624.

7 David Addington, "The Relationship of Selected Vocal Characteristics to Personality Perception," *Speech Monographs,* 35 (1968), pp. 492–503.

8 W. B. Pearce and F. Conklin, "Nonverbal Vocalic Communication and Perception of a Speaker," *Speech Monographs,* 38 (1971), pp. 235–241; W. B. Pearce, "The Effect of Vocal Cues on Credibility and Attitude Change," *Western Speech,* 35 (1971), pp. 176–184.

9 Judee K. Burgoon, Thomas Birk, and Michael Pfau, "Nonverbal Behaviors, Persuasion, and Credibility," *Human Communication Research,* 17 (Fall 1990), p. 140.

10 S. Chaiken, "Communicator Physical Attractiveness and Persuasion," *Journal of Personality and Social Psychology,* 37 (1979), pp. 1387–1397.

11 See, for example, P. G. Zimbardo, M. Weisenberg, I. Firestone, and B. Levy, "Communicator Effectiveness in Producing Public Conformity and Private Attitude Change," *Journal of Personality,* 33 (1965), pp. 233–255; J. Cooper, J. M. Darley, and J. E. Henderson, "On the Effectiveness of Deviant- and Conventional-Appearing Communicators: A Field Experiment," *Journal of Personality and Social Psychology,* 29 (1974), pp. 752–757.

12 A. H. Eagly and S. Chaiken, "An Attribution Analysis of the Effect of Communicator Characteristics on Opinion Change: The Case of Communicator Attractiveness," *Journal of Personality and Social Psychology,* 32 (1975), pp. 136–144; E. E. Sampson and C. A. Insko, "Cognitive Consistency and Performance in the Autokinetic Situation," *Journal of Abnormal and Social Psychology,* 68 (1964), pp. 184–192.

13 H. McGinley, R. LeFevre, and P. McGinley, "The Influence of a Communicator's Body Position on Opinion Change in Others," *Journal of Personality and Social Psychology,* 31 (1974), pp. 686–690.

14 Dale G. Leathers, *Successful Nonverbal Communication: Principles and Applications* (New York: Macmillan Publishing, 1986), pp. 152–163.

15 M. S. Sommers, D. W. Greeno, and D. Boag, "The Role of Nonverbal Communication in Service Provision and Representation," *Service Industries Journal,* 9 (1989), pp. 162–173.

16 E. T. Hall, "A System for the Notation of Proxemic Behavior," *American Anthropologist,* 65 (1963), pp. 1003–1026.

[17] Edward T. Hall, *The Hidden Dimension* (New York, Doubleday Publishers, 1969), passim.

[18] J. C. McElroy and L. J. Loudenback, "Personal Space and Personal Selling: Customer Reactions to Personal Space Invasions," *Proceedings of the Educator Seminar,* (1981), pp. 38–52.

[19] Herbert Simons, "The Carrot and the Stick as Handmaidens of Persuasion in Conflict Situations," *Perspectives on Communication in Social Conflict,* G. R. Miller and H. W. Simons, eds. (Englewood Cliffs, NJ: Prentice-Hall, 1974), p. 177.

[20] R. J. Pellegrini, "Some Effects of Seating Position on Social Perception," *Psychological Reports,* 28 (1971), pp. 887–893.

[21] M. Koneya and A. Barbour, *Louder than Words . . . Nonverbal Communication* (Columbus, OH: Charles E. Merrill Publishing Company, 1976), pp. 58–59.

[22] T. Hoult, "Experimental Measurement of Clothing as a Factor in Some Social Ratings of Selected American Men," *American Sociological Review,* 19 (1954), pp. 326–327; J. Mills and E. Aronson, "Opinion Change as a Function of the Communicator's Attractiveness and Desire to Influence," *Journal of Personality and Social Psychology,* 1 (1965), pp. 73–77.

[23] L. Bickman, "The Effect of Social Status on the Honesty of Others," *Journal of Social Psychology,* 85 (1971), pp. 359–360.

[24] H. S. Freedman, "Nonverbal Communication Between Patients and Medical Practitioners," *Journal of Social Issues,* 35 (1979), pp. 82–99.

[25] E. W. Miles and D. G. Leathers, "The Impact of Aesthetic and Professionally Related Objects on Credibility in the Office Setting," *The Southern Speech Communication Journal,* 49 (1984), pp. 361–379.

[26] Robert Lucky, "Robert Lucky, Engineer," in *Bill Moyers: A World of Ideas II,* ed. Andie Toucher (New York: Doubleday, 1990), p. 202.

[27] J. C. Horn, "The Scentimental Perfume Put-Off," *Psychology Today,* 12 (May, 1980), p. 16.

[28] W. B. Key, *Media Sexploitation* (Englewood Cliffs, NJ: Prentice-Hall, 1976), p. 78.

[29] See, for example, M. F. A. Montague, *Touching: The Human Significance of the Skin* (New York: Columbia University Press, 1971), p. 292.

[30] F. N. Willis and H. K. Hamm, "The Use of Interpersonal Touch in Securing Compliance," *Journal of Nonverbal Behavior,* 1 (1980), pp. 49–55.

[31] Peter J. DePaulo, "Applications of Nonverbal Behavior Research in Marketing and Management," *Applications of Nonverbal Behavioral Theories and Research,* Robert S. Feldman, ed. (Hillsdale, NJ: Lawrence Erlbaum Associates, 1992), p. 74.

[32] Shearon A. Lowery and Melvin L. DeFleur, *Milestones in Mass Communication Research,* third edition (White Plains, NY: Longman Publishers, 1995), p. 13.

[33] Steven Chaffee, "The Interpersonal Context of Mass Communication," *Current Perspectives in Mass Communication Research,* F. G. Kilne and P. J. Tichenor, eds. (Beverly Hills, CA: Sage, 1972), pp. 107–137.

[34] Lowery and DeFleur, *Milestones,* p. 402.

[35] Ibid., p. 403.

[36] See Plato, *The Republic,* Book VII.

[37] Scott Cutlip, Allen Center, and Glen Broom, *Effective Public Relations,* seventh edition (Englewood Cliffs, NJ: Prentice-Hall, 1994), pp. 282–283.

[38] John A. Finley, "Special Report: Reading," *Presstime,* (September, 1984), p. 22; M. R. Samuelson, R. Carter, L. Ruggels, "Education, Available Time, and Uses of Mass Media," *Journalism Quarterly,* 40 (1963), pp. 491–496.

[39] Roger Wimmer and Joseph R. Dominick, *Mass Media Research* (Belmont, CA: Wadsworth Publishing Company, 1983), p. 267.

[40] Joseph Klapper, *The Effects of Mass Communication* (New York: The Free Press, 1960), passim.

[41] Virginia Kidd, "Happily Ever After and Other Relationship Styles: Advice on Interpersonal Relations in Popular Magazines, 1951–1973," *Rhetorical Dimensions in Media,* Martin J Medhurst and Thomas W. Benson, eds. (Dubuque, IA: Kendall/Hunt, 1984), p. 267.

[42] Howard Koch, *The Panic Broadcast: Portrait of an Event* (Boston, MA: Little, Brown, 1970), passim.

[43] Cutlip, Center and Broom, *Effective Public Relations,* p. 290.

[44] Martin Medhurst and Thomas Benson, "Rhetoric of Television," *Rhetorical Dimensions in Media* (Dubuque, IA: Kendall/Hunt Publishing, 1984), p. 1.

[45] Joseph R. Dominick, *The Dynamics of Mass Communication* (New York: McGraw-Hill, 1990), pp. 464–465.

[46] Lowery and DeFleur, *Milestones,* p. 373.

[47] S. Chaiken and A. H. Eagly, "Communication Modality as a Determinant of Message Persuasiveness and Message Comprehensibility," *Journal of Personality and Social Psychology,* 34 (1976), pp. 605–614.

[48] V. Andreoli and S. Worchel, "Effect of Media, Communicator, and Message Position on Attitude Change," *Public Opinion Quarterly,* 42 (1978), pp. 59–70; S. Chaiken and A. H. Eagly, "Communication Modality as a Determinant of Message Persuasion: The Role of Communicator Salience," *Journal of Personality and Social Psychology,* 45 (1983), pp. 241–256.

[49] Cited in Dominick, *Dynamics of Mass Communication,* p. 468.

[50] Orson Welles, New York *Herald Tribune* (12 October 1956).

For Further Thought

1. Analyze advertisements using the six functions of nonverbal communication. In what ways do the nonverbal elements of the ads serve to repeat, contradict, substitute, accent, complement, or regulate the verbal content?

2. Videotape a televised infomercial. Carefully analyze the way that the sales agents use nonverbal communication to sell the product.

3. Take one of Lowrey and DeFleur's ten principles of mass media. Using that principle, explain how a supposedly informative newscast may actually serve to persuade the viewers.

4. Television appears to be less effective than print channels at delivering complex messages but more effective at engendering emotions. Cite specific examples of television programs that support or refute that generalization.

5. Cite examples of the ways in which an advertisement or a political campaign may use different channels to reach different audiences and to achieve different effects.

For Further Reading

Burgoon, Judee K., D. B. Buller, and W. G. Woodall. *Nonverbal Communication: The Unspoken Dialogue.* New York: Harper & Row, 1989.

Feldman, Robert S., ed. *Applications of Nonverbal Behavioral Theories and Research.* Hillsdale, NJ: Lawrence Erlbaum Associates, Publishers, 1992.

Knapp, Mark L. *Nonverbal Communication in Human Interaction,* second edition. New York: Holt, Rinehart and Winston, 1978.

Leathers, Dale G. *Successful Nonverbal Communication: Principles and Applications.* New York: Macmillan Publishing Company, 1986.

Lowery, Shearon A. and Melvin DeFleur, *Milestones in Mass Communication Research: Media Effects,* third edition. White Plains, NY: Longman, 1995.

Malandro, Loretta and Larry Barker. *Nonverbal Communication.* Reading, MA: Addison-Wesley Publishing Company, 1983.

Chapter Eight

RECEIVERS

Receivers, as we noted in Chapter One, are the audiences for persuasive messages. They may be listeners like people listening to a politician's campaign speech on their car radios. They may be readers like subscribers reading a newspaper editorial. They may be viewers such as audiences watching an infomercial on television. Belgian philosopher Chaim Perelman, writing about rhetoric, suggested "there is only one rule in this matter, adaptation of the speech to the audience, whatever its nature."[1] Perelman's concept can be extended beyond speech to include all persuasive messages. The source may provide the ideas and the words to express them, but without the receiver's understanding, they are just empty gestures.

AUDIENCE ANALYSIS

Jack Valenti was a key assistant and speech writer for Lyndon Baines Johnson. In explaining how to write a speech he indicated the important role of analyzing the audience.

> Some years ago I was selected to present to John D. Rockefeller III the prestigious Jefferson Award of the American Institute of Public Service.
>
> I deliberated for a good many hours over the theme of that presentation. My aim was to encapsulate, in less than five minutes, the life of Mr. Rockefeller, and to do so in a fashion calculated to enlighten the audience not only about his work, which all were familiar with, but more notably about the form and force of his character.
>
> My audience would be largely Washingtonian, men and women experienced in politics, literate and informed about current affairs. They would be people who either knew Rockefeller personally or at least were knowledgeable about his life work. Therefore I wanted to give

© David Young-Wolff/PhotoEdit

Persuaders must adapt to diverse audiences.

some emotional weight to what I said, above and beyond relating the specifics of his personal performance.

I determined that my theme would be the genetic code of the Rockefeller family, and that family's persistent acceptance of their obligation to a country that had provided them with the means to enormous wealth.[2]

Valenti carefully considered the nature of his receivers and adapted what he said to that audience. If his audience had consisted of a different group with alternative knowledge and expectations, his introduction of Rockefeller would have been much different.

As Valenti and other speech writers know, understanding the audience and adapting the message to those listeners is the key to effective public speaking. To analyze the audience requires asking and answering questions about the nature of the listeners in the group. Box 8.1 is a list of the typical questions speech writers ask about their audiences.

These questions are easily adapted to other persuasive channels. For example, in a direct mail campaign, the "speaker's" physical condition mentioned in Box 8.1 may be adapted to the state of the mailed brochure after it has been processed by the postal system. Other questions may also be related to the television medium, a written message, or a series of messages in a persuasive campaign.

Asking questions about the audience is relatively easy. Getting answers to those questions is more difficult. There are several sources of information persuaders can tap to do a detailed audience analysis. Here are some of the most common sources of information.

1. *Use your knowledge of the typical audiences.* From your own experience and from previous chapters you know how people usually react to persuasion and the general expectations that audiences have. For example, unless there are unusual circumstances, you can expect that most college classes are pretty evenly divided between men and women, that many of the group will be between 18 and 23 years of age, and so on. Adapting your material to the nature of your audience will help your receivers follow and retain your message. The better you know your audience the easier it is to adapt.

2. *Seek additional information from the organizers.* Being invited to deliver a speech means that someone offered the invitation. Ask the organizers of the event the relevant questions about the audience in Box 8.1.

Box 8.1

TYPICAL QUESTIONS TO ASK IN ANALYZING THE AUDIENCE

Physical Characteristics

Of the audience:

1. How large will it be?
2. What age groups will be present—and in what proportion?
3. Which sex will predominate—and to what extent?
   a. Will they be tired from a day of hard labor?
   b. Will they be tired from a long preceding program?
   c. Will they be lethargic from having just eaten heartily?
   d. Will they be alert and excited, eager for action?

Of the occasion:

1. In what kind of auditorium will the meeting be held?
   a. What is the actual size?
   b. What is the size in relation to the number of auditors?

(continued)

(continued from previous page)

      c. What is the shape?

      d. Where will the speaker stand in relation to the auditors?

      e. How are the acoustics?

      f. Will the speech be delivered from a platform?

      g. What kinds of symbols, if any, will be in the auditorium?

2. What kind of program will precede (and follow) the speech?

      a. What will be its length?

      b. What will be its type (music, games, speeches, movies)?

      c. What will be the audience's participation in it?

3. What is the purpose of the meeting?

      a. To celebrate an anniversary or an event?

      b. To constitute one unit of a campaign or series of programs?

      c. Specifically to hear the invited speaker?

Of the speaker:

1. Will he be physically fit?

      a. Could he rest prior to the meeting, or will he have to speak while tired from traveling or working?

      b. Will he have eaten lightly or not at all during the two or three hours preceding the speech?

2. Will he be physically impressive?

      a. Because of his own physique? or

      b. Because of the height or arrangement of the rostrum?

Psychological Characteristics

Of the audience:

1. What is the mental ability of the audience—and with what variation?

      a. General intelligence level?

      b. General educational level?

      c. General background of experience?

      d. Special knowledge of the speaker's subject matter?

2. What predisposing tendencies will influence the audience?

      a. Special beliefs?

      b. General and specific attitudes?

      c. Group loyalties?

      d. Previous relationships with the speaker?

      e. The probable mood of the audience?

(continued)

(continued from previous page)

    f. Degree of liberalism, or flexibility of mind?
      1. How directly is the self-interest of the audience involved in the proposal?
      2. Does the audience believe its self-interest will be affected favorably or unfavorably?
    g. How much and what kind of public opinion have been evidenced regarding the proposal?

Of the occasion:

    1. Who are the sponsors of the meeting?
      a. What prestige do they have in the community?
      b. What, if any, relationship do they have to the speaker's proposal?
      c. What is their attitude toward the speaker and his proposal?

    2. How appropriate will the speech be to the function of the meeting?
      a. In subject matter?
      b. In aim?
      c. In general tone or style of composition and delivery?

    3. What relationship is the speech expected to have to the function of the meeting?

Of the speaker:

    1. What is the prestige of the speaker with this particular audience?

    2. Is the speaker fully prepared?
      a. Intellectually?
      b. Emotionally?

SOURCE: Robert T. Oliver, *The Psychology of Persuasive Speech* (New York: David McKay Company, Inc., 1968), pp. 81–82.

3. *Examine written sources of information.* Read the local newspapers and magazines the audience is likely to read. For example, the student newspaper can identify the important issues on campus, local newspapers can provide examples of current events and key people of local renown. Read any brochures or handbooks about the organizations that the audience belongs to. The motto of the school, the history of the campus, and other information in the catalogue can offer details that enhance a persuasive campaign on a college campus. The credos of organizations provide

an indication of the particular values endorsed by the group. The specific examples used in a message can be linked to these values to maximize the impact of the message on the audience.

4. *Conduct a site visit.* Personally interviewing the members of the rhetorical audience can provide valuable insights into their thoughts and feelings. This is the approach that many advertisers use when they conduct "focus group" sessions. "Focus groups involve assembling a group of customers or potential customers in a group meeting, showing them alternative ad concepts or other marketing materials, and then having them discuss their reactions to each of the choices. The group is moderated by a focus group specialist. A trained observer takes notes on the reactions or the group is videotaped and the observations are documented later. Focus groups don't provide conclusive evidence, but they are excellent tools for evaluating the impact of alternative choices among ad concepts or other communication marketing tools, such as packaging, product names, or corporate image programs."[3] The value of the focus group depends on how well the focus group reflects the actual audience's values and ideas and the willingness of the focus group to be open and honest in its discussions.

5. *Make use of professional databases of information about audiences.* Marketing research groups provide demographic and psychographic information—such features as their lifestyles, purchasing patterns, family orientation, and cultural traits. The Stanford Research Institute, for example, provides consumer profile information based on consumer responses to questionnaires. They classify nine "VALS" (Values and Lifestyle) types into four categories: Need Driven, which includes survivors and sustainers; Outer Directed, which includes belongers, emulators, and achievers; Inner Directed, which includes I-am-me, Experientials, and the societally conscious; and Integrated.[4] The four lifestyles categories and nine types are summarized in Box 8.2.

The Need Driven group is made up of people with very limited resources. As a result, the type termed survivors is so poverty stricken that most of its income is spent on basics like food and shelter. Sustainers are at the edge of poverty and may include determined people who may be angry at the "system."

Outer Directed people take their value orientation from others. This group includes belongers who seek to preserve the status quo. The

---

Box 8.2

VALUES AND LIFESTYLE (VALS) STANFORD RESEARCH INSTITUTE

Category I Need Driven	Category II Inner Directed
Survivors	I-am-Me
Sustainers	Experientials
	Societally Conscious

Category III Outer Directed	Category IV Integrated
Belongers	Integrated
Emulators	
Achievers	

---

category also includes emulators who are trying to make it big and model themselves on those groups they seek to join. Achievers are the leaders who tend to be confident and efficient in their activities.

Inner Directed people tend to develop their values from within themselves. The I-am-me type tends to be extremely individualistic, often to the point of narcissism. Experientials are people who seek direct experience but who are more inclusive of other people than the I-am-me type. Finally, this category includes the societally conscious. These people have a sense of responsibility and support causes like environmentalism and consumerism. They tend to be both impassioned and knowledgeable.

The final category is the Integrated. These people, like Maslow's self-actualized people, are a small group. "They are fully mature in a psychological sense—able to see many sides of an issue, able to lead if necessary, and willing to take a secondary role if that is appropriate."[5]

Audience analysis is a matter of asking and answering questions about the nature of the target receivers. Specific features that influence receiver responses can be divided into two broad categories: demographic factors and psychological factors.

DEMOGRAPHIC FACTORS

Business people clearly recognize the need for demographic analysis in marketing products and services. Business writers Marvin Nesbit and

Arthur Weinstein argued that demographic information "is the most accessible and cost-effective way to identify a target market, and it is within practically everyone's budget. Even if demographic statistics are a less than perfect marketing tool, they frequently can provide you with a competitive edge."[6] Such factors as the size of the target audience, the typical age, the proportion of males and females, the economic income, geographic background, marital status, and ethnic or cultural heritage of the listeners can influence what to say and how to say it. In the next few pages we shall explore some of the major demographic features of audience analysis and how those factors influence the content, style and delivery of persuasive messages.

SIZE

Sometimes a persuasive message speech will be narrowly focused on a small group of people—when a sales representative interacts with a couple, for example. Sometimes persuasive messages are addressed to moderate-sized groups—for example, a direct mail campaign may be limited to customers who have filled out entry forms in a local drawing. Sometimes the size of the audience is large enough to qualify as a large group—televised advertisements may reach millions. In any of these cases, the size of the audience plays a part in shaping the content of the persuasive message.

Obviously, the larger the audience, the more likely it is that there will be more diverse views, experiences, and interpretations. George Campbell, a rhetorician discussed in Chapter Two, writing in 1776 noted that "the more mixed the auditory [audience] is, the greater is the difficulty of speaking to them with effect. The reason is obvious—what will tend to favor success with one, may tend to obstruct it with another. The more various therefore the individuals are, in respect of age, rank, fortune, education, prejudices, the more delicate must be the art of preserving propriety in an address to the whole."[7] In other words, audiences are composed of individuals but the persuader must try to adapt to *all* of the individuals in the target group. This challenge looms larger with larger audiences. With a few people, it is possible to know enough about their backgrounds to use examples they will relate to, but with a larger group it is harder to generalize about their experiences. As a result, persuading a larger audience may require broader rather than narrower appeals, the use of more inclusive examples, and broader themes.

The larger the audience, the less likely there is to be interaction between the source and the receivers. In a small group people do not feel that they have to raise their hands and be recognized before asking a question and are therefore more likely to interact with the speaker on a less formal level. In a larger group even a live presentation is likely to restrict interaction between the speaker and the audience. Of course, in mediated communication—communication over radio, television or print media—there is likely to be little, if any, interaction between the receiver and the copywriter of the print ad.

AGE

The most widely circulated magazine in the United States is *Modern Maturity*, a publication of the American Association of Retired People.[8] There is no question that the age demographic is important in American society.

The age of the receivers makes a significant difference in how they respond. A group of high school sophomores, for example, may be primarily interested in getting a driver's license whereas a group of college sophomores is more likely to be interested in settling on a career path. As one research report noted, older communicators have poorer self-perceptions of their own language performance and "awareness of limited memory, hearing, or ability to process information quickly can lead to selection of different cognitive and social strategies, to altered levels of motivation and anxiety, to avoidance of challenging situations, and to lowered expectations for subsequent performance."[9]

Age also makes a difference in terms of examples a persuader can use. To illustrate the impact of vivid experience on memory, an instructor could once rely on where one was when John Kennedy was assassinated, but some college students were not even born in 1963 and the same lecturer would have to use the Challenger accident to adapt the example to a younger audience.

GENDER

There is no question that there are gender-linked differences in styles of speaking and listening. Men and women both express their ideas and perceive the world differently.

Communication studies demonstrate that gender differences play a role in how a person communicates. According to a study of the first speeches of college students, "generally the female speakers in this public context were comparatively complex, literate, tentative, and attentive to emotional concerns. Their discourse suggested a relatively powerless condition. By contrast, the males were egocentric, nonstandard, active, controlling, and intense. Their discourse focused on the here-and-now."[10]

Age is an important demographic factor that influences how people react to persuasion.

Similar principles apply to the more important role that gender differences can play in how an audience interprets persuasive messages. Consider, for example, these two passages from a popular book on communication between men and women.

John Gray, a noted psychologist, claims that women "value love, communication, beauty, and relationships. They spend a lot of time supporting, helping, and nurturing one another. Their sense of self is defined through their feelings and the quality of relationships. They express fulfillment through sharing and relating."[11] By contrast, Gray claims that men "value power, competency, efficiency, and achievement. They are always doing things to prove themselves and develop their power and skills. Their sense of self is defined through their ability to achieve results. They experience fulfillment primarily through success and accomplishment."[12] As a result, when approaching the issue of either speaking or listening, men and women will often take different routes.

While both men and women are influenced by emotion as well as evidence, in general women will tend to consider the emotional overtones of a message whereas men typically feel more comfortable with facts and figures. In assessing a proposal, men will analyze whether the proposed solution will quickly and easily accomplish the goal. Women, on the other hand, will tend to be more open-minded about a variety of solutions with the best solution being the one that benefits the most people with the least harm to others and the environment.

Knowing the predominant gender of the audience can help in adapting material to the particular needs and interests of the receivers. This makes the message more relevant and therefore more effective with that audience. For example, some films, like *Mortal Combat*, are clearly aimed at male audiences while others, like *Thelma and Louise*, are aimed at attracting the attention of female audiences.

INCOME

Income is another demographic feature that can be important in audience analysis. Most college students are in a relatively low economic bracket during their college years, but their education will pay off later in higher disposable incomes. That is why credit card companies are particularly eager to enroll college seniors.

A financial advisor seeking to enroll a client in a program would recognize that people in higher income brackets will be concerned with investment rather than savings. Potential clients in a lower economic bracket, on the other hand, would probably be more interested in goal-directed savings plans with protection of principal and decent interest. These factors would indicate the type of program most attractive to the particular type of client.

Financial goals of receivers change with changing economic circumstances. Recent college graduates may want to pay off college loans, build a nest egg, purchase a car, and save for a vacation. A young married couple may be seeking to build a down payment on a house, pay off the costs of having children, and start saving for the children's education. The "empty nesters" will probably want to focus on maintaining a comfortable lifestyle, caring for aging parents, and saving as much as possible for a rapidly nearing retirement. If a person suddenly comes into wealth, these goals rapidly change. Andrew Tobias quotes Gail Sheehy, who suddenly became very wealthy with the publication of her book *Passages*. "Sheehy, with great good sense, is trying hard to avoid what she calls, 'that classic American trap—which is, you suddenly get a windfall and then, instead of living pretty much as you have, only a little better and with a lot more security behind you—with money there to do something amazing every once in a while when it really counts—you suddenly leap up to meet that income level and always bubble over it, and then are constantly running to keep up with this tremendous overhead you've established.'"[13]

Persuaders should look to the demographic factor of income in analyzing the fiscal dimensions of their case. Knowing such features as disposable income, risk tolerance, and financial goals can be tremendously important in assessing an audience and directing the appropriate message to the appropriate audience.

Geography

The geographic location of the audience makes a significant difference in their perceptions. People raised in New York City do not have the same perspective as people raised in Cedar Falls, Iowa. Despite the leveling influence of national television, living in a large metropolitan area in the East is radically different in everyday experiences from living in a small city in Middle America.

Even when size of the city is constant, geography can make a difference. For example, the Fourth Congressional District of Arizona has a population of 610,708. Here is how the area is described:

> From Camelback Mountain, 1800 feet high above the Valley of the Sun, you can look north over one of America's fastest growing and most affluent metropolises, spread out over what was clumps of sagebrush

three or four decades ago. That was what Frank Lloyd Wright saw from his Talisin West home and studio when he looked out toward the Biltmore Hotel he designed in the 1930s. Now the same area—northern Scottsdale, the town of Paradise Valley, the northern section of Phoenix between Camelback and Lookout Mountains includes many of the most upscale parts of the fast-growing metropolitan Phoenix. There is still very much of a Western air to these neighborhoods: grass is discouraged, when not prohibited by subdivision covenant; planting anything but desert flora is frowned upon; the architecture of the house tends toward unadorned stucco with picture windows facing away from the sun; the idea is to suggest that there is a horse corral over in the next lot and sometimes, especially in the northern edges, there is.[14]

The Ninth Congressional District of Ohio includes Toledo and has a comparable population of 570,911. Here is how the same authors describe this location.

Seventy years ago Toledo was one of America's boom towns. The 1920s here was 'a decade of fabulous figures,' Harlan Hatcher wrote: the Willys-Overland plant employed 25,000 workers and turned out an auto every 30 seconds; the city built $20 million coal and iron ore docks; the Libbey–Owens–Ford merger made Toledo, with good local supplies of natural gas and sand, the nation's biggest glass manufacturer; the city built a new museum and transcontinental airport. Toledo had long been well-situated, where the Maumee River empties into Lake Erie, where two dozen rail lines connected it with the East Coast and Chicago and the coal fields of Kentucky and West Virginia. It was well-positioned to be one of the centers of the brash rising auto industry, a national leader when it produced the Jeep in the 1940s. But in the late 1970s and early 1980s, auto company management allowed the union to bid wages and benefits too high while the union allowed management to let quality get too low, to the point that consumers would not buy enough American-made cars for the industry to survive without vast subsidy or major shrinkage. Subsidy, beyond the temporary Chrysler loan and a few small trade barriers, was not forthcoming, and so Toledo and other auto-dependent cities went through tough times: contrast the confident, growing city of the 1920s with the Toledo that sadly saw the tasteful Portside Festival Marketplace close in 1990.[15]

Information about the influence of geographic background of audiences can be vitally important. By knowing the influence of such features on the audience, persuaders can choose topics, examples, and expressions that closely fit the nature of the audience. For example, given the analysis of two cities of nearly equal size, a persuasive speech in Scottsdale might use an analogy with a horse but in Toledo the automobile analogy would be more appropriate. Persuading an audience to adopt an urban planning proposal should take a developmental approach in Scottsdale but a revitalization approach in Toledo.

MARITAL STATUS

Single, married, divorced, separated, living together, dual income with no kids, single head of household, and a variety of other conditions characterize the contemporary American family. This type of background can make a difference in how an audience relates to a source and the topic.

Consider, for example, what a direct mail copywriter would need to do to adapt an ad for safety devices to different groups. A group of unmarried college students are not likely to be vitally concerned with motion detectors and other home security devices but they may be interested in personal protection devices. Single parents and parents with young children would be much more concerned with home safety devices to protect their children. Such demographic features can influence how a persuader must adapt material to the receivers.

CULTURAL BACKGROUND

Cultural background means that the audience's cultural heritage influences their responses to persuasion.

> Culture is an agreed-upon set of rules that consist of components ranging from seemingly inconsequential edicts about how to shake hands or dress on a date to more cosmic ideas about the existence of God or the nature of man. Some of the components of culture are: general style of behaving, etiquette, values, language, tastes and preferences, traditions and customs, food, dress, and musical taste, belief systems and world views. . . .
>
> Just as culture tells us how to behave, it also colors our interpretation of the behavior of others. Because mainstream Americans associate a hearty handshake with strength and purpose, they are likely to assume incorrectly that the more gentle grasp of the Asian is a sign of weakness or indecisiveness. Such ethnocentrism can create harmful misunderstandings in the multicultural business environment.[16]

The Bureau of Census estimated that in 1995 the U. S. population was 83.2 percent Caucasian, 12.9 percent African-American and 4 percent other races. By 2015, the proportion is projected to be 79.9 percent Caucasian, 14 percent African-American, and 6 percent other races.[17] These demographic features clearly show that ethnic background is a variable of growing importance in persuading audiences now and in the future.

Cultural background is not limited to race, of course. As a demographic variable, cultural background means that the audience's cultural heritage influences their responses to communication. For example,

Table 8.1

Samli's Response Hierarchy Models for Four Cultures

Response Hierarchy Models for Four Cultures

	Japanese	Chinese	American	Korean
Cognitive Stage	Receive info from: friends, knowlegeable people. Read brochures and sales literature.	Receive info from: family, co-worker, knowledgeable people.	Receive info from: friend, brochures and sales literature.	Receive info from: knowledgeable people. Read brochures and sales literature.
Affective Stage	Develop interest and confidence in product because the brand is very strong.	Develop interest and confidence in product because the brand is very strong and there is trial warranty.	Develop interest and confidence in product because the product can be returned.	Develop interest and confidence in product because the brand is very strong and there is trial warranty.
Behavior Stage	Product will be tried a few times and will be purchased very quickly by those who have above-average income and are well-educated.	Product will be tried many times and will be purchased quickly by those who are open-minded.	Product will not be tried at all and will be purchased somewhat quickly by educated, open-minded risk-takers who have above-average income.	Product will be tried a few times and purchased slowly by inner-directed people who have above-average income.

SOURCE: A. Coskun Samli, *International Consumer Behavior: Its Impact on Marketing Strategy Development.* Reprinted with permission of Greenwood Publishing Group, Inc. Westport, CT. Copyright 1995, Quorum Books.

sharing personal information during a persuasive presentation may be viewed by a listener from one ethnic group as sympathetic and open while listeners from another ethnic group may feel very uncomfortable that such information is discussed so openly with strangers. A remark in the presentation that indicates the source has used alcohol may be irrelevant to some receivers, accepted and even held as evidence that the person is a "regular guy" by others, but it may indicate that the speaker and consequently his ideas are suspect by members of ethnic groups who believe alcohol use is related to weak character and muddled thinking. In selling a product, an ad with a public display of affection may be offensive to one cultural group but acceptable to another.

A. Coskun Samli conducted a study of consumer behavior in four cultures: Japanese, Chinese, American, and Korean.[18] His "response hierarchy" for these four cultures is reproduced in Table 8.1.

As sensitive individuals, persuaders need to be aware of subtle differences between the source and audience members of other ethnic backgrounds. Both source and receiver may have a heritage as Americans in common and experiences such as the Challenger tragedy, the LA riots, and the O. J. Simpson trial in common. However, the audience's interpretations of such experiences may diverge from the source's interpretations. For example, gift giving may be an important practice in a collective culture,[19] but Fortune 500 companies have ethics policies concerning gifts. If we assume that everyone thinks exactly as we do, we may unwittingly alienate our receivers. The following guidelines should help in adapting to the diverse ethnic backgrounds of audiences.

1. *Avoid ethnic jokes and epithets.* As a persuader, it is important to keep the audience on your side. Using an ethnic joke or epithet runs the risk of alienating both members of that group as well as other members of the audience who are offended by "poking fun" at others. Even though the *intent* may be to inject humor into the persuasive situation, the *impact* will be injurious.

2. *Be aware of different value systems.* While most people share common values like the need for respect, ethnic backgrounds imply differences in value systems and the expression of values. For example, it is easy to assume that most Americans are Christians, but a significant number of Americans are Jewish; therefore a holiday reference that fails to recognize both Christmas and Hanukkah or Easter and Passover creates an unnecessary barrier between the source and the receivers. There are also over 5,500,000 adherents of the Moslem religion in North America,[20] so religious references should recognize the significant numbers of the many recognized religions.

3. *Study languages and cultures to avoid unintentional* faux pas. Most people do not mean to alienate their audiences, but ignorance of language and cultures create problems. The classic examples of this problem are found in advertising. In Taiwan Pepsi Cola's slogan "Pepsi Comes Alive" was translated into Chinese as "Pepsi brings your ancestors back from the grave." In Latin American markets, in one country the Spanish term *bola* means "ball" but in another country it means "revolution," and in another it means "a lie or fabrication."[21] Careful study of other languages and cultures makes you more aware and sensitive to the needs and interests of the global community. Some of the references at the end of this chapter offer additional insight into intercultural communication.

PSYCHOLOGICAL FEATURES

An audience's responses are influenced by psychological as well as demographic factors. The most important psychological factors of audience analysis for persuaders to consider include the intelligence of the audience, the open-mindedness of the audience members, and how ego-involved they are in your topic.

INTELLIGENCE

Intelligence is linked to vocabulary. In persuading a more highly educated audience, rhetors can use more esoteric vocabularies. A less educated audience might have difficulty understanding if the rhetor uses overly complex language.

Compare the language choices in the two selections in Boxes 8.3 and 8.4. One is from *The Encyclopedia Britannica,* a reference work geared toward grade-school-level readers; the other is the same topic from *The World Book Encyclopedia,* a work intended for a younger, less educated audience.

Note that while both passages provide information, *The Encyclopedia Britannica* provides more detailed examples as well as more complex language, including foreign words and references to religion and history. The authors of these two articles unquestionably adapted both the content and the style of their articles to the expected experience of the readers.

OPEN-MINDEDNESS

How open-minded the audience is will influence their thinking about the topic. Dogmatic or closed-minded people are more likely to respond to authorities they respect than arguments presented in the message.[22]

Dogmatism is a key factor in persuasion. There are several approaches persuaders can take in dealing with dogmatic attitudes. In addition to citing authorities the dogmatic receiver respects, persuaders can seek to use interactive channels. This will permit greater feedback and flexibility in responding to dogmatic responses. Careful selection of examples and vocabulary are particularly important in dealing with highly dogmatic receivers. Remember, too, that receivers may be dogmatic about some issues but quite open-minded about others; a given audience may be more or less receptive to the message, depending on how dogmatic they are about the particular topic of the message.

Box 8.3

Certain poetical passages of the biblical Old Testament refer to a strong and splendid horned animal called *re'em*. This word was translated "unicorn" or "rhinoceros" in many versions of the Bible, but many modern translations prefer "wild ox" (auroch), which is the correct meaning of the Hebrew *re'em*. As a biblical animal the unicorn was interpreted allegorically in the early Christian church. One of the earliest such interpretations appears in the ancient Greek bestiary known as the *Physiologus*, which states that the unicorn is a strong, fierce animal that can be caught only if a virgin maiden is thrown before it. The unicorn leaps into the virgin's lap, and she suckles it and leads it to the king's palace. Medieval writers thus likened the unicorn to Christ, who raised up a horn of salvation for mankind and dwelt in the womb of the Virgin Mary. Other legends tell of the unicorn's . . . purifying of poisoned waters with its horn so that other animals may drink.

Cups reputedly made of unicorn horn but actually made of rhinoceros horn or narwhal tusk were highly valued by important persons in the Middle Ages as a protection against poisoned drinks. Many fine representations of the hunt of the unicorn survive in medieval art, not only in Europe but also in the Islamic world and in China.

EGO INVOLVEMENT

Ego involvement is another factor that affects how audiences respond to messages. Ego involvement is a matter of how salient or relevant the topic is to that audience. Some people may treat a given topic as a mere preference whereas others take the same topic quite to heart. For example, while fashion may be a matter of relative indifference to some, for fashion mavens, clothing styles are critically important.

To make the appropriate adaptation, persuaders must carefully analyze how ego-involved their audiences are with the topic. Advocating reform in the income tax system to an audience of full-time students assumes a different amount of involvement than persuading that same group four years later when they are employed full-time.

Part of ego involvement is experience. Teenagers, for example, do not need to know the same things about health insurance that older people do. Persuaders should also consider the audience's reaction to

---

Box 8.4

From *The World Book Encyclopedia*, © 1996 World Book, Inc. By permission of the publisher.

Unicorn is a legendary, one-horned animal described in ancient and medieval literature. Although there is no evidence that such an animal ever lived, many people believed in unicorns.

About 2,400 years ago, a Greek physician named Otesias wrote about a strange animal said to live in India. This animal resembled a wild ass and had a white body, blue eyes, and a single horn on its forehead.

In early Christian legends, the unicorn was as small as a goat but so fierce that no humter could capture him by force. The only way to catch a unicorn was to send a maiden alone into the forest. When the unicorn found her, he would rest his head in her lap and fall asleep.

During the Middle Ages, stories about unicorns became increasingly popular. Many medieval paintings and tapestries featured images of these animals. Nobles purchased objects believed to be unicorn horns for extremely high prices. Most of these objects were the tusks of walruses or of unusual whales called narwhals. Today, the unicorn remains a popular character in fantasy literature.

---

the source's age. Source credibility will vary depending upon the age of the listeners, for example. Consider how different a commercial would be if the same content on tennis shoes were delivered by a young person, a middle-aged person, or an older person.

TEN GENERALIZATIONS ABOUT RECEIVER PSYCHOLOGY

Given the diversity of receivers, it is difficult to make generalizations about their psychology. Nonetheless, a few things can be said to be generally true of people. Here is a list of ten.

1. *Receivers expect rational support.*

Since human beings are rational creatures who think about experiences, persuaders can expect that audiences will require a rational approach to the material presented. In persuasive campaigns sources should not expect an audience merely to take their word; effective persuaders provide the proof to support what they claim. An ad campaign for an expensive item like an automobile must provide considerable amounts of documentation and cannot rely solely on quick, attractive television spots.

2. *Audiences respond to emotions.*

Human beings are not just thinking machines; to be fully human is also to be a creature of emotions. This means that the audience's feelings influence their perceptions of messages. The implication here is that persuaders must be aware of the potential role of emotional connotations attached to the words. While a joke about drunks may be intended to be funny, an audience member who lost a loved one to a drunk driver may respond with tears rather than laughter.

The principle of emotional connotations also applies to the individual words used in persuasion. Most of us have very positive associations with the word "mother" because our mothers are comforting, nurturing, and loving people. But to some, the term mother may actually have negative emotional loadings. Christina Crawford in *Mommie Dearest,* and the matricidal Menendez brothers, for example, did not have positive emotional reactions to their mothers.

3. *Receivers react to both the source and the message.*

As we noted in Chapter Five, Aristotle in 354 B.C. wrote that speakers must be concerned with their credibility in the eyes of the audience. Aristotle's principle of *ethos,* the perceived credibility of the speaker, still applies to persuasion. Receivers respond not just to the message but also to the source of that message. It is important, then, to pay attention to how the source comes across to the receivers. Both the content and the presentation of the message should be geared to enhancing *ethos.*

It is important to note that the content of the message enhances the source's credibility. The substance of what is said should demonstrate expertise on the topic; the message can also subtly cite the source's qualifications in the topic. Notice, for instance, how Susan Au Allen established her credibility at the international Asian Expo in Anaheim, California.

"We are going to start with a little make believe. For the next twenty minutes or so, we are going to pretend that all of you have just joined the United States Pan Asian American Chamber of Commerce. . . . [My] primary responsibility is to do what I can to make you successful, either as importers from Asia or exporters to Asia. Having been born in China, and having been involved in trade most of my professional life, I know about the

Imagine SMELLING your father two miles away, finDing your dinner in the pitch dark, and Being aBLe to hear the paint dry on your bedroom wall.

Now you can actually experience for yourself the amazing hyper-real world of animal senses. All you have to do is visit the Animal SuperSenses exhibit exclusively at The Witte Museum in San Antonio. It's interactive, hands-on fun and learning for the whole family. It's Animal SuperSenses. See it. Hear it. Feel it. Unless you're not human, you don't know what you're missing.

Open daily at The Witte Museum in San Antonio. Call 210-820-2111 for more information. Sponsored by Southwestern Bell.

Visual factors like typeface and artwork affect receivers' responses to written communication.

subject. So in a sense, I am going to be your teacher, and you are going to be my students. And I want all of you to get A Plus on our report cards."[23] Ms. Allen established her background and expertise on Asian trade in the opening of her speech.

Visual production and vocal delivery can also enhance credibility. People are more likely to respond positively to a well-groomed person speaking in a direct manner with a lively voice; they are likely to tune out a disheveled person speaking in an evasive manner with a dull monotone voice. People respond to the appearance of written messages; visual factors like the typeface and artwork influence the reputation of a company's written communication. In short, both the form and the substance of the message should seek to improve the source's image in the minds of the audience.

4. *Receivers expect a source's ideas to fit with their own experiences.*

We use Coleridge's principle of the willing suspension of disbelief to enjoy works of fiction. We are willing to accept that dinosaurs can be genetically reconstructed and enjoy *Jurassic Park* or that aliens would attack Earth in *Independence Day*. In real life, however, audiences are not willing to suspend disbelief.

In most cases, we expect persuaders to provide fact not fantasy, and we expect those facts to fit in with our experiences.

Persuasive messages must fit the arguments into the receiver's existing beliefs and values. To make a case that UFOs have extraterrestrial origins, a persuader must be able to cite credible evidence from reliable sources and prove, not just to assert, that a given incident was the result of contact with alien creatures.

5. *Receivers respond to other receivers.*

If a few people in the audience give a performer a standing ovation, we feel the urge to rise to our feet as well, even if we didn't think the performance was *that* great. This common experience indicates that other receivers can influence another receiver's response. People are reluctant to act inconsistently with the prevailing mood of the audience. As a result, you should be aware of the influence of members of the audience on each other in a live speaking engagement.

6. *Receivers generally want the source to succeed.*

It is a myth to think that audiences are hostile enemies of persuaders. The vast majority of the time the audience actually wants the source to succeed. Of course, if a gun control advocate is trying to persuade members of the National Rifle Association or if a chiropractor seeks to persuade the American Medical Association, it is likely that the source will encounter hostility, but most situations are not that extreme. Persuaders are more likely to encounter apathetic rather than hostile audiences.

7. *Receivers will cooperate with the source.*

Receivers typically will cooperate with the source, especially in face-to-face situations. If a speaker talking about the difficulty of getting the House to work with the Senate demonstrated the problem by asking people to pat their heads while trying to rub their stomachs, most audience members would try it. However, that same speaker would probably find an individual reluctant to stand up before the crowd and do the same thing. If a sales agent asks the client to jot down the figures for the cost of the job, the client will generally be willing to help out. As we shall see in Chapter Eleven, receiver involvement is a highly recommended sales tactic.

Persuaders can count on the cooperation of the audience as long as the request is reasonable and does not single out an individual.

8. *Receivers need structure.*

When the patterns are not in the stimulus, our minds tend to create them. Notice how your mind puts the pieces together to create a whole image in Figure 8.1.

Similarly, audiences need structure in what they perceive. The structural imperative is obvious at the level of sounds and words. For example, "north" consists of four sounds /n/ /o/ /r/ /th/ and "thorn" consists of those same four phonemes in a different order. "The Ford smashed into the Chevy" has a very different meaning from "The Chevy smashed into the Ford" even though the words in the two sentences are identical—only the order of the words changed.

The need for structure also applies to the level of ideas in a message. Audiences need to follow the plan of the message just as they need to be able to follow the plot of a movie.

9. *Receivers will tend to go on mental holidays.*

Ralph Nichols, a pioneer in listening research, coined the expression "mental holiday" to describe what happens when a person's attention wanders. This tendency is a problem for speakers. An audience member may appear to be smiling at your wit but that person is actually thinking about the romantic evening spent

Figure 8.1
Gestalt Figure

SOURCE: Tom Porter and Sue Goodman, *Designer Primer.* (New York: Charles Scribner's Sons, 1988), p. 15.

the night before. Given the short attention span and the great temptation to go on a mental holiday, persuaders must periodically seek to refocus the receiver's attention on the subject at hand. Here are some techniques to help to accomplish that.

Pay close attention to the content of the message. Offer internal summaries to review briefly what went on before. Internal summaries reinforce the points in the presentation for anyone who may have gone on a mental holiday and are now trying to figure out what is going on. Explicitly label points and use transitions as verbal signposts that help receivers track what is said. Explicit expressions like "The main point I am trying to make . . ." or "Before moving to the next step, it is critical to remember that . . ." are internal transitions that help to redirect attention to the critical point of the persuasive message.

Use short, simple, declarative sentences. These are easier to grasp in a limited time. Because an inattentive receiver takes a moment to refocus attention, the key word used may have been missed; therefore use a few introductory words. The key word of a sentence should not be the first word of the first utterance about the topic.

C-ISBN2F-9-1456

C S N2F 9 1456

Location: Default Location
Entered By: RF
Edited Date: 02/2010
ISBN: 0155023565
Title: Procedure, Elements and Types of Persuasion

Use visual channels and vocal delivery to recapture attention. Revealing a visual aid attracts the wandering attention of receivers. A quick cut to another point of view can help to redirect attention in a commercial. Sound qualities of voice or music can also regain attention.

In the written media, the problem of gaining and maintaining attention is even more difficult. Most people will try to appear interested, even if they are bored by a speaker. For written messages, where the source is not present when the message is being delivered, the problem is compounded. Copywriters and commercial artists use boldface words or unusual typefaces to attract a reader's attention. They also use color and contrast to attract attention.

Whether orally or in writing, persuaders choosing to emphasize words in persuasive messages should select verbs over nouns because it is the verb that provides the "news" in the sentence and emphasizes action in the composition.

Persuaders have at their disposal the ability to vary the content and the style of the message to attract the audience's attention and interest in written messages. Here are three features that can be used to attract and hold an audience's attention: the novelty of the message, its relevance to the receivers, and the understandability of the words.

Novelty

Persuaders can make their messages more interesting by focusing on original or striking content. People are curious and enjoy new experiences; they are interested in the latest developments.

If the topic is already well known, finding a new slant will make it more interesting. For instance, the receivers may be all too familiar with the parking problem on campus, but if the source can come up with a unique solution (e.g., satellite parking with shuttles, valet parking with proceeds going to campus organizations, short-term parking lots restricted to the length of one class session), the receivers will be more interested in the message.

Persuaders can also use novelty by making the message more interesting by using original or striking language. The style of the language can add interest or it can bore. A receiver is more likely to continue to attend to the interesting ideas in a message when they are couched in interesting language. For instance, use a novel expression rather than a cliché. The tired style of a cliché "we should avoid it like the plague" is uninteresting, but Ross Perot's "that dog won't hunt" was considered novel, gained people's attention, and kept them asking for more.

Relevancy

Relevancy, a second factor, is the quality of being salient or important to the receiver. Target audiences are more interested in (and more likely to attend to) stimuli or ideas that they consider relevant whereas things they deem irrelevant are more likely to be ignored or quickly forgotten. As kids, for example, we tuned out the "mushy stuff" in movies because it was irrelevant. As adults, we tune out stuff that is boring, although that may no longer be the "mushy" scenes.

Persuaders not only have to grab the audience's attention but they have to hold it. To maintain attention, the material must be directly related to the needs and interests of our specific group of receivers. Finding the "hook" to make the message relevant to the receiver requires a careful audience analysis.

Understandability

The third factor, understandability, means that persuaders must make the content of the message, the material that the receivers have never encountered before, understandable to them. Since people follow the path of least resistance and avoid difficult and tiring listening situations, it is the source's responsibility to make new or difficult material understandable.

Consider this sentence from a computer magazine column: "By integrating a Mips R4x00—compatible CPU with an advanced memory architecture that obviates the need for conventional SRAM (static RAM) cache—a Silicon Valley startup has created a unique upgrade board that turns VL-Bus PCS into high-performance RISC systems for Windows NT."[24] Unless a reader is fairly knowledgeable about computer jargon, that sentence is incomprehensible. There are three major ways to make your message understandable for the audience, even if they are unfamiliar with the topic.

First, use appropriate vocabulary. This does not mean using short, simple words, but rather that jargon or technical words that are beyond the experience of the audience must be used sparingly and, when used, must be defined clearly. In our computer example, it would help to know the meaning of technical terms like Mips, CPU, SRAM cache, RISC, and VL-Bus.

Second, limit the complexity of the sentences. Long, convoluted sentences may be acceptable in academic writing, but most people will not spend the time deciphering convoluted sentence structures. For maximum impact, sentences should be easily understood without talking down to your audience. Consequently, short, simple sentences are preferred for ease of listening. While compound and complex sentences may be necessary occasionally, limit the use of compound–complex sentences.

Third, make new material understandable to audiences by relating the new concepts to experiences they have had.

10.   *Receivers need stylized redundancy.*

There is an adage for public speaking that says, "In the introduction you tell them what you're going to tell them; in the body you tell them; in the conclusion you tell them what you told them." The point of this adage is that an audience requires redundancy.

In communication parlance, redundancy is not superfluous repetition, it is the use of reiteration in different forms to compensate for potential loss of audience attention through distracting physical noise. Just as a spacecraft has backup systems to ensure against failure, persuaders should use redundancy to ensure against failure. For example, a sales agent may prepare a salesbook to repeat the important points covered in the pitch. The visual images provide the clients with a backup system for any points that were missed when physical noise distracted their concentration or when their minds wandered to pressing personal problems that create psychological noise.

Straight repetition without variation is boring. That is why practicing the scales, drilling vocabulary words, and rerunning basketball plays is so dull. Similarly, long persuasive messages should not just repeat the same point over and over. Communication professor Gerald Phillips coined the term "stylized redundancy"[25] to indicate that the repetition must be presented with variations to avoid losing the audience's interest and attention. Here are ways you can introduce stylized redundancy into your messages.

Use different words to express the same point. In writing about a newspaper, for example, one can use paper, journal, periodical, tabloid, chronicle or a host of other expressions.

Don't rely on just one form of material. Persuaders can add variety, depth, and interest in the topic by using several forms of supporting material.

In summary, remember that redundancy is particularly important but mere repetition is not enough. Effective persuaders use stylized redundancy to help their audiences observe and preserve the ideas.

Summary

Effective persuaders know that the most clear and vivid message delivered in a direct and lively manner is only a rehearsal unless there is an audience. The receivers are a vital but often overlooked part of the persuasive process. This chapter has examined the issues of why and how a persuader can analyze an audience and adapt to the specific nature of the receivers.

We began by examining questions typically asked in audience analysis. We also considered sources that can provide answers to those questions. Persuaders can answer the audience analysis questions by using their knowledge of the group they will be targeting. Additional information about the nature of the audience can be gleaned by asking people in the group or the organizers of the persuasive event. Examining written sources of information, such as newspapers and printed brochures, about the group can also provide useful answers to the audience analysis questions. Finally, persuaders may make use of site visits and professional databases of information about audiences.

Persuaders should investigate both demographic features and psychological features. Demographic factors include the size, age, gender, income, marital status, and ethnic background of the receivers. Psychological features include the intelligence, open-mindedness, and ego involvement of the audience.

We also noted ten generalizations about the psychology of audiences: (1) Receivers expect rational support. (2) Audiences respond to emotions. (3) Receivers react to both the source and the message. (4) Receivers expect a source's ideas to fit with their own experiences. (5) Receivers respond to other receivers. (6) Receivers generally want the source to succeed. (7) Receivers will cooperate with the source. (8) Receivers need structure. (9) Receivers will tend to go on mental holidays. (10) Receivers need stylized redundancy.

Notes

[1] Chaim Perelman and L. Olbrechts-Tyteca, *The New Rhetoric: A Treatise on Argumentation*, trans. John Wilkinson and Purcell Weaver (Notre Dame, IN: Notre Dame University Press, 1969), p. 25.

[2] Jack Valenti, *Speak Up with Confidence* (New York: William Morrow and Company, 1982), p. 143.

[3] Kim Baker and Sunny Baker, *How to Promote, Publicize, and Advertise Your Growing Business* (New York: John Wiley and Sons, 1992), p. 40. Permissions granted by John Wiley & Sons, Inc.

[4] See, for example, Arnold Mitchell, *The Nine American Lifestyles* New York: Macmillan, 1983.

[5] Judith Nichols, *By the Numbers: Using Demographics for Busienss Growth in the '90s* (Chicago, IL: Bonus Books, Inc, 1990), p. 24.

[6] Marvin Nesbit and Arthur Weinstein, "How to Size Up Your Customers," in Diane Crispell, ed., *The Insider's Guide to Demographic Know-How*, second edition (Ithaca, NY: American Demographics Press, 1990), p. 15.

[7] George Campbell, *The Philosophy of Rhetoric* (Carbondale, IL: Southern Illinois University Press, 1963), p. 102.

[8] *The 1994 Information Please Business Almanac and Desk Reference*, Seth Godin, ed. (New York: Houghton Mifflin Company, 1993), p. 532.

[9] Ellen Bouchard Ryan, Sheree Kwong See, W. Bryan Meneer, and Diane Trovanto. "Age-Based Perceptions of Language Performance Among Younger and Older Adults," *Communication Research*, 19 (August 1992), p. 437. Copyright © 1992. Reprinted by permission of Sage Publications, Inc.

[10] Anthony Mulac, Torborg Louisa Lundell, and James J. Bradac, "Male/Female Language Differences and Attributional Consequences in a Public Speaking Situation: Toward and Explanation of the Gender-Linked Language Effect," *Communication Monographs*, 53 (June 1986), p. 124.

[11] John Gray, *Men Are from Mars, Women Are from Venus* (New York: HarperCollins, 1992), p. 18.

[12] Ibid., p. 16.

[13] Andrew Tobias, *Still the Only Investment Guide You'll Ever Need* (New York: Bantam Books, 1987), p. 142.

[14] Michael Barone and Grant Ujifusa, *The Almanac of American Politics 1994* (Washington, DC: National Journal, 1994), p. 50.

[15] Barone and Ujifusa, p. 1007.

[16] Sondra Thriederman, *Profiting in America's Multicultural Marketplace* (New York: Lexington Books, 1991), pp. 2–3. Copyright 1991 by Sondra Thiederman.

[17] *The World Almanac 1993* (New York: Scripps Howard, 1992), p. 385.

[18] A. Coskun Samli, *International Consumer Behavior: Its Impact on Marketing Strategy Development* (Westport, CT: Quorum Books, 1995), p. 111.

[19] J. Breslin, "Cultural Diversity and Intercultural Communication" teleconference, October 19, 1994.

[20] *The World Almanac and Book of Facts 1996* (New York: World Almanac, 1995). Reprinted with permission from the World Almanac.

[21] Roger E. Axtell, *The Do's and Taboos of International Trade* (New York: John Wiley & Sons, 1991), pp. 219–221.

[22] J. Rohrer and M. Sherif, eds. *Social Psychology at the Crossroads* (New York: Harper & Row, 1951), *passim;* I. Steiner and H. Johnson, "Authoritarianism and Conformity," *Sociometry*, 26 (1963), 21–34; F. A. Powell, "Open and Closed-Mindedness and the Ability to Differentiate Source and Message," *Journal of Abnormal and Social Psychology*, 65 (1962), pp. 61–64.

[23] Susan Au Allen, "Bountiful Voyages: Doing Business in Asia," *Vital Speeches of the Day*, 60 (February 1, 1994), p. 254.

[24] Tom R. Halfhill, "Turn Your PC into a Powerful RISC Machine," *BYTE*, 19 (July 1994), p. 44.

[25] Gerald M. Phillips and J. Jerome Zolten, *Structuring Speech* (Indianapolis, IN: The Bobbs-Merrill Company, Inc., 1976), p. 32.

For Further Thought

1. Look through a magazine and stop at the advertisements that catch your attention. What are the factors of attention (novelty, relevance, pleasantness, etc.)? How can these features be adapted to oral rather than visual communication?

2. Select a speech from *Vital Speeches of the Day*. What did the speaker do to assure that the speech was interpreted correctly, remembered accurately, and retrieved easily?

3. Assume that you are a speech writer for your local representative. Develop a demographic analysis of the U.S. House of Representatives that your representative might use in giving a speech on the federal deficit.

4. All generalizations have exceptions. For each of the ten generalizations about the psychology of audiences, cite a specific situation or topic that would be an exception to the generalization.

For Further Reading

Caernarven-Smith, Patricia. *Audience Analysis & Response*. Pembroke, MA: Firman Technical Publications, 1983.

Clevenger, Theodore. *Audience Analysis*. Indianapolis, IN: The Bobbs-Merrill Company, 1966.

De Mente, Boye Lafayette. *How to Do Business with the Japanese*. Lincolnwood, IL: NTC Business Books, 1993.

Greenbaum, Thomas L. *The Handbook for Focus Group Research*. New York: Lexington Books, 1993.

Holtzman, Paul D. *The Psychology of Speaker's Audiences*. Glenview, IL: Scott, Foresman, 1970.

Samovar, Larry A. and Richard E. Porter, *Intercultural Communication: A Reader*. (Belmont, CA: Wadsworth Publishing Company, 1982.

PART THREE

TYPES OF PERSUASION

Chapter Nine

PERSUASIVE PRESENTATIONS

Sitting at a table trying to convince the campus parking committee, standing before a client making a pitch for venture capital, talking to a group of potential voters at a town hall meeting—we have all been in situations that challenged us to speak. And we will all face public speaking challenges in the future as well. This chapter first offers an overview of designing and delivering effective persuasive presentations. Next we examine how to be a critical evaluator of rhetorical presentations.

PRODUCING PERSUASIVE PRESENTATIONS

An athlete does not just run out in the arena to compete; athletes must prepare and practice before competing. When the competition is over, the athlete and the coach review the performance to learn how to be more effective in the future. Just as becoming an effective athlete requires practice, competition, and review of the performance, becoming an effective speaker requires preparation, practice, performance, and review.

PREPARE THE SPEECH

In his autobiography Lee Iacocca wrote, "Public speaking, which is the best way to motivate a large group, is entirely different from private conversation. For one thing, it requires a lot of preparation. A speaker may be very well informed, but if he hasn't thought out exactly what he wants to say *today, to this audience,* he has no business taking up other people's valuable time."[1] Iacocca, like all effective speakers, recognizes the important role of careful preparation.

Persuasive presentations require careful preparation.

Because preparation is so important, the following pages will devote considerably more space to this stage than to the other stages of persuasive presentations. There are seven steps in the preparation stage:

- choose your topic
- select the main points
- organize your ideas into an interesting and understandable speech
- develop the points of the speech
- invent openings
- create conclusions
- choose words to use

Choose Your Topic

The initial step in preparing a persuasive speech is often the most difficult—selecting the topic. In classroom situations you may have to generate your own topic. In this case your task is to select a topic that you know something about. For example, if you can talk about a topic for a class, you should choose a familiar topic, one that you have some experience with. Perhaps you know something about computers, perhaps you want to make a plea for more workplace safety measures because you saw dangerous situations in your part-time job.

In many cases, however, your topic is predetermined. Your teacher may assign the topic; you may be designated by your company to pitch a new proposal to clients; you may be bidding on a contract that requires a persuasive presentation. In these cases, the circumstances dictate the topic area.

In some cases you must generate your own topic. To come up with a topic for a speech, you might think about a recent experience—leaving the classroom and walking across campus to the dorm, going up the stairs, and sitting down at the desk in the room. This process can lead to topics like walking as exercise, why architects select different types of doors, campus safety at different times of the day, stairs versus escalators versus elevators, keys and locks, incandescent versus direct light, sunlight and vitamins, posture and chairs, sitting versus standing at desks, and how dorm life differs from apartment life. Any of these topics could be developed into a speech.

In either situation you should focus your topic by identifying a **goal.** "Goal setting," wrote Stephen Covey, a professor of business management and author of *Seven Habits of Highly Effective People*, "is obviously a powerful process. . . . It's a common denominator of successful individuals and organizations."[2] The goal is your specific topic in relationship to your particular audience. This is also called your **specific purpose,** a clear and attainable goal that is compatible with your general purpose. There are three qualities that make an effective specific purpose. A good specific purpose is:

- focused on an audience response
- operationally defined
- realistic

In the last chapter you learned how to analyze an audience. That is a critical key to persuasive presentations because the goal in speaking, the specific purpose, should always focus on what you want to accomplish with your audience. In other words, your presentation is a means to an end, and that end is to gain an audience response.

To illustrate how important it is to word your goal with your audience in mind, consider these two specific purpose statements.

Number One: I plan to give a persuasive speech about the National Collegiate Athletic Association's "no pass, no play" rule.

Number Two: after listening to my persuasive speech on the National Collegiate Athletic Association's "no pass, no play" rule, my listeners will write letters of protest to the Board of Directors at 6201 College Blvd., Overland Park, KS 66211.

In the first specific purpose statement, you could give the speech to an empty room and still accomplish the goal. The second specific purpose statement is better because it focuses on gaining a specific effect with your audience.

When your specific purpose is well written, it focuses you on your audience's reaction to your speech. It is *your audience* that must remember and use the information in your informative speech, *your audience* that must be influenced by your persuasive speech to do something about the issue, *your audience* that must be moved by your speech to socialize. No matter what your general purpose may be, your specific purpose must focus on the definite response you are seeking from your specific audience.

In addition to being audience centered, your specific purpose must be operationally defined. An operational definition is a statement that specifies concrete activities necessary for measurement.[3] For example, the abstract, conceptual definition of learning is "knowledge or skill acquired by instruction or study" but an operational definition of learning is "the score on the Scholastic Aptitude Test." In other words, an operational definition makes an abstract concept concrete and measurable. Your specific purpose statement should be concrete and measurable.

An operationally defined specific purpose makes your goal clear and objective. To illustrate the benefit of operationally defined specific purpose statements, consider the goals in Box 9.1.

Note that in each case, specific purpose statements that are operationally defined are clear and concrete. Conceptually defined statements are fuzzy and we have no way to determine whether the speech achieved the goal. Using operational definitions, on the other hand, makes our purposes explicit, and we can objectively determine whether we achieved our stated objective.

The third quality of an effective specific purpose statement is that it must be realistic. While public speaking is a very powerful tool, it is not omnipotent. You can use public speaking to describe how a dentist works, but you cannot cure a toothache by talking about it. You can persuade City Council to put in a traffic light, but you cannot control the speed of traffic in the school zone by shouting at the cars. You can make people care about AIDS victims, but you cannot cure the disease with your speech.

Box 9.1
OPERATIONAL DEFINITIONS

Conceptually Defined Persuasive Goal	Operationally Defined Persuasive Goal
After listening to my persuasive speech on the homeless, my audience will be persuaded to help them.	After listening to my persuasive speech on the homeless, at least half of my audience will sign up to volunteer at the Aimes shelter.
I am going to persuade my audience to change their minds about drinking and driving.	After hearing my 10-minute persuasive speech on driving under the influence of alcohol, my listeners will designate a driver for their next party.
My audience will be persuaded by my speech on Galaxy computers.	After hearing my 30-minute presentation comparing Galaxy computers with the two leading competitors, my listeners will sign the purchase contract for three dozen Galaxy 6060s.
My audience will be inspired by my speech on the flag.	After listening to my speech on the flag as an emblem, my audience will demonstrate appropriate respect for the flag.

Your specific purpose statement must be realistic. It is unrealistic to expect that you can convince the American public to convert to the metric system in a single persuasive speech, no matter how good it is. A good goal is attainable and recognizes the limitations of time, attention, and the medium of the message.

Select the Main Points

Once you have selected a topic and identified a specific purpose for your audience, your next step is to determine the main points in the body of the presentation. The average adult attention span is roughly fifteen minutes, so you cannot count on covering twenty or thirty ideas with any hope of success. Furthermore, we forget nearly 75 percent of what we hear, so you cannot expect your audience to remember long lists of ideas.[4]

To focus your listeners' attention on the major ideas of your speech, select those few ideas that embody the residual message, which is the message that is remembered, the ideas that remain after your listeners have forgotten most of what you have said. To illustrate the point, think about a course you took a year ago. You may recall a few important ideas, but you do not recall everything you knew when you took the final examination. What you remember is the residual message of that class.

Organize Your Ideas

Humans are organizing creatures. We organize the day around hours. We organize society around laws and governments. We organize games around rules. We even organize parties. In addition to partitioning your speech, you need to organize the material into a coherent structure.

Quintilian, a famous speech teacher of the first century A.D., noted that without proper organization your speech "will be like a ship drifting without a helmsman, will lack cohesion, will fall into countless repetitions and omissions, and, like a traveler who has lost his way in unfamiliar country, will be guided solely by chance without fixed purpose or the least idea either of starting point or goal."[5]

While there are many different organizational patterns, the most useful for persuasive presentations is the motivated sequences. In 1935 Professor Alan H. Monroe proposed a pattern of organization that included these five steps: attention, need, satisfaction, visualization, and action.[6] Monroe's Motivated Sequence is based on the concept that your audience must be moved to attend to your ideas, that they must next perceive a need for your ideas, that those needs must next be satisfied, that you must also help them to visualize the resolution of the needs, and, finally, you must urge them to act. Consequently, you may wish to organize your presentation by providing these steps: gain attention through an interesting anecdote or similar device, provide a clear picture of the need for taking action, offer a straightforward resolution of the need in the satisfaction step, use vivid depictions to help the listeners visualize the consequences of doing nothing or the benefits of accepting your proposal, and, finally, urge them to action.

Develop Your Points

Once the main ideas of the speech have been selected and ordered, consider ways to develop those ideas. To bring the point home, to make your speech memorable, or to make the idea appealing, you need to offer **supporting material** that impresses your listeners. Common forms of support include the following.

- examples that illustrate a particular point
- descriptions that create mental pictures of your ideas

- testimony that cites the words of an expert or witness
- numerical data that quantify the concept
- audio or visual aids that help your audience hear or see the material more clearly.

By Giving Examples   Examples are specific instances that represent a larger idea. Examples may be brief or detailed, real or hypothetical. They are always geared to make a concept more understandable or a persuasive point more acceptable.

Here is how a mother of a child with multiple handicaps used a specific example to illustrate her point when she addressed the local school board to consider an extended school year for children in special education.

> Ask any teacher in special education. Children regress over the summer when they are not in school. My Joey [not the child's real name] is in special education. He has problems in speaking and reading. But after working hard all last year, he could read 25 words by June and could speak understandable sentences. For the three months of summer he received no speech therapy or other schooling. In September, his teacher said his speech is worse and she has trouble understanding him. She also said he forgot most of the words he could read last June. He is starting over to learn what he already knew last June. If our school district had an extended school year for special education, my Joey would not now be working on those same 25 words he learned last year but would be learning something new—something more.

A specific, detailed example makes an argument more persuasive.

By Offering Description   Another type of supporting material, vivid description, is a word picture that helps the audience to visualize the main idea. In a speech to the student therapists of the campus chapter of the National Student Speech-Language-Hearing Association, a recovered stroke victim described vividly what it was like to suffer a stroke and be unable to speak.

> I was scared, cold in the hospital. All of these doctors would come out of this gray fog—come toward me very fast—and peer into my face. I'd watch their mouths move, I'd hear the sounds and words. But it was as if they were speaking a foreign language. I knew they were talking English, but I just couldn't quite figure out what the words meant. They went by so fast.

Providing a vivid description makes the argument more persuasive and memorable.

By Quoting Testimony   A third form of supporting material is testimony. Testimony is a matter of directly or indirectly quoting the words of another to support the point you are making. Remember that your audience will attribute credibility, or lack thereof, to the source you cite as evidence. For instance, in a speech on judicial reform, a student used testimony to make her point.

> And in the words of Justice William O. Douglas, "There are only two choices: A police state in which all dissent is suppressed or rigidly controlled; or a society where law is responsive to human needs. If society is to be responsive to human needs, a vast restructuring of our laws is essential."[7] I know which system I want to live under.

Using testimony from a revered judicial figure is more persuasive than quoting a literary figure on the same issue.

By Using Numerical Data   Still another type of supporting material is numerical data. We live in an age of numbers, and quantifying ideas can make them more understandable. Here is an example of how a student in a beginning public speaking class began a speech on violence in America.

> According to FBI statistics, an average of 49 persons are murdered in this country every day. Two are murdered by rifles, three by shotguns, and 21 by handguns. Another ten are stabbed and six are beaten to death every day. Strangulation and other forms of violence account for the remainder.

By Employing Audiovisual Aids   Audiovisual aids support your talk and can bring your presentation to life. Photographs, slides, graphs, recordings, audiotapes, videotapes, and models all offer sights and sounds that can reinforce your words. Remember the impact of viewing the Rodney King videotape for the first time followed, later, by the videotape beating of Reginald Denny? No amount of verbal description could have had the visceral impact of watching those tapes.

Not all visual aids are as striking or as emotionally involving as the Rodney King and Reginald Denny videotapes. Most visual aids are used to clarify the meaning of verbal discourse. Imagine giving a speech on tying nautical knots without a visual demonstration to accompany your words. That is why so many companies now provide videotape demonstrations of their products and use rather than to rely solely on written directions and descriptions.

Persuaders often employ visual aids for support.

Invent Your Opening

Having structured and developed the main ideas of your talk, the next task is to devise an introduction. The introduction is critical. It must grab the attention of your audience and establish rapport, a feeling of unity, with your listeners. Your opening must also give a preview, a sense of what is to come in your speech. Common opening strategies include quotations, humorous anecdotes, rhetorical questions, and startling statements that grab the audience's attention.

Employ Quotations   Someone else's words may help you express an important theme and may provide a starting point for your own ideas. Be certain the quotation you have selected to open a speech is both interesting and relevant. Use the words of the person being quoted, thereby reflecting the credibility of the source of the quotation onto you, the speaker, in order to gain the initial attention of your listeners and to set the scene for the body of your speech.

Here is an example of how a student used a quotation to begin her speech on bio-ethics:

> Albert Schweitzer speaks for all of us when he cautioned, "Until he extends his circle of compassion to all living things, man will not himself find peace." Dr. Schweitzer who spent his life providing medical services

to people in this country and in Africa, did not limit his compassion to one species—human beings. He considered all life to be sacred.

Relate Anecdotes   While not all anecdotes are funny, you can use humorous anecdotes effectively to gain attention. An anecdote need not be riotously funny, but it should be amusing. As a speaker, you should not use a joke just to be telling a joke—the anecdote must be relevant to what you say. Off-color humor or derogatory jokes are inappropriate. Use humor to put your listeners in a receptive frame of mind for the body of your speech, not to shock or offend them.

As you know, parking is a perpetual problem on campus. To begin his speech on this universally irritating subject, Miguel used a light touch.

> On the way into class today, as I circled the student parking lot hunting for an open parking space, I watched as a person drove up, parked his car on the side of the driving lane, took out his jack, hoisted up the car, took off the tire, threw the tire in his trunk, and put a "be back soon" note on his windshield before he ran off to class. I applaud his ingenuity, but must we all be reduced to tricks to find a place to park?

Ask Rhetorical Questions   The example of Miguel's introductory remarks on parking not only used a humorous example, but ended with a rhetorical question. Rhetorical questions are questions that the speaker poses, not intending to get the listeners to answer aloud but seeking instead to get the listeners to think about the topic. Since people are accustomed to ask and answer questions in conversation, you can invite your audience's interest by emulating the dialogue form. By posing a question or series of questions to get the audience thinking about the issue, you set the stage to follow up the questions with a speech that addresses those issues.

Here is how Joanne sparked interest in the proceedings of city council:

> Do *you* rent an apartment in town? Do *you* know that, if they have their way, the city council will tax *you* for the "privilege" of paying tuition to be a student? That's right. There is a bill before city council for an "occupational privilege" tax that will be assessed on all students who live in town.

Create Your Conclusion

The introduction puts the audience in a receptive frame of mind and previews what is to come by alluding to the specific purpose of the speech. The body of the speech covers the sequenced ideas and develops them with supporting material. The conclusion of the speech reviews the main ideas and provides a sense of finality.

Speeches that end abruptly startle the audience, while speeches that dwindle away leave the audience dissatisfied. Just as we expect a dessert to finish off a fine meal, audiences expect a conclusion to complete a fine speech. When reading an essay, a reader can go back over the material to recollect the writer's main points. On the other hand, a listener has only the fleeting moment to absorb a speaker's thoughts. Take every opportunity to reinforce your ideas. Your final opportunity to reach out to the audience is in the conclusion of the speech. Make your final words appropriate and memorable. Common devices for conclusions include reviewing the main points covered in the body, urging the audience to thought or action, and offering a pithy quotation from another source.

Review Ideas   A review of your speech's main ideas will leave a lasting impression on an audience. Here is how Catherine Ahles, vice president for college relations at Macomb Community College in Warren, Michigan, concluded her speech to a college sorority:

> As you go forward to discover your world of possibilities, I challenge you to think about the seven questions I've posed tonight:
>
> > Are you creating your own opportunities?
> > Can you make informed choices?
> > How keenly are you paying attention?
> > How daring are you?
> > What are your convictions?
> > How strong is your confidence?
> > What is your personal philosophy?
>
> > And I give you another challenge: to select one or two of these dimensions, and make a commitment to use your Phi Theta Kappa experience to discover your full capabilities in that dimension.[8]

Notice that Catherine Ahles did not merely offer a factual summary of her points. As an effective speaker, she recognized that the conclusion of her speech both summarized and challenged her audience.

Urge Action   Challenging the audience or urging them to action is another device used to conclude a speech. The challenge is not an aggressive assertion but rather a warm invitation for the listeners to join the speaker in a way of thinking about the topic. Notice how masterfully this was done in John F. Kennedy's well-known inaugural address:

> And so, my fellow Americans: ask not what your country can do for you—ask what you can do for your country.
> My fellow citizens of the world: ask not what America will do for you, but what together we can do for the freedom of man.

Finally, whether you are citizens of America or citizens of the world, ask of us here the same high standards of strength and sacrifice which we ask of you. With a good conscience our only sure reward, with history the final judge of our deeds, let us go forth to lead the land we love, asking His blessing and His help, but knowing that here on earth God's work must truly be our own.[9]

Use Relevant Quotations   If a challenge seems inappropriate for your speech, you may decide to employ a relevant quotation. Sometimes another speaker or writer has so eloquently expressed a theme you have emphasized that he or she merits quotation. Be sure to give appropriate credit when using another person's words. Note how Harriet Michel, in her speech entitled "King—From Martin to Rodney," effectively finished her address by using a relevant quotation:

> I'd like to leave you with a quote from the late Whitney Young, president of the National Urban League.
> "I do have faith in America not so much in a sudden upsurge of morality nor in a new surge toward greater patriotism.
> "But I believe in the intrinsic intelligence of Americans.
> "I don't believe that we forever need to be confronted by tragedy or crisis in order to act.
> "I believe that the evidence is clear.
> "I believe that we as people will not want to be embarrassed or pushed by events into a posture of decency.
> "I believe that America has the strength to do what is right because it is right.
> "I am convinced that given a kind of collective wisdom and sensitivity, Americans today can be persuaded to act creatively and imaginatively to make democracy work.
> "That is my hope, this is my dream, this is my faith."
> Ladies and gentlemen, thank you very much.[10]

Choose Your Words Carefully

Once you have discovered material, generated and structured the main points, developed those points and worked out an introduction and a conclusion, you must try to choose the best words to express your thoughts. Your goal is to select words that clearly and memorably express your thoughts to your audience. In other words, an effective oral style is both clear and impressive.

Try to select the words that most clearly express your ideas. Las Vegas has been described as a "shimmering oasis" by one speaker and the "capital of glitz" by another. Although "shimmer" and "glitz" both have meanings connected with glitter and reflected light, each speaker created a different concept of Las Vegas by the words chosen to encode the message.

Impressiveness, a second quality of effective style, is that characteristic of language that makes words memorable. Many novice speakers believe that the road to impressiveness is to use obscure words, and the longer the better. In reality, the impressiveness of a message is not a function of a thesaurus or of the length of the words. We recall vivid passages from John Kennedy's inaugural address when the longest word in "Ask not what your country can do for you but what you can do for your country" is two syllables. Rather than trying to impress the listeners with your ability to use long, unfamiliar words found in a thesaurus, select the words that most vividly portray the idea you are seeking for your audience. Select words that have concrete, sensory appeal. "The silverware clattered and the plates shattered in the steamy restaurant kitchen" is more memorable than "He had an accident" because it details sensory experiences.

PRACTICE THE SPEECH

Just as pilots run through situations in flight simulators, public speakers should run through simulations of the actual speech. Rehearsing is an effective way to try out your material before the real event.

Arrange to rehearse your speech well before the time you present it. To the extent possible, try to create a setting that resembles the size and arrangement of the actual event. The acoustics of a dormitory room are quite different from those of a classroom. Rehearsing in a room approximately the size of the actual setting will make the rehearsal more realistic and more profitable.

A speech should always be rehearsed out loud. Merely skimming over your notes or mumbling to yourself will not allow you to formulate the timing and delivery that are crucial to effective presentations.

Speakers are often surprised when a speech they expected to deliver in five minutes actually took a considerably longer or shorter time than it did in rehearsal. Usually that surprise comes about because the rehearsal consisted of quietly reading over the speech. Practice out loud and stop only for the pauses you plan to make in the actual speech, and your rehearsal will come much closer to the timing of the actual event.

If at all possible, rehearse your speech in front of another person. Practicing before a mirror is a second choice, but the mirror will not give you feedback about content and delivery that a live listener can provide.

DELIVER THE SPEECH

The third stage of public speaking is delivery. While this is the central and often the only focus of popular books on public speaking, delivery is only one of the factors that contribute to an impressive presentation. It is, however, the most noticeable aspect. Therefore it deserves special attention.

In Chapter Seven, we discussed channels of communication. For most public speeches we can divide delivery factors into two channels: how you look and how you sound.

Visual Aspects

When you first step in front of an audience, your listeners will first notice your face, and the most important part of your face is your eyes. It is therefore critical that you pay particular attention to maintaining **eye contact** with your audience.

The eyes capture your listeners' attention and open channels of communication. To open and maintain communication with your audience, you cannot be note dependent or gaze at the ceiling or floor. You must look at your audience. Try to scan the faces of all of your audience from time to time; this generates a personal sense of being in touch with them.

Eye contact also allows you to read and react to the feedback your audience provides to you during your speech. If you didn't look at your listeners, you would not see the encouragement or agreement on their faces nor would you be aware if some listeners were confused by a point you were making or disagreed with an argument you presented.

Gestures are another important visual feature of public speaking. Too often novice speakers encumber themselves by holding notes that inhibit their natural tendency to reinforce ideas with gestures. Some speakers stand stiffly rooted behind the lectern, grasping onto it as if it were a life preserver in a stormy sea.

Gestures can add liveliness and emphasis to your words. Keep your gestures open and natural so the audience can see them. Remember that the lectern may block your audience's view, so bring your gestures up for visibility.

Awkward, stiff gestures look rehearsed and unnatural. Remember, too, that anything you do that distracts from your words hinders your audience's attention. Don't nervously fiddle with notes, jewelry, hair, or jingle the change in your pocket; these are common nervous distractions that must be controlled for the few minutes you are speaking.

A third feature of **visual** delivery is the overall **appearance** of your body. Be sure to dress appropriately. Control nervous rocking or shifting of your weight from foot to foot to enhance the overall impression of your speech. As mentioned earlier, the opposite extreme, standing ram-rod stiff and locked behind the lectern, is as much a distraction as uncontrolled rocking. Try to relax but avoid slouching. Your objective is to achieve the desirable middle ground of natural-looking delivery.

Auditory Factors

The goal of the effective speaker is to sound conversational. To sound relaxed and to sound as though you are conversing with your listeners, use inflection as well as a rate of speed that approximates how you naturally speak. Unfortunately both beginning and experienced speakers often fail to speak naturally when talking in public.

Speak loudly with enough **volume** to be heard in the back of the room. Acoustics are important because the size and shape of the room and the types of walls and ceilings all can affect how your voice is carried through the room. All of the work you devoted to preparing and rehearsing your speech will be wasted if the audience cannot hear what you have to say. Don't force your listeners to strain to hear you.

Use vocal variety to make your speech interesting and natural. **Pitch** refers to the highness or lowness of your voice. When you speak casually, you alter your pitch and add vocal variety as a natural act. Oddly enough, some people drop into a monotone when they stand up to speak. We don't speak in monotones when we see a friend and say, "Hi, Todd! It is *really* good to see you again." Yet speakers often drop into that flat, uninflected monotone when they say, "Hello. It is a real pleasure to be here today to talk about this important topic." You may not define giving a speech as a "pleasure" but the topic *is* important and you do have something valuable and interesting to share with your listeners. If you speak in a monotone, your audience will consider you insincere and your arguments uninteresting and unimportant. You cannot persuade your audience if you do not sound sincere and interested yourself.

To sound more natural and to add interest to your voice, you can animate your voice by raising the **inflection** at the end of questions while dropping the pitch at the end of statements and by stressing the key word or words in a sentence. Talk to your audience just as you would talk to close friends. Use the same animation in your voice in talking to a room full of people as you would use in talking to one person.

Of course, pitch variation can be overdone. People who use too much animation in their voices sound frantic or phony. Just as you would want to strike a balance between a stiff and formal delivery as opposed to a nervous or slouching one, you will want to strike a conversational balance between an uninspiring monotone and an overly dramatic vocal delivery.

Consider the speed **rate** of your speech. Studies have demonstrated that people ordinarily speak at about 125 words a minute. While listeners can understand over 180 words a minute, they generally report that such speech is too fast for comfortable listening.[11] You are not in a race, so there is no need to rush through the talk. Conversely, if you drop too much below the normal rate you invite impatience and daydreaming on the part of your audience. Plan to provide deliberate pauses to highlight important points and give your audience time to mull over those important points. Say the main points slower and with more weight and the supporting material with more speed. This tactic will help you to vary the velocity of your speaking.

It is difficult to get the **timing** down precisely in a speech, but practice and experience will help to hone your skills as a speaker. Eventually vocal variety will become as natural in your public speaking as it is in your conversations.

Some speakers fill their speeches with nonmeaningful sounds or phrases. If you fill your speeches with **vocalized pauses** like "um" and "uh" or fillers such as "like" and "you know," you will distract your audience's attention and sound nervous. As we discussed in Chapter Five, this decreases your credibility with the audience. Remember, you do not have to fill every second with a sound. Eliminating distracting vocalized pauses or overused, nonmeaningful fillers go a long way toward enhancing delivery and making you sound confident and persuasive.

Finally, remember that audiences determine credibility on the way that speakers sound, as we noticed in Chapter Five. If you want to maximize your persuasive impact, take care to pronounce words properly and use correct grammar.

REVIEW THE SPEECH

With sighs of relief, speakers return to their desks after giving their speeches. "Thank heavens that is over," they mutter to themselves. But it is not over when the speech is finished. If you really want to become a better speaker, you have to think about doing an even better job next time. There are three sources for learning to improve.

One source of improvement is to learn from **others.** Listen and learn from the other speakers in the class and in all speaking situations. Analyze what other speakers are doing. Try to determine what works and what doesn't work. Learning from your colleagues is a great source of ideas.

Another way to learn from others is to observe great speakers and to read great orations. Watching speakers on C-SPAN or attending a live presentation can offer valuable tips on improving your own speaking. The next time you are in a lecture or in church, notice what the speaker is doing and seek to emulate the positive and eliminate the negative. You can also learn valuable lessons by reading great orations. Collections of speeches such as those found in the "For Further Reading" section at the end of this chapter can provide inspiration and insight into effective speaking. Look for ways to open and close a speech, for patterns of organization, for effective expression of ideas in the language. In short, let the experts guide and inspire your own progress in speaking.

A second source of learning is **experience.** Classroom experience is valuable because you gain immediate experience and helpful commentary from your teachers and classmates. But classroom experience is not the only experience. Rehearse your speeches in front of friends or family; they can give you valuable ideas for improvement. Purchasing an inexpensive tape recorder to tape and replay your speech can be a valuable investment. Listening to a recording of your rehearsed speech can be a beneficial learning experience, but don't be shocked by your first experience with a tape recorder. People rarely like the way they sound over the small speakers of a tape recorder.

A third source of information for improvement is **training.** The remainder of this book and your classroom course of instruction will help you attain the skills and techniques of speaking in public. Training programs are also available from groups such as the Toastmasters or from commercial enterprises such as the Dale Carnegie courses. Training to be a good speaker is no less rigorous than training to be a good athlete. Both require time, attention, good coaching, and determination, and both are worth the effort.

ANALYZING AND EVALUATING PERSUASIVE PRESENTATIONS

Having examined the presentational process from the source's point of view, we can turn our attention to the other lane of the communication interchange—how to listen effectively to persuasive presentations. In this section we will focus on consumers of persuasive presentations and how the persuasive speaker can help the listeners.

Your listening abilities involve three interrelated activities of the listening process:

- hearing
- perceiving
- thinking

Each is necessary, and no single activity is complete in itself. The relationship of hearing, perceiving, and thinking to listening is illustrated in Figure 9.1.

Listening and Hearing

Hearing is a physical process of reception. It is a mechanical part of listening that is necessary for the reception of sounds. Therefore, it is important for us to pay attention to delivery factors that directly affect our hearing. The three most important factors are volume, competing noise, and articulation. Consider each of these in turn.

Volume is the loudness of the speaker's voice. If the speaker's voice is too soft, you will not be able to hear the message clearly.

Imagine that you see a friend you want to talk to but she is on the other side of a noisy street. You have to shout to be heard, and your friend might turn around and cup a hand to her ear to try to improve the reception of the sound of your voice. If the message was important enough and the sound of your voice too soft to be heard clearly, either you or your friend will probably become sufficiently frustrated to cross the street so that you may be heard more easily. Reducing the distance between speaker and listener makes talking and hearing easier.

The same principles apply in presentational situations. One technique to ensure volume is to give feedback to the source to indicate that the volume is too soft. Another technique is to try to reduce the distance between you and the speaker.

You may find that **noise** competes for your attention. A class across the hall is noisily dismissed just as the speaker reaches the climax of the speech. The punch line from a hilarious joke is drowned out by the excited shout of the crowd attending a wedding in the ballroom next door.

One way to compete with noise is to ask the speaker to repeat a missed point. If the interference is likely to be a single, temporary interruption, you can ask the speaker to reiterate the point that you missed. You can also rely on redundancy to compensate for any lapses

Figure 9.1
The Three Activities of Listening

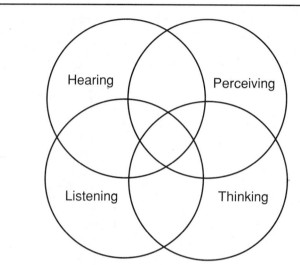

of attention. For example, many speakers prepare an overhead projection to repeat the important points covered orally. The overhead transparency provides a backup for any points that were missed when physical noise distracted concentration or when our minds wandered as a result of psychological noise. Cupping your hand behind your ear is a good feedback signal to let the speaker know you are having trouble hearing the presentation.

The third factor that affects your hearing is **articulation.** The English language consists of forty-three meaningful sound units called phonemes, listed in Box 9.2.

You combine phonemes to form meaningful words and sentences. Speakers need to enunciate these sounds clearly if the audience is to hear the message easily and without distortion.

Sometimes speakers will have unusual articulation for words. Accents can be quite distracting—either hard to understand or so interesting that listeners forget to listen to the content. To compensate for a speaker's articulation, you can focus on listening for the main points. Resist being distracted by the difficulty of making out what is being said. Resist focusing on your frustration. Instead try to get out of the presentation what you can. If the points are important enough, you can always seek out the presenter after the presentation for further clarification.

Box 9.2
THE SOUNDS OF ENGLISH

Consonants	Vowels
p as in *p*in	a as in p*a*t
b as in *b*in	ai as in p*ar*k
t as in *t*ank	e as in n*e*t
d as in *d*ank	i as in p*i*t
k as in *k*ate	ee as in f*ea*t
g as in *g*ate	o as in p*o*t
m as in *m*ope	au as in f*or*t
n as in *n*ope	u as in p*u*t
ng as in di*ng*	oo as in b*oo*t
l as in *l*ight	uh as in b*u*t
r as in *r*ight	i as in ch*ir*p
f as in *f*at	a as in *a*bout
v as in *v*at	ay as in d*ay*
th as in *th*ere	ai as in m*y*
s as in *s*ap	oy as in t*oi*l
z as in *z*ap	ow as in p*ou*t
sh as in *sh*are	oa as in g*oa*t
zh as in a*z*ure	ee as in sm*ea*r
h as in *h*ear	ae as in st*a*re
ch as in *ch*eck	oe as in n*ew*er
j as in *j*amb	
w as in *w*inner	
y as in *y*esterday	

So far we have considered listening and the physical process of hearing, but listening is more than just a physical activity. It is also a psychological process that involves mental factors such as attention and interpretation.

LISTENING AND PERCEIVING

Listening is more than the physical process of hearing. The psychology of communication emphasizes that meaning in the minds of sources and receivers is created by the perceptual process. It is entirely appropriate, then, to consider aspects of perception in the listening process.

To enhance listening, consider the rate of your speech.

We cannot attend to all the sensory input that bombards us. Close your eyes and listen carefully. What did you hear? I heard the hum of the fan in my word processor, traffic noise from outside the window, footsteps of people walking around, doors opening and closing, and myriad other audible sensations. Those sounds are still bombarding me, but now that I am again concentrating on you the reader, I have filtered out those extraneous sounds—I have selected some sounds to attend to and have ignored others.

Audience members also filter out auditory stimuli and select specific sounds to listen to. We *choose* to listen. As a result, we must choose to concentrate on the presentation rather than to other sounds (physical noise) or to our own thoughts (psychological noise).

One way to improve our listening is to be prepared to listen. If we approach a listening situation with a preconceived notion that the presentation will be dull, we often find a self-fulfilling prophecy. If we plan to spend the energy and to concentrate on the speaker's message, we improve our listening ability dramatically.

Another technique that improves listening is to give the source a fair chance to be heard. Sometimes we prejudge a source or a message. If we dislike a particular speaker's mannerisms, we may be deaf to the arguments in the message. If we disagree with the source's position on an issue, we may be closed-minded about hearing anything that competes

Listeners must be able to retrieve memories.

with our preexisting views. In every listening situation we should be at least willing to consider the communication without spending our mental time constructing refutations of the speaker's points.

LISTENING AND THINKING

To listen truly you must be actively engaged in thinking about the presentation. Thinking involves at least three features:

- interpreting
- storing
- retrieving

In other words, thinking consists of attaching meaning to the words, holding the ideas in memory, and accessing those stored ideas when needed.

Interpreting

Audiences interpret messages. That is, we put the message in a frame of reference, which helps us understand the data being presented. Just as a television program will focus on a building before cutting to a room in order to establish the location of the room, listeners will pass messages through a frame of reference to establish the meaning of the words.

Typically we filter information through several frames of reference. The four most typical ones are the following:

- cognitive frames
- value frames
- syntactic frames
- free association frames

Cognitive frames of reference mean that we have mental images of the words we hear. Some symbols have many cognitive associations. When a person says "chip," for example, we may associate the word with a salty snack, a break in a cup, a person's nickname, a computer component, or a variety of other images. Which image is selected depends upon the context in which it is said. If someone said, "the chip in the computer" rather than "the chip in the teacup," we would have the image of an electronic component rather than a nick in a drinking vessel. In any case, we attach cognitive associations or meanings to the words we hear. These cognitive associations are usually called the denotative meaning of words.

To listen effectively, we need to be aware that a single word may have a variety of cognitive possibilities and that we can often understand unknown words without the use of a dictionary. We must seek to expand our vocabularies so that we are familiar with a variety of words. We can also listen for the context of the unfamiliar word; often a term will be clarified by its use in the sentence. A good speaker will use an unfamiliar word in such a way that we can determine the word's meaning from the context in which it is used.

We human beings are not just mental organisms; we are also feeling creatures, and therefore we attach emotional loadings to the words that we hear as well. Our **value frames** provide emotional perspectives on the words we hear. For example, the word "mother" or "marriage" may have different associations for one person than another. The subject of Rush Limbaugh may raise negative reactions from some members of the audience and positive reactions from others. The emotional loading of words and ideas, the connotations, are more individually based than the denotative definitions.

To compensate for the impact of connotations, remember that your emotional loadings for a word may not be the same as those of the speaker. For instance, the same speech on archery for hunting would elicit very different values and emotional responses depending upon your orientation as an animal rights activist, an NRA member, or an archery enthusiast.

Syntactic frames of reference mean that the sequencing of phonemes, words, sentences and ideas makes a difference in the way we interpret what we hear.

Listen for transitions or verbal signposts during the speech to make it easier for you to follow the speaker's train of thought. Such cues as "and now we'll move from the educational accomplishments of women in the 1990s to the disparity between women's and men's salaries in the professions for the past decade" are cues that the speaker is moving from one point in the speech to the next. A good speaker uses preparatory statements and summaries to cue you, the listener, to the changes in the focus of the speech.

Free association frames of reference mean that we can make new and unique associations in unexpected ways. We should make use of the ability to create new and unusual ideas while we listen. Sometimes, by modifying the speaker's proposal in a creative way, we can find a compromise that is even better than the proposal. Such creative synthesis is not possible if we are not fully engaged in thinking about the speaker's communication.

Storage

In addition to interpreting the message, listeners must store the information for future reference. We know that most people listen inefficiently. A study by Ralph Nichols, a pioneer in listening research, indicated that college students remembered only 68 percent of the material they heard in lectures.[12] Here are three practical suggestions for making speeches you hear more memorable.

First, make sure that the point or points in the speech are clear to you. Try to identify the overall claim of the speech and how the rest of the ideas relate to that overall point. Even if the speaker has not made it explicit, try to see the presentation in light of the overall issue being advocated. That way you can more easily assess whether the support is adequate and sufficient to make the case.

Second, you can make use of redundancy. When we study for a test we "overlearn" by repeating the information so often that even if we forget some of it (and we will), residual material remains. Likewise, by using redundancy, by mentally rephrasing and paraphrasing the main points in several different ways, you can be sure that you retain the important points. Since we can think much faster than a speaker can speak, we can use the extra mental time to work on recollection of the speaker's message.

The third technique you can use is to access the information through more than one channel of communication. While the old adage indicates that "a picture is worth a thousand words," you can improve the chance that you will remember the speaker's points by taking careful notes. Look at the visual aids. Get involved in the communication process—think of ways to visualize what the speaker is saying even if there are no visual aids for the point. By hearing *and* seeing, you reinforce the message.

Retrieving

After interpreting and storing words, listeners must be able to retrieve the memories. It is not enough that a presentation be remembered, listeners must also be able to retrieve the memories when they are needed. Effective listeners seek specific ways to help their recall of the message. There are three typical ways in which you can help to retrieve ideas from a speech.

- apply the information
- use mnemonic devices
- integrate new information with old

Let's consider each of these in more detail.

First, make the information **applicable.** Usable ideas that are relevant and immediately applicable in your life are easier to recall. Think about ways to apply the presentation so that you can recall the material at a later time.

Second, use **mnemonic devices.** These are memory aids that can be created from the material in presentations. For example, in music we remember the lines of the treble staff with *Every Good Boy Does Fine.* We remembered the order of the planets in our solar system (Mercury Venus Earth Mars Jupiter Saturn Uranus Neptune Pluto) with *My Very Elderly Mother Just Sat Under Nellie's Porch.* Telephone numbers, for example, frequently spell out the name of the company or a related idea to make the telephone number more memorable. To illustrate, people can order federal IRS forms and schedules by calling 1-800-TAX-FORM. In numerical form that is 1-800-829-3676, but TAX-FORM is easier to retrieve from memory than 829-3676. Similarly, you can create your own mnemonic devices to recall the main points of a presentation.

Third, **integrate** the new information with the known. We recall the familiar more easily than the unfamiliar. Therefore, you can make explicit links between what you already know and what you need to know to retrieve the ideas. For example, an instructor trying to help you remember and retrieve information for a test in acoustics might explain the Doppler effect (the change in frequency of a wave that occurs whenever there is a change in the distance between the source and the receiver) by linking it to something in your experience—a car horn that sounds like it changes its pitch as it approaches you. If your speaker does not create this linkage for you, as a good listener, you can create it for yourself. By linking the unknown or abstract to the known or concrete, you can recall the ideas more readily.

Listening is a complicated process involving both physical and psychological processes. As a listener you can improve your skills by being aware of both the physical and the psychological factors that affect your listening and actively participating in the listening process by modifying the physical environment and by involving your mental skills in listening to the speaker's message.

Summary

This chapter discussed specific techniques for preparing and delivering persuasive presentations. You have examined the preparation stage in which topics are selected, main ideas generated and organized, supporting material developed, specific language selected, and the speech rehearsed. You have looked at techniques to use in the practice stage for rehearsing your speech. You learned some of the techniques of delivery including visual features like eye contact and gestures as well as vocal features like volume, rate, and vocal inflection. Finally, you know how to improve your speech performance by learning from experience, learning from others, and learning from training.

In this chapter you also explored the important concept of listening. Listening is both a physical and a psychological process. The physical process of hearing means that you must pay particular attention to the volume and clarity of the speaker's delivery to assure that the speech can be heard comfortably.

In addition, you must pay attention to the psychological aspects of listening, perceiving. This means that you must choose to listen and should remain objective in persuasive listening situations.

Finally, since listening also involves your thought processes, you can listen more effectively by using appropriate frames of reference, by conserving the message in mental storage, and by linking the thoughts for easier retrieval.

Notes

[1] Lee Iacocca with William Novak, *Iacocca: An Autobiography* (New York: Bantam Books, 1986), p. 58. Copyright © 1984 by Lee Iacocca. Used by permission of Bantam Books, a division of Bantam Doubleday, Dell Publishing Group, Inc.

[2] Stephen R. Covey, A. Roger Merrill, and Rebecca R. Merrill, *First Things First* (New York: Simon and Schuster, 1994), p. 136.

[3] For a full explanation of operationalizing, see Mary John Smith, *Contemporary Communication Research Methods* (Belmont, CA: Wadsworth Publishing, 1988), Chapter 3.

[4] There are many different ways of measuring attention and attention span in listening. See Carl H. Weaver, *Human Listening: Processes and Behavior* (Indianapolis, IN: Bobbs-Merrill, 1972), Chapter 2.

[5] Quintilian, *The Institutes of Oratory*, trans. H. E. Butler (Cambridge, MA: Harvard University Press, 1966), VI.

[6] Alan H. Monroe, *Principles and Types of Speech* (Chicago, IL: Scott, Foresman and Company, 1935), vii and passim.

[7] William O. Douglas, *Points of Rebellion* (New York: Random House, 1970), p. 92.

[8] Catherine B. Ahles, "The Dynamics of Discovery," *Vital Speeches of the Day*, LIX (March 15, 1993), p. 352.

[9] John F. Kennedy, "Inaugural Address," *Selected Speeches from American History*, eds. Robert T. Oliver and Eugene E. White (Boston: Allyn & Bacon, 1966), p. 287. Copyright 1966. Allyn & Bacon. All rights reserved.

[10] Harriet R. Michel, "King—From Martin to Rodney," *Vital Speeches of the Day*, LIX (March 1, 1993), p. 308.

[11] Charles M. Rossiter, "The Effects of Rate of Presentation on Listening Test Scores for Recall of Facts, Recall of Ideas, and Generation of Inferences," unpublished dissertation, University of Ohio, 1970, quoted in Weaver, *Human Listening*, p. 146.

[12] Ralph G. Nichols, "Factors in Listening Comprehension," *Speech Monographs*, 15 (1948), pp. 154–163.

For Further Thought

1. Make your own list of "rules" for public speaking; make one list of "Dos" and one list of "Taboos" for public speakers.

2. Review examples of great speeches. Some anthologies of speeches are listed in the "For Further Reading" section. Review two examples of great speeches from those anthologies or other collections of speeches. What did the best speakers do to develop their ideas? Seek examples of how famous speakers use examples, description, testimony, numerical data, and audiovisual aids.

3. Interview someone who regularly gives speeches (e.g., a teacher, politician, minister). Find out what training that professional speaker had in public speaking. Inquire about special techniques the speaker uses to prepare a persuasive address. Ask him or her about the best speech he or she ever gave; what made it so successful?

4. Select a speech from *Vital Speeches of the Day*, a periodical found in most libraries. What did the speaker do to assure that the speech was interpreted correctly, remembered accurately, and retrieved easily?

5. Think about a time when you were moved by a speech. Use the principles of effective listening and persuasion to explain how the speaker achieved that effect for you.

For Further Reading

DeVito, Joseph. *Elements of Public Speaking*. fifth edition. New York: Harper-Collins, 1995.

Fletcher, Leon. *How to Speak Like a Pro*. New York: Ballantine Books, 1983.

Johannesen, Richard L., R. R. Allen, and Wil Linkugel. *Contemporary American Speeches*. seventh edition. Dubuque, IA: Kendall/Hunt Publishing, 1992.

Safire, William. *Lend Me Your Ears: Great Speeches in History*. New York: W. W. Norton & Company, 1992.

Sprague, Jo and Douglas Stuart. *The Speaker's Handbook*, fourth edition. Fort Worth, TX: Harcourt Brace College Publishers, 1996.

Steil, Lyman, Larry L. Barker, and Kittie W. Watson. *Effective Listening*. Reading, MA: Addison-Wesley Publishing Company, 1983.

Wilson, John F., Carroll C. Arnold, and Molly Meijer Wertheimer. *Public Speaking as a Liberal Art*, sixth edition. Boston: Allyn & Bacon, 1990.

Wolvin, Andrew and Carolyn Gwynn Coakley. *Listening*, third edition. Dubuque, IA: William C. Brown Publishers, 1988.

Chapter Ten

ADVERTISING

The numbers are always staggering. The average American is exposed to one thousand ads a week. American networks show over six thousand television commercials a week. The automotive industry alone spent more than one billion dollars on advertising in 1992. The average cost for a 30-second prime time spot was over $217,000 in 1992 and more for special programs like the Super Bowl. A full-page ad in the *Wall Street Journal* cost $110,627 in that same year. Sixty-two percent of households earning over $30,000 watch infomercials, program-length TV commercials.[1] With figures like those, is it any wonder that advertising is a major area of concern for businesses, that marketing is a key part of the business school curriculum, and a growing number of serious studies are being conducted on advertising and its impact on consumers?

But the numbers are merely an abstract representation of the extent of advertising. They do not tell the whole story. They do not examine the ways persuasion is used in advertising nor do they examine the impact of that persuasion on consumers.

In this chapter we shall explore the role of persuasion in advertising. We shall begin by looking at general principles of advertising. Next we shall focus on specific advertising media including print, radio, and television. Finally, we shall explore persuasion in advertising from the consumer's point of view.

PRINCIPLES OF AD COPY

The heart of the advertising agency is the creative department. In this division, copywriters and artists generate the basis for the ads that will

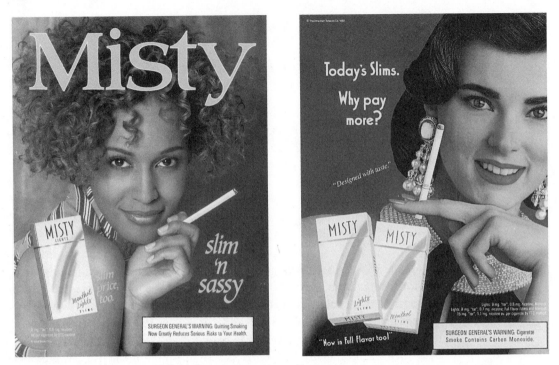

Advertising platforms carefully define their target audiences.

appear on billboards, radio, television, in newspapers, magazines, circulars, and product displays. The famous writer Aldous Huxley once wrote, "I have discovered the most exciting, the most arduous literary form of all, the most difficult to master, the most pregnant in curious possibilities. I mean the advertisement. . . . It is far easier to write ten passably effective sonnets, good enough to take in the not too inquiring critic, than one effective advertisement that will take in a few thousand of the uncritical buying public."[2] There are some general principles that these copywriters and artists follow in constructing advertisements.

In advertising terms, the **platform** is the statement of the principles for the ad—the central themes. A. Jerome Jeweler divided the platform into five parts: objectives, target audience, key consumer benefit, other usable benefits, and creative strategy statement.[3]

The **objective** is the goal of the ad. Just as a persuasive speech must have a specific purpose, a platform must have a clear statement of the expected outcome. Some ads are intended to introduce a new product. Some are geared toward maintaining product loyalty. Still others are aimed at "positioning" what Al Ries and Jack Trout explained this way: "To succeed in our overcommunicated society, a company must create a position in the prospect's mind, a position that takes into consideration not only a company's own strengths and weaknesses, but those of its competitors as well."[4]

The **target audience,** as you might expect, are the specific buyers expected to purchase the product or service being advertised. As we discussed in Chapter Eight, the audience is the key to effective persuasion. Advertising platforms carefully define their target audiences in terms of both the influential features of demographics and the psychological features that influence the receivers' reactions.

The **key consumer benefit** is also called the "unique selling proposition." The platform must identify the aspects that make the product or service desirable for the target audience and different from the competitors. Advertisers need to identify what makes their product or service uniquely beneficial for the buyers. Perhaps the product will save money, make the buyers more attractive, work more efficiently. Perhaps it tastes better, smells fresher, looks cleaner, feels softer, or sounds brighter. Whatever the positive qualities of the product or service may be, they must be clearly identified and linked to the needs and desires of the target audience.

Other usable benefits refer to the additional qualities of the product or service that can benefit the target audience. A good, long list of additional benefits provides additional ideas for use in constructing the ad. For example, the shampoo being pitched may have a unique selling proposition in that the product is made from all natural products and contains no artificial chemicals, but there are additional benefits that might be stressed. The ad might also emphasize that only one application is needed, or that it conditions as well as cleans, or that no animals were harmed in testing the product. Such additional benefits may well be worked into the ads in addition to the unique selling proposition.

Finally, Jeweler suggested that the platform should contain a **creative strategy statement.** This is the list of persuasive tactics to be used in the advertisements. Suppose, for example, that we know the product is a new tool that can be used as a hammer, screwdriver, and wrench. The objective is to persuade the target audience that this new product provides a convenient tool set combined into a single tool. It is intended to appeal to the people, mostly men, who must make minor repairs on an almost daily basis. The tool is not intended for people facing major jobs nor for the died-in-the-wool home handyman. Most people do not want to have to make three trips to the garage to get different tools when they are involved in minor home repairs. Other usable benefits include its lifetime guarantee, its design that allows it to be stored conveniently in a drawer, and its ergonomic feel. The creative strategy would emphasize that people in the targeted audience are busy people faced with minor projects, like hanging pictures, repairing a curtain rod holder, or tightening a doorknob. When they start such projects, they don't realize it will require two or three tools. They are annoyed by having to stop, dash out to the garage for another tool, and return to the project. The ad will emphasize the convenience of a three-in-one tool. The audience will be left with the idea that this is a convenient, sensible way to complete small home repair projects quickly.

After establishing the platform, it is necessary to construct the ad itself. Exactly what will appear in the advertisement depends on the type of media to be used. A radio spot, for example, requires different copy than does a billboard. In the following sections, we shall explore some of the persuasive principles of ads in the various media.

PRINT

Print has proven to be an effective medium for persuasive advertising. Peter Wright, for example, studied 160 homemakers using an advertisement for a new product equivalently presented in print and in broadcast form. He found that homemakers who read the print advertisements were more interested in purchasing the product when it was available than were the homemakers who viewed the broadcasted advertisment.[5]

The content of print ads, like other forms of advertising, generally follows the principles described earlier in this chapter. Research on the effectiveness of advertising was summarized this way: "[A]ll forms of promotions (other than TV advertising) generally obtain a strong and immediate positive from consumers. Information-oriented promotions, such as newspaper features and store displays, are most effective in getting consumers to switch brands, the former out of store and the latter in-store. On the other hand, price-oriented promotions, such as discounts, coupons, and cents-off, are most effective in getting consumers to buy in larger quantities."[6]

David Crystal is a British linguist who has studied the language of advertising. He summarized the nature of language used in advertising by dividing it into lexical or semantic elements and grammatical elements.[7]

SEMANTIC ELEMENTS

Advertising uses vivid words. As we discussed in Chapter Six and elsewhere, vivacity is an important linguistic quality of persuasive messages. Vivid words appeal to the senses and generate strong emotional impressions.

IT'S EASY TO SEE THE ADVANTAGES OF OUR V8 ENGINE WHEN THE HOOD IS RAISED.

THE NEW JEEP. GRAND CHEROKEE

At Jeep, we've always had a slightly different slant on driving. Of course, due to some of the most advanced technology ever to hit the road, that slant is usually caused by a steep mountain face.

With 220 horsepower and 300 foot-pounds of torque, the new Grand Cherokee Limited 4x4 offers the most powerful V8 engine available in its class.* A power plant made even more impressive by the new "on-demand" exclusive Quadra-Trac® four-wheel drive system that can detect wheel slippage and transfer power to the wheels with the most traction. As for feeling safe, dual front air bags,† side-door guard beams, and four-wheel anti-lock brakes all come standard.

To find out more, visit your Jeep dealer. If you prefer, call 1-800-925-JEEP, or visit our Web site at http://www.jeepunpaved.com You'll discover that its advantages are easy to see—from every angle.

T H E R E ' S   O N L Y   O N E

*Source of Class: *Automotive News,* 5/95. †Always wear your seat belt. Jeep is a registered trademark of Chrysler Corporation.

Semantic elements like vivid, concrete, positive, and unreserved language are vital to print ads.

Ads employ concrete language. Language that is concrete has more detail and is clearer. For example, dog is more concrete than pet, and Fido is more concrete than dog. According to research conducted by Rossiter and Percy, visual imagery is critical to both short-term and long-term response to advertising and "[t]he single most important variable affecting visual imagery as a response to linguistic stimuli is *concreteness.*"[8]

The language of advertising is positive. This means that the language used in advertising seeks to associate positive words with the product or service being pitched. "Improved," "maximum," and "ready" are examples of the kind of positive words typically found in advertising.

Ads use unreserved language. In other words, superlatives are the typical form of words used. Look carefully at ads in your favorite magazine. Aren't products referred to in superlative terms like "first," "finest," and "perfect"?

Grammatical Elements

In addition to being vivid, concrete, positive, and unreserved, Crystal also claims that there are distinctive features of the grammar of advertising. Here are four elements:

Advertising English "is typically conversational and elliptical—and often, as a result, vague."[9] In other words, ads typically use phrases and sentence fragments—the same grammatical forms we typically use in ordinary conversations. As a result, the claims made in ads may be vague. "With Spencers you get more!" "Own Your Own!" are vague expressions. Does Spencer's give the consumer more in a package than the competition, more value for the price, more problems, or what? "Own Your Own" is a play on words but makes a very vague claim about the product or service.

In addition, advertising uses highly figurative language. Metaphors ("Put a tiger in your tank"), similes ("Its like a thousand vibrating fingers"), as well as other literary stylistic devices abound in advertising language.

Crystal also found "deviant graphology" to be a common feature of ads. For example, an advertiser may spell words in unusual ways, like "krystal klear" or "nu-brite." Such peculiar spelling has a definite impact on receivers. People have come to think that "lite" means "light."

Finally, Crystal claimed that advertising uses "strong sound effects, such as rhythm, alliteration, and rhyme. . . ." Memorable slogans frequently use such auditory effects to great effect. For example, "I like Ike" was an excellent slogan in the 1952 presidential election because it

How To Get Past Tense.

Think of all the things you have to do in a day. Mundane, but necessary things. Doesn't it make sense to make them a little more exciting if you can...This is the Pontiac® Grand Am® Sport Sedan. The car that turns the ordinary four-door into something extraordinary. It's more than dual air bags and ABS. Its all-new Twin-Cam engine and sport suspension are the perfect antidotes for boredom.

Gotta make a pizza run? Grand Am will make it spicier. Picking up your dry cleaning? "Wear" something exciting on your way there. The whole idea behind Grand Am is to make the ordinary... extraordinary. If you've got demands that put a lot of stress in your life, Grand Am is how you get past tense. **For more information, please call 1-800-2PONTIAC or check out our site on the World Wide Web at http://www.pontiac.com.**

PONTIAC GRAND AM
WE ARE DRIVING EXCITEMENT.

*Grand Am SE
Sport Sedan*

USA Proud Sponsor of the 1996 U.S. Olympic Team

Grammatical elements like this play on words make print ads memorable.

contained a memorable sound effect. The components of a "Big Mac" ("two all beef patties, special sauce, lettuce, cheese," etc.) is still memorable after all these years because of its rhythmic qualities.

Compare Crystal's elements with the advice that is typically given to copywriters. Box 10.1 contains a representative example of the rules for writing ad copy.

In addition to the linguistic elements that Crystal identified, the print medium also employs elements of visual communication. Features like pictures, typeface, and layout are critical to effective persuasion in print advertising.

Visual Elements

There is clear evidence that visual elements are influential in print advertising. Mitchell and Olson tested "verbal" ads for a facial tissue against "visual" versions for the same product that emphasized pictures over written content. They found that two of the three visual versions (one showing a kitten and another a sunset) showed significantly greater change in product attitude than did the verbal version and the visual version using an abstract picture.[10] Sandra Moriarity examined 222 advertisements drawn from the Starch Readership Service in one year. She concluded that "in 97% of the advertisements, the noted score for the ad as a whole was identical to the seen score for the visual" which "suggests that the advertisement's impact is certainly a function of the power of its visual."[11]

Visual aspects are more than just pictures used in ads. Of equal importance are visual factors like the typeface, use of all capitals versus uppercase and lowercase letters, color contrast, and the use of white space to focus attention and to highlight important points. While novel type in advertising is less legible, it is more effective in attracting attention among readers.[12] Finally, design of the layout, or placement of the elements in the ad, also affects advertising effectiveness. In a study of 168 magazine ads published between 1973 and 1982, researchers concluded that "magazine ads which employ copy-heavy and type-specimen layout designs are less effective at attracting the attention of male readers than seven alternative layout designs."[13]

While it is impossible to detail all of the potentially influential aspects of design in advertising, we can identify a few of the important elements of visual communication. In *The Graphics of Design*, Turnbull and Baird identify six principles of design for visual presentation of advertisements: (1) Proportion refers to size or dimension relationships.

Box 10.1
ADVERTISING WRITING STYLE

Make it easy on your reader. Write short sentences. Use easy, familiar words.

Don't waste words. Say what you have to say—nothing more, nothing less. Don't pad, but don't skimp. If it takes a thousand words, use a thousand words. As long as not one is excess baggage.

Stick to the present tense, active voice—it's crisper.

Avoid the past tense and passive voice—these forms tend to drag. Exceptions should be deliberate, for special effect.

Don't hesitate to use personal pronouns. Remember, you're trying to talk to just *one* person, so talk as you would to a friend. Use "you" and "your."

Clichés are crutches; learn to get along without them.

Bright, surprising words and phrases perk up readers, keep them reading.

Don't overpunctuate. It kills copy flow. Excessive commas are the chief culprits. Don't give your readers any excuse to jump ship.

Use contractions whenever possible. They're fast, personal, natural. People talk in contractions. (Listen to yourself.)

Don't brag or boast. Everyone hates a bore. Translate those product features you're so proud of into consumer benefits that ring the bell with your readers. Write from the reader's point of view, not your own. Avoid "we," "us," "our."

Be single-minded. Don't try to do too much. If you chase more than one rabbit at a time, you'll catch none.

Write with flair. Drum up excitement. Make sure the enthusiasm you feel comes through in your copy.

SOURCE: David L. Malickson and John W. Nason, *Advertising—How to Write the Kind That Works* (New York: Scribner's Sons, 1982), p. 81.

(2) Balance is the sense of equilibrium among the elements. (3) Contrast is the matter of emphasis in the ad. (4) Rhythm is the repetition of some element in the ad. (5) Unity means that all of the elements of the ad are coherent. (6) Harmony is a balance of "strong visual impact" with a "unity of effect."[14]

Consider the ad in Figure 10.1. Evaluate it in terms of proportion, balance, contrast, rhythm, unity, and harmony.

Figure 10.1
Sample Print Ad

Proportion, balance, contrast, rhythm, unity, and harmony are the key visual factors in a print ad.

Visual ads like this one emphasize pictures over written content.

Notice, for example, that the proportion focuses our attention on the facial expression of the firefighter, that balance is maintained between the brim of the helmet and the text beneath the chin with the visual emphasis creating an inverted triangle that points to the company's logo at the bottom of the page.

RADIO

Radio, with its exclusive focus on the auditory aspects of communication, is nevertheless a potent force in advertising.

Bob Schulberg in *Radio Advertising: The Authoritative Handbook* indicated that among light television viewers, radio represented 65 percent of media use and that even among heavy television viewers, radio represented 28 percent of the media use compared to 8 percent of their media time spent reading newspapers and 5 percent devoted to reading magazines.[15]

Linda Coleman conducted a qualitative study of advertisements. She studied prosodic, or sound, qualities, in a variety of ads. She concluded that prosodic cues "direct our processing of information presented in the utterance. Cues such as voice tone, pitch, tempo, and duration are used to draw attention to certain segments, to de-emphasize others, to convey the speaker's attitude toward the subject matter, and to indicate the function of a particular segment within an utterance. The importance of prosodic cues is demonstrated by the fact that the hearer of a commercial can arrive at very different conclusions about what is being said than will the reader of a transcript not analyzed for intonation."[16]

Robert Bly is an advertising copywriter and business consultant. He offered fourteen tips for writing radio copy. These principles are reproduced in Box 10.2. Notice that while many of the principles are similar to the advice offered for print advertising, there are some important difference that emphasize the unique qualities of radio.

While many people emphasize how to write effective ads, Bob Schulberg addressed an important counterpoint. He wrote, "Radio is the ultimate personal advertising medium. In most cases, the communication is between the advertiser and *a single person*. Although this is assuredly one of radio's great strengths, it can work against the advertiser whose commercial, for whatever reason, turns the listener off. It isn't necessary for the listener to switch stations. All he or she has to do is mentally tune out. And it happens far too often."[17] Among the reasons radio spots fail, Schulberg cited the following:

Overproduced radio commercials confuse the listener. A visual work can be so ornate that it is difficult to comprehend it. In a similar vein, a radio spot can have so much going on in it that it is confusing. Overproduction means there is too much going on at once for a listener to easily comprehend.

Another reason why radio ads fail is a poor differentiation of sounds. Imagine, for example, trying to listen to an ad that uses lyrics in the background music while the advertising message is also being read. Even if the ad itself doesn't have such conflicting sounds, sometimes the ad will sound "muddy" because the studio conditions are different from the listener's conditions which might include traffic noise and automobile sounds when listening to a car radio.

Humorous commercials that aren't funny are a disaster. While humor can work to help differentiate a product from its competitors,

Box 10.2
ROBERT BLY'S FOURTEEN PROVEN COPYWRITING TECHNIQUES

1. *Stretch the listener's imagination. Voices and sounds can evoke pictures in the mind.* . . .

2. *Listen for a memorable sound or voice.* A distinctive voice, a jingle, a solution that will make your message stand out.

3. *Present one idea.* Be direct and clear or your message may become subject to distractions.

4. *Select your customer quickly.* Get the attention of your customer fast.

5. *State your product/service and promise early.* Radio spots that do so get higher awareness. And be sure to repeat the product name at least six times in a one-minute commercial.

6. *Capitalize on local events.* Tie in with fads, fashion, news events, weather, or holidays.

7. *Music helps.* It's great for reaching teenagers who prefer the "now sounds.". . .

8. *Ask listeners for action.* You can't make a sale unless you ask for the order. . . .

9. *Use the strength of radio personalities.* They have steady listeners. Have them deliver the radio spot live. . . .

10. *Have more than one spot ready for broadcast.* Radio is a high frequency medium. You need to have variety in your sales message.

11. *Special messages can reach ethnic groups.* Special messages to special groups do very well. It pays to design radio spots for ethnic groups and even produce them in that group's language (e.g., Spanish for Hispanic marketing).

12. *Use radio for special promotions.* A holiday sale, a grand opening, an anniversary sale or a "this week only" promotion all work well on radio.

13. *Don't evaluate radio copy by reading a typed radio script.* The spoken word is different than the printed word. . . .

14. *Get help if you need it.* You can write the spots yourself. But, if you are not an expert in radio advertising, get help from a professional who has experience in the field.

SOURCE: Robert Bly, *Advertising Manager's Handbook* (Englewood Cliffs, NJ: Prentice-Hall, 1993), pp. 300–301.

Schulberg recommended that serious and/or high-priced items probably should not use humor, especially "unfunny funny" spots.[18]

Finally, there is the problem of the sponsor serving as the commercial talent. Radio requires special training and experience to make it work well. Just listen to the difference between the sound of the professional announcer and an interviewee or a caller. We all have our favorite example of business owners who insist on producing the most amateurish commercials—either over-hyped hard sell or dead monotone. It is rare that the client can actually carry off an effective radio spot.

TELEVISION

There is no question that television advertising is effective. Television has the ability to combine the imaginativeness of radio with the visual interest of print but enhances print visuals with action. Print can be animated and move across the screen; print can be made larger, sharper, more colorful in television. Furthermore, television ads have become an art form. "Looking at the ads of the 1950s," wrote Paul Rutherford, "provokes laughter in present-day audiences because their primitive visuals, simple-mindedness, and earnest enthusiasm so often make them seem camp. . . . Since then, not only have ad-makers exploited the ever-improving technology of video, they have mastered the power of the metaphor, the play of contrasts, the motif of transformation, and the strategy of irony. What I've called the commercials of distinction are among the most ingenious, compact, and effective means of communication around."[19]

Television is used extensively in political persuasion as well as in product advertising. Donald Cundy conducted a study of the effect of television on voters and replicated it in two different regions of the country. He concluded that "under conditions of low viewer involvement, even a single exposure to a televised spot can have a substantial effect on targeted components of viewer imagery."[20]

To take advantage of television's possibilities, Thomas Bivins suggested five guidelines for writing a television ad. These guidelines appear in Box 10.3.

Linguist Michael Geis divided the dialogue of most television ads into two classes: interviews and minidramas. An interview is a dialogue between an interviewer and an interviewee. The interviewer "conducts some sort of product test, questions a Consumer about why he or she prefers the product, or 'lectures' a consumer on the virtues of a product,

Box 10.3
GUIDELINES FOR SCRIPTS

1. Open with an attention-getting device: an interesting piece of audio, an unusual camera shot, or a celebrity. The first few seconds are crucial. If your viewers are not hooked by then, you've lost them.

2. Open with an establishing shot if possible—something that says where you are and intimates where you are going. If you open in a classroom, for instance, chances are you are going to stay there. If you jump too much, you confuse viewers.

3. If you open with a long shot, you should then cut to a closer shot, and soon after, introduce the subject of the spot. This is especially applicable if you are featuring a product or a celebrity spokesperson.

4. Vary shot composition from M[edium] S[hot] to C[lose] U[p] and a super (superimposition) of logo or address. (A *super* involves placing one image over another.)

5. Don't call for a new shot unless it adds to the spot. Make your shots seem like part of an integrated whole. Be single-minded and try to tell only one important story per shot.

SOURCE: Thomas Bivins, *Handbook for Public Relations Writing,* second edition (Lincolnwood, IL: NTC Business Books, 1991), pp. 159–160.

etc."[21] The interviews with consumers in unusual situations for a plastic bag are good examples of this form. The minidrama, on the other hand, is a "slice of life" in which the people in the ad engage in conversations rather than interviews. The coffee commercial involving neighbors who get romantically involved is such a minidrama that it actually produced a fiction book based on the exploits of the main characters.

In constructing and placing television advertising, research in advertising effectiveness indicates that novel design, positioning, and timing are additional features to consider.[22] Novel design means that new products and new approaches to established products are most likely to benefit from television advertising. Television is particularly good at introducing new products and services through advertising. It is also particularly good at introducing new forms of familiar products. For example, the blue color of a popular candy was introduced primarily through television ads.

Positioning a television ad means having it run where it is most likely to reach the target audience. For example, advertising children's toys on Saturday mornings.

Timing is a related matter of scheduling the advertisements in the peak selling seasons for the product or service—for example, scheduling air conditioning repair service in the summer rather the winter months.

So far we have discussed persuasion in advertising from the producer's point of view. It is, however, equally important to consider advertising from the consumer's point of view.

CONSUMING ADVERTISING

In this section we shall look at consuming advertisements in two areas. First, we shall consider how consumers interpret advertisements. Finally, we shall explore how consumers assess persuasion in advertising.

INTERPRETING MEDIATED PERSUASION

Charles Atkin and Gary Heald interviewed a representative sample 323 voters in a congressional campaign.[23] While they focused on a political advertising campaign, their findings can be extended to five areas for consumers to consider in interpreting advertising messages.

First, a political campaign can "increase the electorate's level of knowledge about the candidate and his featured issue positions." Therefore, advertising can be used as a teaching tool. Consumers can discover not only what products are available, but what features are important to look for in a product by carefully attending to various advertisements.

Second, Atkin and Heald found that political advertising campaigns could "elevate emphasized issues and attributes higher on the voters' agenda of decisional criteria." In other words, the political campaign broadcasts had the effect of setting an agenda for public decision making. In a similar vein, product advertising can serve to set the agenda for consumer products and services. Consumers were not concerned about carbon monoxide poisoning in the home until a product like a smoke alarm was widely advertised to detect carbon monoxide leaks in the home. As Judith Williamson wrote in *Decoding Advertisements*, "Advertisements are one of the most important cultural factors moulding and reflecting our life today."[24]

Consumers should carefully consider the importance of the products, services, and ideas touted in advertisements. The key is to decide where the matter really stands in the hierarchy of importance for the individual consumer.

Ads like this can help to set the agenda of receiver interests.

Third, the study of political advertisements found that the campaign could "stimulate the electorate's interest in the campaign." While it is true that advertisements are designed to sell the product, service, or candidate, it is also true that there is an entertainment value in advertisements as well. Advertisements can be beneficial by stimulating interest in what is going on. For example, interest in ecology and the environment can be promulgated by products advertising their ecological sensitivity.

Fourth, the researchers found that political campaign advertising could produce more positive affect toward the candidate as a person. While this is a feature peculiar to "selling" a political candidate, it also indicates a little recognized value of advertising. By recognizing positive qualities in the spokesperson for the product, consumers can come to agreement on appropriate social behavior. By seeking positive relationships in advertising portrayals and by rejecting negative portrayals, consumers can influence what they consider to be appropriate interpersonal relationships.

Finally, Atkin and Heald found that political advertising campaigns could "intensify polarization of evaluations of the candidate." In other words, the political advertisements forced voters from neutral and indifferent positions to stronger positions of liking or disliking. In political terms this is actually a beneficial effect since voter apathy and indifference is a notorious problem in a democratic society. In a more commercial sense, advertising plays an important role in consumer motivation. We should view advertisements for their ability to stimulate us to action, to force us to commit to a course of action and contribute to the growth of the economy rather than sit by passively accepting the way things are.

ASSESSING MEDIATED PERSUASION

While it is important to interpret the meaning of advertisements in terms of their ability to inform, set agendas, stimulate interest, generate positive role models, and activate us as consumers, it is also important to have criteria available to evaluate or assess the advertisements we encounter. There are three areas to consider in the assessment of advertisements: subliminal persuasion, deceptive practices, and criteria for evaluating products, services, and politicians.

Subliminal Persuasion

The concern about subliminal persuasion seems to wax and wane. In 1957 James Vicary spliced frames reading "Drink Coca-Cola" and "Hungry? Eat popcorn" into a popular motion picture. Vicary claimed

There is no conclusive evidence that subliminal perception has any long-term effect. This ad shows a take off on subliminal perception.

that this significantly increased the sale of Coke and popcorn.[25] Periodically the issue reappears. In the 1970s, for example, Wilson Key claimed that erotic images were included in magazine ads to appeal to consumer sex drives.[26]

The impact of such claims was sufficient to cause the Federal Communications Commission to bar the practice from radio and television advertising. Ethicists condemn the practice "because hidden use of subliminal persuasion circumvents and undermines capacities and freedoms that are essential to human self-fulfillment."[27]

However, there does not appear to be any conclusive evidence that subliminal perception actually has any effect on consumers beyond a few seconds. By definition, subliminal perception would have to work subconsciously, which makes testing it a tricky proposition. Furthermore, even if the persuasive message were "perceived" by consumers, there is no evidence that it actually affects the beliefs, attitudes, values, or behaviors of the receivers.[28]

Deceptive Practices

As we noted in Chapter Four, the power to persuade implies the power to deceive. As a result, there are a number of deceptive, albeit legal, practices that consumers should be aware of. The two most important are the use of weasel words and the inconclusive claims made in advertisements.

Carl Wrighter coined the term "weasel word" to refer to terms used in advertisements that allow copywriters to weasel their way out of actually making a false argument.[29] For example, the word "helps" weasels the product out of actually saying that it prevents tooth decay or cures colds. Another weasel word is "virtually" which does not mean that a product *actually* is or does anything.

Wrighter also recommended that consumers pay close attention to the claims being made in advertisements. For example, note that a question is not a statement; therefore, when an ad uses a question as a claim, it is not really asserting the claim. For example, an ad that says, "Don't you want your children to be safe? Use ultra-tite locks" is not really saying that "ultra-tite" locks actually keep your children safer than any other brand of locks. Another common claim is the mysterious ingredient claim in which the product is touted to be better because there is some special formula that makes it superior. In reality, many products work pretty much the same and a "powerful" magic formulation is not demonstrably superior to a competing product that does not have that "secret ingredient."

Criteria for Evaluating Ads

In addition to being aware of the need to pay close attention to the ad so that decisions are made consciously, and to being critical of the language and claims made in advertising, consumers should also apply specific criteria to evaluating ads.

First, consumers should carefully separate image from substance. Ads are deliberately constructed to present a positive image of the product. For example, food is "made up" with photographic techniques to make it appear more appetizing than it actually appears. The next time you are in a restaurant, compare the photographs in the menu with the reality on your plate to understand the power of form over substance. In other words, consider what is said not what is implied in any ad. By carefully separating the image being promoted from the product you are purchasing, you can be better assured of getting what you pay for.

Second, be sure to determine what you really want from what you merely think you want. Advertisers are attempting to create a demand for a product or service. In doing so, as we have seen, they systematically attempt to determine how to link their products or services to your needs and desires. They often rely on you to "process" the ad through the peripheral route rather than the central route we discussed in Chapter Three. Take the time and expend the energy to really think about what is being advertised. Even a relatively inexpensive item should be purchased because you can benefit from having it not because it appears to be popular or in short supply.

By attending to advertisements, by checking our interpretations of advertisements, and by applying critical thinking techniques to all purchases, we consumers can get the most from the ads that bombard us. Failing to do so can be hazardous to our wealth.

Summary

Advertising is the genuine paradigm of persuasion. It is probably the most pervasive form of persuasion in American society.

We began this chapter by examining general principles of creating ad copy. We noted that advertisements are constructed from a platform consisting of objectives, target audience, key consumer benefit, other usable benefits, and a creative strategy statement.

Next we examined specific persuasive features of the print media. Specifically, we considered semantic elements, grammatical elements, and visual elements of advertising copy.

In radio advertising we noted fourteen techniques for writing radio copy. We also explored four reasons why radio advertisements fail: over-production, poor differentiation of sound, humor that isn't funny, and using the sponsor as talent.

Finally, we looked at television advertising. We noted guidelines for generating a television script and constructing dialogue.

In the consumer section we began by considering how consumers interpret the mediated persuasion of advertising. We extended research on political advertising to commercial advertising. We noted five principles. Ads can teach. Ads can set a commercial agenda. Ads can entertain. Ads can instill positive values. Ads can stimulate consumers to action.

In assessing mediated persuasion. We noted that there is no clear evidence that "subliminal persuasion" has an impact on consumers. We also noted some of the forms of legal deception in advertising, including weasel words and peculiar claims. Finally, we developed two criteria for assessing ads. (1) Consumers should separate image from substance. (2) Consumers should determine what they really want rather than what the advertisers try to instill as needs.

Notes

[1] Paul Rutherford, *The New Icons? The Art of Television Advertising* (Toronto: University of Toronto Press, 1994), p. 169; Seth Godin, ed. *1994 Business Almanac and Desk Reference* (Boston: Houghton Mifflin Company, 1994), pp. 533, 545, 550, and 565.

[2] Aldous Huxley, "Advertisement," *On the Margin* (New York: George H. Doran Company, 1923), pp. 123–124.

[3] A. Jerome Jeweler, *Creative Strategy in Advertising* (Belmont, CA: Wadsworth Publishing Company, 1981), p. 14.

[4] Al Reis and Jack Trout, *Positioning: The Battle for Your Mind* (New York: Warner Books, Inc, 1986), p. 24.

[5] Peter Wright, "Analyzing Media Effects on Advertising Responses," *Public Opinion Quarterly,* 38 (Summer, 1974), p. 201.

[6] Gerald Tellis, "Modeling the Effectiveness of Advertising in Contemporary Markets: Research Findings and Opportunities," *Attention, Attitude, and Affect in Response to Advertising,* Eddie Clark, Timothy Brock, and David Stewart, eds (Hillsdale, NJ: Lawrence Erlbaum Associates, Publishers, 1994), p. 61.

[7] David Crystal, "Advertising English," *The Cambridge Encyclopedia of the English Language* (New York: Cambridge University Press, 1995), pp. 388–399. Reprinted with permission of Cambridge University Press.

[8] John Rossiter and Larry Percy, "Visual Communication in Advertising," *Information Processing Research in Advertising,* Richard Jackson Harris, ed (Hillsdale, NJ: Lawrence Erlbaum Associates, Publishers, 1983), p. 98.

[9] Crystal, *Cambridge Encyclopedia of the English Language,* p. 388. Reprinted with permission of Cambridge University Press.

[10] A. A. Mitchell and J. C. Olson, "Cognitive Effects of Advertising Repetition," *Advances in Consumer Research IV,* W. D. Perrault, ed. (Atlanta: Association for Consumer Research, 1977).

[11] Sandra A. Moriarity, "A Content Analysis of Visuals Used in Print Media Advertising," *Journalism Quarterly,* 64 (1987), p. 554.

[12] Sandra A. Moriarity, "Novelty vs. Practicality in Advertising Typography," *Journalism Quarterly,* 61 (Spring, 1984), pp. 188–190.

[13] Leonard Reid, Herbert Rotfeld, and James Barnes, "Attention to Magazine Ads as Function of Layout Design," *Journalism Quarterly,* 61 (Summer, 1984), p. 441.

[14] Arthur T. Turnbull and Russell N. Baird, *The Graphics of Communication* (New York: Holt, Rinehart and Winston, 1964), pp. 179–190.

[15] Bob Schulberg, *Radio Advertising: The Authoritative Handbook* (Lincolnwood, IL: NTC Business Books, 1989), p. 71.

[16] Linda Coleman, "Semantic and Prosodic Manipulation in Advertising," *Information Processing Research in Advertising,* Richard Jackson Harris, ed. (Hillsdale, NJ: Lawrence Erlbaum Associates, 1983), p. 238.

[17] Schulberg, *Radio Advertising,* p. 126.

[18] Ibid., p. 117.

[19] Rutherford, *The New Icons?,* pp. 194–195.

[20] Donald T. Cundy, "Image Formation, the Low Involvement Viewer, and Televised Political Advertising," *Political Communication and Persuasion,* 7 (1990), pp. 41–59.

[21] Michael L. Geis, *The Language of Television Advertising* (New York: Academic Press, 1982), p. 131.

[22] Tellis, "Modelling," p. 62.

[23] Charles Atkin and Gary Heald, "Effects of Political Advertising," *Public Opinion Quarterly,* 40 (1976), pp. 216–228.

[24] Judith Williamson, *Decoding Advertisements* (London: Marion Boyars, 1978), p. 11.

[25] See, for example, Sarah Trenholm, *Persuasion and Social Influence* (Englewood Cliffs, NJ: Prentice-Hall, 1989), pp. 47–49; Timothy Moore, "Subliminal Advertising: What You See Is What You Get," *Journal of Marketing,* 46 (1982), pp. 38–48.

[26] W. B. Key, *Subliminal Seduction: Ad Media's Manipulation of a Not So Innocent America* (New York: Signet Books, 1973).

[27] Richard Johannesen, "Perspectives on Ethics in Persuasion," *Persuasion: Reception and Responsibility,* seventh edition by Charles U. Larson (Belmont, CA: Wadsworth Publishing Company, 1995), p. 43.

[28] See, for example, M. Trainer and M. Simonson, "Subliminal Massages, Persuasion, and Behavior Change," *Journal of Social Psychology,* 128 (1987), pp. 563–565; T. E. Moore, "The Case Against Subliminal Manipulation," *Psychology and Marketing,* 5 (1988), pp. 297–316.

[29] Carl Wrighter, *I Can Sell You Anything* (New York: Ballantine Books, 1973), passim.

For Further Thought

1. Select an unusual product like curry powder (spice) or fingernail clippers. Create advertising copy using the principles of advertising platforms like the unique selling proposition.
2. Use the principles of writing style in Box 10.1 to analyze and evaluate a print ad. Explain how the copywriter met or failed to meet the standards of effective copy.
3. Listen to the radio for half an hour; watch television for half an hour. Make careful notes on the ads you hear and see. What do the two different media do similarly in their ads? What do the two media do differently in their ads?
4. Consider different forms of advertising like billboards and T-shirts. In what ways are these similar to the traditional forms of advertising discussed in this chapter? In what ways are such forms of advertising unique? What are the principles of persuasion that apply to these forms of advertising?
5. Make a list of deceptive practices you encounter in advertising. How can consumers be alerted to such forms of persuasion?

For Further Reading

Clark, Eddie M., Timothy C. Brock, and David W. Stewart, eds. *Attention, Attitude, and Affect in Response to Advertising.* Hillsdale, NJ: Lawrence Erlbaum Associates, 1994.

Levinson, Jay and Seth Godin. *The Guerrilla Marketing Handbook.* Boston: Houghton Mifflin Company, 1994.

Myers, Greg. *Words in Ads.* London: Edward Arnold, 1994.

Wernick, Andrew. *Promotional Culture: Advertising, Ideology, and Symbolic Expression.* Newbury Park, CA: Sage Publications, 1991.

Chapter Eleven

SALES INTERVIEWS

"Behaviorists stress the importance of immediate feedback and positive reinforcement as necessary consequences to shape our actions," said master salesman Bruce White. "Salespeople are reinforced constantly, and closing a sale is definitely the tangible result of successful effort. And since most salespeople receive commissions or bonuses in relation to their sales, incentive increases with the rate of success."[1]

Sales is the most direct application of persuasion in the business world. In no other field do we find the principles and elements of persuasion so clearly at work to the mutual benefit of the source and the receiver.

In this chapter we shall examine the application of persuasion in an interview setting. Since sales work is a form of interviewing, we shall begin by examining the special characteristics of interviews. Then we shall turn to a specific description of the persuasive aspects of creative sales. Finally, we shall look at the sales process from the consumer's point of view.

PERSUASIVE INTERVIEWS

An interview is a relatively formal type of interpersonal communication in which the parties pursue preconceived goals by questions and answers.[2] This means that interviews are more structured than, say, a casual conversation with a friend.

Interviews are also goal directed. A reporter conducting an interview is pursuing a goal of acquiring information to be used in a news report. A car sales agent dialoguing with a potential customer is, in fact, conducting an interview. In each case, the goal of the interview is persuasion.

Finally, an interview involves dialogue through questions and answers. While some sales situations involve a persuasive presentation, or monologue, most sales involve interaction between the parties through dialogue. In our previous example of the automobile sales agent interacting with a customer, the interaction is designed to uncover the customer's needs, base the ensuing persuasive efforts on those needs, answer questions about the automobile's performance, and respond to any skeptical questions posed by the buyer. To achieve these goals, sales agents both ask and answer questions. Since this is a crucial technique for sales, we need to take a closer look at types of questions used in sales interviews.

Types of Questions

Research in interviewing indicates that there are at least three different types of questions: open, closed, and leading. **Open questions** invite a wide response. For example, a real estate salesperson might ask a prospective client, "What sort of a setting are you looking for in your new home?" **Closed questions** are more directed and call for a more limited range of response. "What are the ages of your children?" is an example of a closed question. An extreme form of closed question is the "yes–no" question that allows only two possible responses, for example, "Are you familiar with the Greenwood area?" **Leading questions** have the expected answer incorporated in the wording of the question. "This is a convenient location, isn't it?" is a leading question. A more neutral way of phrasing that question is "What do you think of this location?" Each of the types of questions has a specific purpose.

Open questions are used to elicit a developed or complicated response. Sales agents will frequently use this type of question to analyze the prospective client. "How would you rate the quality of the merchandise you have purchased this year?" explores how satisfied the client is with the product. "What sorts of problems are you having with your current vendor?" seeks to determine the areas of discontent that may exist in the current service. "What do you think of the prices of your current supplier?" tries to uncover how the client feels about the cost of the merchandise.

Open questions are also useful in getting a reluctant client to open up. Some people are suspicious of salespeople and may be reticent in talking to the agent. Because open questions require more than a minimal response, they can be employed to get the client to talk more about the topic. "Tell me a little bit about what you are looking for in a vendor" requires the respondent to say more than yes, no, or maybe.

Closed questions are used to get at specific information. A salesperson might ask, for example, "How long does it typically take for the product to arrive after you have placed your order?" This closed question establishes a definite time frame for delivery. "Do you know anyone else who might be interested in this product?" is an example of using a closed question to get leads on potential clients.

Closed questions are also used to check for listening accuracy. For example, a sales agent might ask, "You currently place orders quarterly, is that right?" to check whether information heard earlier is understood correctly.

Yes–no questions, the extreme form of closed questions, are frequently used in sales interviews to develop a yes response in the receiver, to put the client in a positive frame of mind. For example, a sales person may ask, "Now I just want to check my understanding of your needs. You want a computer that is powerful enough to handle account spreadsheets. Correct?" "Yes." "And you want a model that can be easily upgraded to keep up with the changes in the technology, yes?" "Uh-huh." "And the computer must also be able to run your current programs but also the new software you plan to purchase?" "Yes." "So our Abacus 6000 would meet all of those requirements, right?" "Sure looks like it."

Leading questions are particularly useful in sales interviews. Because they steer the respondent in a predetermined direction, leading questions can be used to move into particular areas. "Do you get frustrated by the planned obsolescence of most products?" leads the interview into a specific area the sales agent estimates to be a potential motivator for this client.

Leading questions may also be used to get the respondent to participate in a positive way. For example, a sales agent may ask, "Your competitors have said that this product has been really useful. What advantages do you see in this product?"

Leading questions must be used with caution in a sales interview. People resent being manipulated. Using blatantly leading questions may be perceived as seeking to trick the client into a purchase.[3]

Questions may also be primary or probing. Primary questions open a new topic area. Probing questions follow up on the current topic. For example, a sales agent may ask a primary question like "Our insurance policy guarantees delivery on time, every time. Have you had problems with delayed delivery in the past?" "Yes." The agent may then want to follow up with a probing question like, "Can you give me an example of the last time this happened?"

Primary questions should be planned in advance to cover specific areas the questioner wants to have answered. The agent, for example, will want to plan a strategy for sequencing the topics covered in the interview. As Robert Miller and Stephen Heimen recommended in *Conceptual Selling,* "your goal in thinking about sequence before the sales call begins is to avoid the common error of submitting your customer to a barrage of disconnected queries. . . ."[4] Customers, too, should plan primary questions in advance. As we shall stress throughout this chapter, an interview means that both parties ask and answer questions from time to time. Clients should always have in mind the specific issues that they need to have answered by the sales agent. Clients should also realize that the questions they ask can give the sales agent clues about the needs and issues that are most important to them.

Probing questions function as follow-up questions to explore further a subject raised by a primary question. A salesperson may follow up on a comment by a client by asking, for example, "You've indicated that you are fairly pleased with the service of your current vendor. Have there been any incidents when shipment has been delayed or you've encountered a servicing problem?" Probing questions cannot always be planned in advance. Questioners should stay alert to the possibility that a given area may require additional probing before there will be a full understanding.

A Sales Model

As we noted in the Introduction of this text, a model helps us to visualize the important elements in an abstract process. We can visualize a model of a sales interview as pictured in Figure 11.1.

Let's examine the elements in Figure 11.1 using the sale of an automobile as an example. The source is a car sales agent, Shannon Green. The receiver is a client, Jan Brown.

The exigence, the problem being addressed in the situation, for both Shannon and Jan is the sale of a new car, but each party has a different view of that exigence. Shannon knows that the goal is to sell an automobile, so the task is to use the sales interview to clarify the exigence, to gauge Jan's ability to resolve the exigence, and to dramatize Jan's need for a car. On the other side, Jan may need to have the need clarified, must come to recognize the ability to resolve the exigence, and must come to feel the urgency to purchase a car.

The messages in this case consist of the dialogue, the interaction through questions and answers, between Shannon and Jan. Shannon will use questions to clarify Jan's needs: what make of automobile is best? what features are important? and so on. Shannon will also seek to

Figure 11.1
A Model of a Sales Interview

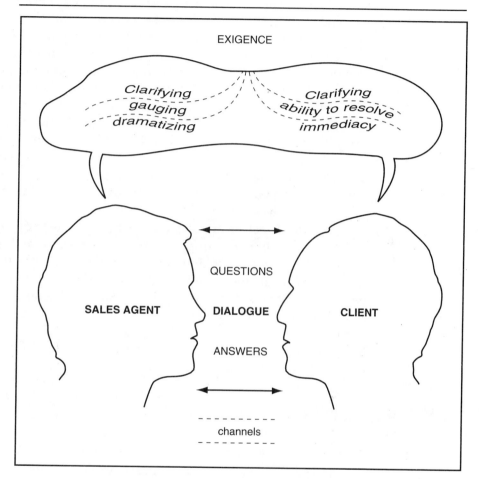

gauge Jan's ability to purchase the automobile: Can Jan afford the payments? will there be another person besides Jan involved in the decision to buy? and so on. Finally, Shannon will use questions and answers to dramatize the exigence: the satisfaction of ownership, the comfort of driving a new automobile, the feeling of safety in protective design qualities, the relief from worrying about breakdowns, and so on.

Jan will also use questions and answers to resolve the exigence. There are goals of clarifying the exigence: which model would best meet the type of driving Jan does? would it be better to buy or to lease? how soon will the desired style and color be available? and so on. Jan will also use questions and answers to recognize the ability to resolve the exigence: which options can be incorporated into Jan's budget? can affordable payments be arranged? and so on. Finally, Jan will use the question-and-answer interaction to make a decision: should the purchase be made now or later in the month when the price might be better? should the decision be postponed until the new models come out? should more comparisons be made before finalizing a decision? and so on.

The channels involved in the sales interview are usually those involved in any face-to-face interview. The verbal interaction includes both sight (pictures, brochures, etc.) and sound (verbal interaction). The appearance of the automobile and both Shannon and Jan's nonverbal behavior are also important. However, because purchasing an automobile usually involves at least one test drive, additional channels come into play: the handling of the car appeals to the tactile sense, the "new car smell" involves the olfactory sense, and so on.

All of these factors are constrained by laws, customs, and traditions affecting the sale. For example, there are laws that mandate a "cooling-off period" during which Jan can cancel the contract without penalty. There are also customs that will affect the sale. For example, there may be a custom of negotiating that calls for Shannon to take any offer made to a supervisor. There may also be traditions involved in the car sale. For instance, it seems to be a ritual tradition to kick the tires of any car being considered for purchase. All such factors affect what can and cannot be said and done in a sales interview.

ASPECTS OF SALES INTERVIEWS

With an overview of the sales interview process in mind, we can now turn to specific aspects of the process. In this section we shall look at the specific elements from the standpoint of the sales agent. In a later section, we shall look at persuasion in sales from the standpoint of the consumer. As we shall see, the parties involved are equally important. Without clients, a salesperson cannot resolve the exigence. Without salespeople, consumers cannot receive the specific data they need to make informed decisions about products and services.

Many people consider sales to be the manipulation of a naive customer by a fast-talking sharper. In reality, most sales interviews are negotiations rather than manipulations. The salesperson attempts to negotiate a recognition that the product is the best available, the item is affordable, and that the time is right to purchase. The customer seeks to negotiate the best price, the appropriate quantity, and the appropriate service for the product. Thus, the customer and salesperson together ne-gotiate through clarification of the advantages and disadvantages, the needs and desires of the two parties.

Business consultants Robert Miller and Stephen Heiman suggested:

> In Win–Win selling both the buyer and the seller come out of the sale understanding that their respective interests have both been served—in other words, they've both Won. It is our firm conviction, based on thou-sands of selling situations, that over the long run the only sellers who remain truly successful are committed to this Win–Win philosophy. . . . In selling, two parties—a buyer and a seller—have to come to an agree-ment before any deal can be made. This means that any sales transac-tion involves *mutual dependence.*[5]

Clearly, this is a view of the sales process fully in keeping with our per-spective of persuasive communication.

The sales agent is a pivotal party in the persuasive process. We will begin our examination of sales interviews with this key aspect.

CHARACTERISTICS OF EFFECTIVE SALES AGENTS

As our model in Figure 11.1 indicates, the sales agent recognizes the na-ture of the problem and seeks to gain the compliance of the client in re-solving the exigence. In achieving that goal, agents use a variety of tactics including moral appeals, warnings, and promising. We shall ex-amine some of those tactics below. For the moment we shall concen-trate on four characteristics that make a successful sales agent: knowing the product, knowing the prospect, developing a sales personality, and communication style.

Knowledge of the product is indispensable in sales. A sales interview involves not only asking question but also answering the client's ques-tions. Most of the client's questions will focus on aspects of the product or service being sold, so sales agents must know their prospects well enough to answer without having to fumble through files looking for the answers.

This does not mean that a sales agent needs to know everything there is to know about the product. Robert Calvin advised that product knowledge should be adapted to the nature of the audience.

> If your sales force offers a technically based product such as industrial robots to plant engineers, the salespeople must possess very complete product knowledge. For example, they must know the alloys and thick-ness of all metals involved. But if your sales force offers a technically based product such as hand held calculators to department store buy-

ers, then the salespeople need only limited product knowledge. They must know how to operate the calculator, its use, and its performance capabilities. However, component and construction knowledge are unnecessary because the department store buyer is not an engineer and his or her concerns pertain to product features, benefits, reliability, and salability. . . . Essentially, then, you must teach the sales force whatever product/service knowledge the customer requires in order to make the buying decision.[6]

The best tactic, then, is to conduct a careful audience analysis as described in Chapter Eight. Agents must know what the customer needs to know.

The second characteristic of effective sales agents is to know the prospect. The prospect is a shorthand term for prospective buyer. In other words, to be effective, a sales agent must think carefully about the nature of the receiver.

Knowing what the prospect needs or wants is critical. It is also vital to know what the prospect is trying to accomplish; what are the goals? Sales agents need to know what motivates the client so that they can link the product or service to those wants, needs, and goals.

Whenever possible, agents need to investigate prospective customers in advance of the sales interview. If information is not available, many successful salespeople suggest holding a preliminary interview before the sales interview. Here is how sales trainer Brian Tracy recommended handling the situation if the agent has no background information on the prospect:

> I say, go in with nothing in your hands. Don't carry a briefcase. If you do, you are immediately classified as a salesperson. Go in with nothing, and the prospect likely will ask where your briefcase is. "I don't need it now. I'm not here to sell you anything. What I want to do today is to ask you a few questions and see if there's a way we can help you." Right away, you have separated yourself from the mediocre salespeople who come in, open a briefcase, pull out the price lists and brochures, then spread them around like a faro dealer.[7]

Tracey suggested that the agent take notes, study them, and return another day with recommendations tailored to the individual client.

Third, a sales agent should develop the kind of personality that encourages sales. This means that sales agents should seek to be engaging, credible, compelling, and dynamic.

Engaging means that a sales agent should seek to be liked. People are more likely to purchase from someone they like, someone they enjoy seeing and talking to. This means that sales agents should be well groomed and friendly, but the most important factor may be a matter of

---

Box 11.1
ROGER DAWSON'S KEY POINTS IN MAKING PEOPLE BELIEVE YOU

1. Never assume they believe you.
2. Tell them only as much as they'll believe.
3. Tell the truth, even if it hurts.
4. Point out the disadvantages.
5. Use precise numbers.
6. Let them know you're not on commission.
7. Downplay any benefits to you.
8. Dress the part of a successful person.
9. If you do have something to gain, let them know.
10. Confront problems head on.
11. Use the power of the printed word.
12. Let them know who else says so.
13. Build and use a portfolio of testimonials.
14. Get endorsements from people they'd know.
15. Use "If they can do it, I can do it."

SOURCE: Roger Dawson, *Secrets of Power Persuasion* (Englewood Cliffs, NJ: Prentice-Hall Publishing, 1992), p. 36.

---

respecting the client. At times this may be difficult. Gallagher, Wilson, and Levinson explained the situation this way. "Everyone wants to be respected, but in selling, your status is clearly lower than your prospects'. You come to them, and they have the right to reject you, to make demands, or to insist that you defer to their schedules. Many salespeople feel uncomfortable with this difference in status. They may try to build themselves up by boasting or putting the competition down. This frustrates the prospect, and both parties become uncomfortable."[8]

Another characteristic to be developed is credibility. We devoted all of Chapter Five to this important element in persuasion. Motivational speaker Roger Dawson has fifteen suggestions for making people believe you. His advice is summarized in Box 11.1.

Still another trait to develop in an effective sales personality is to be compelling. This means being determined so that people will act on your recommendations. Ferdinand Fournies recommends that sales agents should know exactly what they want the client to do and to "close" on that objective. He indicated that:

[O]nce the customer arrives at the 'I'm ready to buy,' there is no rule that says he must buy your product unless you have the only product in the world to satisfy that customer's need or desire. Unfortunately, there are a lot of products in the world that do about the same job reasonably well. If you get a customer to the ready state and don't ask him to take action (the closing action), the next sales person who asks for the business is going to get it. You did all the hard work, but somebody else asked the closing question and got the sale.[9]

A final trait that is involved in the effective sales personality is to be dynamic. To generate this characteristic it is critical that sales agents appear professional, as all sales trainers recommend. It also means that a sales agent must act professional. This means being well organized and using verbal and nonverbal behavior to balance enthusiasm with self-control. It also means adapting to the client during the interview. Take every opportunity to provide an example of genuine caring. Be sensitive to the perceptions of the client, especially if the client is from a different cultural background.

Finally, sales agents need to consider their communication style in dealing with clients. In a study of 160 real estate agents in three different states, researchers John Parrish-Sprowl, Rod Carveth, and Marshall Senk found that "salespeople who perceive themselves as being effective communicators or have a strong and positive communicator image are more successful than those sales people who do not perceive themselves as being effective communicators."[10]

So far, we have examined the practical implications of persuasion in analyzing the sales situations and communicator behavior. Another important skill is for salespeople to carefully analyze the prospective customers.

Analyzing the Prospect

As our model in Figure 11.1 indicated, the goal of a sales agent is to perceive the need to purchase as being a real need, to get the receiver to recognize his or her ability to resolve the exigence, fulfill that need, and bring the prospect to a level of readiness to respond. To accomplish those goals, sales agents must carefully analyze their prospective clients.

To do that, we can apply the techniques discussed in detail in Chapter Eight. To those suggestions we add one additional sales technique. As part of the pre-sales preparation, agents should carefully analyze the values of the client in relationship to the product or service being sold.

In 1968, Wayne Minnick conducted research on American values and used a classification scheme of theoretical values, economic values, social values, political values, and religious values. Although the work is somewhat dated, many of the values he identified apply to contemporary society.

In terms of theoretic values, for example, most Americans respect the scientific method and things labeled as scientific. However, some people fear the advance of science and prefer to rely on friends and other trusted persons to endorse a product. According to Minnick's research, most Americans respect common sense, but the definition of common sense depends upon individual experience. Common sense for an inner-city teenager might be "street smarts," but it might be "the way we did things in the good old days" for a seasoned citizen in a retirement community. It may be common sense to think "I trust a product I already know" for an established homeowner but it may also be common sense to think "it must be good because my uncle uses it" for a young apartment dweller.

With our society becoming a kaleidoscope of color, ethnic backgrounds, and experiences, it is much more difficult to provide generalizations about values that cover everyone. Effective sales agents should consider the prospective customer's age, sex, cultural background, lifestyle, aspirations, and so on. For people who espouse traditional values, family, safety, and happiness may be of paramount concern. For people who are ambitious and primarily motivated by economic values, increased productivity, financial gain, and/or status symbols may be more salient.

The actual sales presentation comes after the preparation stage that we have been discussing. The series of questions and statements in the actual interview are the heart of the sales process. We'll examine the interview itself in the next section.

THE PARTS OF A SALE

Just as the oration described in Chapter Nine has three parts (an introduction, a body, and a conclusion), the sales interview has three parts as well. The opening is often called the approach. The "body" of the interview is frequently called the demonstration, and the conclusion is called the close. In Chapter Nine we also discussed Monroe's Motivated Sequence. This sequence (Attention, Need, Satisfaction, Visualization, and Action) can also serve as the structure of a sales interview. The approach seeks to gain attention. The demonstration generates need, offers satisfaction, and creates visualization. The close is the action step of the interview.

Approach

The opening of the sales interview has two important functions. It should be designed to establish rapport with the client and develop the client's interest in the product.

Rapport is important because the client must feel comfortable talking to the sales agent. The point of the interview is to get the client to open up and take an active part in the discussion. This can best be achieved when the client feels a sense of compatibility with the sales agent. Effective agents should be careful about different perceptions of the initial moments of an interview. Some clients may view "small talk" as important in getting to know each other. However, some may consider the small talk a waste of time or even prying.

The second aspect of the approach is to instill **interest.** Agents must get the client interested in the product or service under discussion. Unless the agent secures the client's attention, little that follows will have any persuasive impact.

Demonstration

As indicated earlier, the demonstration is the main portion of the interview. Questions and answers focus on the specific needs of the client and how the agent's product or service will meet those needs.

The agent's goal in the demo is to guide the interview through the persuasive process. To accomplish this goal, the salesperson must not just launch into a preset monologue. The agent should develop questions that elicit information used in determining what will motivate the client to buy. This is a matter of classifying and dramatizing.

Classifying means that an agent should be able to sort through all of the benefits of the product or service to determine which appeals are most significant for the client. There is a sales adage that goes "You don't sell the steak, you sell the sizzle." This means that people do not purchase products or services just to have them; they purchase products or services to use them, to gain the benefit of having them. By asking questions about the client's circumstances and history, skilled sales agents can determine which benefits are desirable for a specific client.

Dramatizing means that the features of the product are shown to provide the benefit. The demo is the agent's opportunity to show how the client will benefit by purchasing the product or service. According to Jeffrey Gitomer, "[h]aving your prospect physically involved is the single most important aspect of the selling process. Let him run the demo,

---

Box 11.2
STANDARD CLOSING TECHNIQUES

Assumptive Close: assumes the client is going to buy. "When would you like the order delivered?" Must only be tried if the client has indicated a willingness to close.

Alternative Close: offers two positive options. "Will this be check or charge?"

Benjamin Franklin Close: listing the pros and cons on paper (with the pros outnumbering the cons, of course). "Let's list the the advantages and disadvantages of going with our product."

Upgrading Close: offers add-ons to the sale. "Would you like to select the free accessories to go with your purchase?"

Action Close: asks the client to take some closing action, not whether the client wants to buy. "Would you look over this order form to make sure I have your needs listed correctly?"

SOURCE: Adapted from William Bethel, *Questions That Make the Sale* (Chicago, IL: Dartnell, 1992), pp. 141–152.

---

push the button, work the copier, drive the car, hold something, help you put something together, make the call, fax the document. Get the picture?"[11]

By constantly classifying and dramatizing, sales agents can navigate the demo toward the ultimate objective: the close.

Close

At some point, it is will be necessary for the agent to try to close the sale, to get the prospect to place the order or sign the sales contract.

Effective sales agents recognize that clients do not usually interrupt and ask for the contract. It is up to the agent to watch for the signals that the client is ready to buy and then try for a close. The first attempt may be a trial close; if the client is still reluctant, it is necessary to continue the sale and try for a close later. Sometimes it takes several trial closing efforts.

Sales literature offers a wide variety of techniques to use in seeking a close. Box 11.2 provides a description of some of the most common closing techniques.

As we have seen, the sales process is a negotiation between sales agent and client. So far we have looked primarily at the sales agent, but the other party is equally important.

CONSUMERS AND SALES

It is time to switch gears in our consideration of the sales process. We shall look at the process from the consumer's point of view. There are four main differences between sales agents and consumers that we should bear in mind.

First, remember that sales agents are trained and consumers are not. Robert J. Calvin cited an industry study of sales training. He reported that a study of "424 companies showed that 37 percent of the respondents had initial sales force training programs lasting under three months, 21 percent had programs of between three and five months, 20 percent programs of between six and eight months, and 22 percent programs of over eight months."[12] In addition, sales agents receive continuing education in sales tactics and new products.

Consumers, on the other hand, have few, if any, opportunities to receive formal training in understanding the sales process and what to do in sales situations. As we will see, there are some guidelines for sales that consumer groups publish and promote, but most consumers must rely on learning by experience rather than formal training programs.

Second, sales agents know the products, but consumers have limited information at best. In most companies, price and product lists are updated on a regular basis. New models are introduced. Sales and new prices are established on a regular basis. Product specifications are periodically detailed and distributed to agents.

"Knowledge is power," wrote George Eliot in her novel *Daniel Deronda*. Unfortunately, most consumers are at an informational power disadvantage in the sales situation. Even when consumers do their homework and research a product they are considering, the information is often of limited use. The particular model reviewed in a consumer magazine is not the exact model available in the store. The list price is always higher than the street price but determining the street price is often difficult if not impossible. The product specifications that the consumer actually needs may not be readily known or available to the purchaser.

Third, agents know the competition, but consumers may not. Knowing the competition allows sales agents to talk about why their product or service is superior. Here is Miller and Heiman's advice to salespeople about knowing their competition. "You're never going to know as much about your competitors' solutions as you know about your own. But if you are totally in the dark about them, then you are selling from a position of profound weakness."[13]

Consumers, on the other hand, may not be in a position to draw a fair comparison between providers. One may offer a product at a lower price but also be offering a product of inferior quality. Most consumers know that price may or may not be a good indicator of the quality of the product. Status, advertising, or other factors may have inflated the price of a product over its identical competitors. One manufacturer may be planning to abandon a particular product line, making repairs or parts difficult, if not impossible, to obtain. One may provide poorer service or support, a factor consumers don't discover until after they have signed the contract, usually nonrevocable. One may be trying to sell down its stock of a product before an improved version comes out, a plan consumers may not know is in the works.

Finally, there is one very important aspect that consumers too often ignore. The sales agent needs the consumer much more than the consumer needs the sales agent.

There is just no getting around the fact that the consumers are the true rhetorical audience, the only ones capable of doing something about the exigence. After selling to a sympathetic but limited group of friends and family, sales agents must seek clients or they will fail in their careers.

Consumers, on the other hand, are the decision makers. They are the ones who decide whether and how much to buy. Even corporations that have a large share of the market do have competition. Consumers can choose among a variety of sales agents, but agents cannot choose among clients for their products. This gives the consumer an enormous advantage in negotiating a sales interview.

In examining the persuasive process from the client's point of view there are two principles that should always be the operating principles of the negotiation: (1) investigate before investing, and (2) *caveat emptor*, let the buyer beware. We should examine each of these operating principles.

INVESTIGATE BEFORE INVESTING

It is always surprising how otherwise intelligent people will fall into a trap of investing money without fully understanding what they are purchasing. Peter Lynch is a Wall Street superstar who directed the enormously successful Fidelity Magellan Fund. One of his most important principles to "beat the street" in investing reads, "If you don't study any companies you have the same chance of success buying stocks as you do in a poker game if you bet without looking at your cards."[14] Consumers should look at anything they purchase as an investment of their hard-earned money and apply Lynch's principle.

The Better Business Bureau suggests three standards for defining a good bargain: (1) the item should be something the consumer needs or wants, (2) at a price the consumer is willing to pay, (3) from a reliable source.[15] These three rules identify the main elements to be investigated.

First, **prioritize** your needs and wants. Most consumers have a list of wants and needs that exceed their income. Consequently, we must prioritize and decide on which of our wants and needs are most important to us.

Prioritizing is an individual's decision that takes into consideration the importance of the need, the strength of ego involvement in having the want satisfied, and a host of individual factors. Prioritizing might be done in a rough approximation of Maslow's hierarchy described in Chapter Three. However, some may use Lazarus Long's Law "Budget the Luxuries First" as a guiding principle.

Before putting contracts out for bid, large companies and government offices develop a set of specifications, a list of the necessary features to complete the contract. Before investing in anything, individual consumers would do well to make their own list of specifications—wants and needs to be investigated and used as the basis for comparisons.

Second, **identify a budget.** How much can you afford for the product without making uncomfortable sacrifices? The price a consumer is willing to pay should be in range from the lowest reasonable bargain to the maximum price that would still be acceptable. Knowing how high you are willing to go is a vital piece of information to bear in mind when negotiating with a salesperson.

Part of determining the price of an item is determining its actual cost. A jacket in an upscale department store that is discounted by 30 percent may still cost more than the same jacket at regular price in a discount department store. Paying more for options that are not needed on an automobile, even when those options are discounted by 50 percent, may add to the cost of the car but not add to its value if those options are rarely used.

Another important consideration is the cost of a product if it is being financed. Credit cards and revolving credit loans provide immediate access to a product but significantly raise the actual price of the product. A television set, for example, may cost 20 percent more if paid for over a year using credit card interest rates. A house or condominium may cost double the selling price when mortgage rates are spread out over thirty years.

Third, consumers should **investigate suppliers.** Reliable sources are going to back their products. They are willing to provide written bids and guarantees. They offer references that should be checked out and not just glanced at. Ask friends, check with the Better Business Bureau to determine if complaints have been filed, ask for references and follow up on those references.

Caveat Emptor

The Latin phrase *caveat emptor* means "Let the buyer beware." Vigilant consumers recognize their responsibility in the sales process. It is important to recognize some of the less unethical sales practices to watch for.[16]

One dangerous tactic is the "something for nothing" ploy. "Free" offers are often worthless or unnecessary add-ons. Sometimes the "free" item is offset by a commitment to buy more than you actually want. "You have won" usually means you are a target. "Free trip and accommodations" comes with hours spent being subjected to high pressure sales tactics.

The bait-and-switch offer is another unscrupulous practice. This tactic offers a great bargain as an inducement to come into the store. Unfortunately, when you ask for the item, you are told they are out of stock and directed to a more expensive alternative. A variation on the bait-and-switch tactic involves the salesperson pointing out all of the defects of the advertised bargain and directing the customer to more expensive versions that don't have those drawbacks.

Since bait-and-switch is illegal, some merchants will indicate the available quantity or other disclaimers in advertisements. Always read the fine print carefully.

Resisting Sales Pressure

Just as there are standard tactics that salespeople use in persuading customers, there are standard tactics customers can use to resist sales pressure in the marketplace and in other commercial activities. These five principles provide the basis for consumer practice in sales interviews.

First, be prepared for the interview. All too often consumers fail to plan for the sales interview. Sales calls are worked in as a necessary distraction from our regular activities. As a result, we are often ill-prepared for the interview when it happens.

Consumers should do their homework on sales just as they do before any important meeting. Be sure to check out the reputation of the company. Don't even make an appointment with any company that has a shady reputation. As we discussed earlier, develop your specifications—determine your wants and needs and an acceptable price range. Make a list of the questions you want to ask the interviewer. If they haven't been answered, be sure they are answered before committing to anything.

Second, don't be tempted by time constraints. Limited time makes a powerful persuasive tool. Sometimes the ploy is used in an effort to speed up the decision-making process. Sometimes the tactic is used to wear down resistance; the agent may be so persistent that the client buys something just to get rid of the nuisance.

Third, consult others. Take down the names, addresses, and phone numbers of all testimonials and follow up by contacting them. Discuss the issue with other decision makers; seek their perspective and experience with the product or similar products.

Fourth, don't fall for the scarcity scare. "While supplies last" is the paradigm phrase that represents the scarcity ploy. If a product is in such short supply, isn't it logical to assume that you will have great difficulty replacing or repairing it should you purchase it?

Finally, never make a commitment on the first call. The higher the price, the more important this rule becomes. The sales agent will not like this decision, but it is critically important. Be firm and indicate that you must think over the proposal. Establish a time frame for making your decision and stick to it.

Summary

In Chapter Ten we examined cases of persuasion in advertising and focused on mass channels discussed in Chapter Seven. In the current chapter we have explored paradigm cases of persuasion in sales interviews with a focus on personal rather than mass channels.

We began with a discussion of persuasive aspects of interviewing. We covered the use of different types of questions: open, closed, and leading; primary and probing. We also considered a model of persuasive interviews that showed the sales agent and client interacting about an exigence or problem using questions and answers within the constraints of the sales situation.

After the overview of a sales model, we considered specific aspects in the sales interview. We noted that sales agents must know the product, understand the prospect, and develop a sales personality. We also noted that prospects can be analyzed according to the demographic and psychological characteristics of audiences described in Chapter Eight, and added a discussion of values common in sales negotiations. Finally, we considered the specific parts of the sales process: the approach, the demonstration, and the close.

In the consumer section of the chapter we noted differences between sales agents and consumers: (1) Sales agents are trained and consumers are not; (2) sales agents know the products, but consumers have limited information; (3) agents know the competition, but consumers may not; (4) sales agents need the consumer more than the consumer needs the sales agent.

Finally, we developed two important principles for consumers in persuasive sales settings: investigate before investing and *caveat emptor.* We concluded with techniques for resisting sales pressure.

So far, we have examined two specific contexts of persuasion. In Chapter Nine, we explored how to construct a persuasive presentation and how to listen critically to persuasive speeches. In Chapter Ten we noted how to construct advertisements and analyze and evaluate ads. In this chapter we investigated how to construct sales interactions and be an effective receiver in sales interviews. In the final chapter we shall look at persuasion in the context of campaigns.

Notes

[1] Bruce White quoted in Porter Henry, *Secrets of the Master Sellers* (New York: AMACOM, 1987), p. 3.

[2] James Benjamin and Raymie McKerrow, *Business and Professional Communication* (New York: HarperCollins, 1994), p. 109.

[3] Tony Alessandra, Phil Wexler, and Rick Barrera, *Non-Manipulative Selling* (Englewood Cliffs, NJ: Prentice-Hall, 1987), p. 46.

[4] Robert Miller and Stephen Heimen, *Conceptual Selling* (New York: Warner Books, 1987), p. 103.

[5] Ibid., pp. 159–160.

[6] Robert J. Calvin, *Managing Sales for Business Growth* (New York: AMACOM, 1991), pp. 37–38.

[7] Quoted in Robert McGarvey, "Listen Up!" *Entrepreneur*, August 1995, pp. 107–108.

[8] Bill Gallagher, Orvel Wilson, and Jay Levinson, *Guerrilla Selling* (Boston: Houghton Mifflin Company, 1992), p. 67.

[9] Ferdinand F. Fournies, *Why Customers Don't Do What You Want Them to Do—And What to DO About It* (New York: McGraw-Hill, 1994), p. 117. Reprinted with permission of the McGraw-Hill Companies.

[10] John Parrish-Sprowl, Rod Carveth, and Marshall Senk, "The Effect of Compliance-Gaining Strategy Choice and Communicator Style on Sales Success," *The Journal of Business Communication*, 31 (1994), pp. 299–310.

[11] Jeffrey H. Gitomer, *The Sales Bible* (New York: William Morrow Company, 1994), p. 138.

[12] Calvin, *Managing Sales*, p. 35.

[13] Miller and Heimen, *Conceptual Selling*, p. 128.

[14] Peter Lynch, *Beating the Street* (New York: Simon and Schuster, 1993), p. 305.

[15] Better Business Bureau, *Guide to Wise Buying* (New York: Harper & Row, 1980), p. 298.

[16] Reader's Digest, *Consumer Adviser* (Pleasantville, NY: The Reader's Digest Association, 1984), p. 31.

For Further Thought

1. Listen carefully to a sales interview, for example, pitched in selling a used car or or a stereo. Identify the types of questions used in the interview. Did the agent use a variety of questions in focusing the sale? What types of questions could have been asked to create a more persuasive effect?

2. Who is the best salesperson you have ever encountered? What qualities did that person display that made him or her so effective?

3. Imagine that you were selling an insurance policy to your roommate or next-door neighbor. What sorts of appeals would be most effective with that client? How could you demonstrate and dramatize those appeals?

4. Make your own list of priorities for major purchases like buying a home, purchasing a new car, and so forth. Consider what you must do to resist the persuasive efforts of agents selling your highest priority item.

5. Refer to Chapter Ten on advertising. How do sales agents take advantage of advertising in constructing their sales messages?

For Further Reading

Alessandra, Tony, Phil Wexler, and Rick Barrera, *Non-Manipulative Selling*. Englewood Cliffs, NJ: Prentice-Hall, 1987.

Leonard, Walter B. *Consumer Reports Money-Saving Tips for Good Times and Bad*. Yonkers, NY: Consumer Reports Books, 1992.

Rackman, Neil. *S. P. I. N. Selling*. New York: McGraw-Hill, 1988.

Stewart, Charles J. and William B. Cash. *Interviewing: Principles and Practices*, seventh edition. Dubuque, IA: Brown and Benchmark, 1994.

Chapter Twelve

PERSUASIVE CAMPAIGNS

In the 1980 presidential race, Ronald Reagan was running against incumbent Jimmy Carter. Long before he sadly contracted Alzheimer's disease Reagan's

> inclination to make offhand remarks to please his audiences produced a series of minor crises. . . . He said the United States was "energy rich" even though it was becoming dangerously dependent on foreign oil. He blamed trees (not automobiles) for smog, leading students at one of his rallies to attach a sign to a tree saying, "Chop me down before I kill again." . . . One slip, though, Reagan turned to his advantage. When economists criticized him for calling the recession the economy was undergoing a "depression," he began telling audiences: "I'm told I can't use the word *depression*. Well, I'll tell you the definition. A recession is when your neighbor loses his job and a depression is when you lose your job. Recovery is when Jimmy Carter loses his!"[1]

That anecdote about Reagan illustrates an important issue about campaigns, the topic of this chapter. A single persuasive effort is not sufficient to achieve a persuasive objective; persuasion takes a concerted campaign.

It is an empirically established principle that a single attempt at persuasion is not sufficient to accomplish a long-term objective. For example, Watts and McGuire found that the impact of a single persuasive message decayed fairly steadily over a six-week period of time, and Cook and Insko found that reexposure to a persuasive message generated more persuasive persistence than did no reexposure.[2] When messages are put together systematically, we refer to the series as a campaign.

A campaign, then, can be defined as a systematic series of persuasive events conducted over an extended period of time and designed to achieve a predetermined objective. There are four qualities in that

Political campaigns use a variety of persuasive appeals to achieve specific goals.

definition that distinguish a campaign from other persuasive efforts we have described in this book. First, campaigns are systematic. Second, campaigns involve a variety of persuasive events. Third, they are conducted over a period of time. Fourth, they are geared toward accomplishing an objective. We can consider each element in turn.

First, campaigns are **systematic.** This means that they have a structure, an organizational pattern. The structure of campaigns has been described in various ways. Dan Nimmo, for example, described the structure of a campaign in terms of a drama involving the dramatic elements of: introduction, rising action, turning point, falling action, and conclusion. He suggested that presidential campaigns involve a similar structure. The introduction is addressed during the period of conjecture about potential candidates who might accept the nomination of the party. Rising action is reflected in the early organizational efforts in which candidacy is announced and funding is sought. The caucuses and primaries which precede the convention and the party's nomination provides the pinnacle and turning point of the action; the falling action occurs during the period of the general election campaign including all of the speeches and political advertising that accompany the campaign. Finally, the campaign concludes with the election.

An alternative structure was described by Leland Griffin. He suggested that there is a period of inception, in which either a "pre-existing sentiment" flowers into public attention or in which a striking event initiates a movement; a period of rhetorical crisis in which the opposition to the movement disrupts the balance "in the mind of the collective audience"; and a period of consummation when the crisis is resolved.[4]

Whether we describe campaigns in dramatic terms or organic terms, there is no doubt that the series of persuasive events in a campaign are not a haphazard hodgepodge. They have a form that defines the events as a campaign rather than random phenomena.

Second, campaigns involve a **series** of persuasive events. Unlike a single speech, a single television advertisement, or a single sales interview, campaigns employ a variety of persuasive events. The launch of Microsoft's Windows 95, for example, involved a series of persuasive events with television advertisements, newspaper announcements, and staged media events like Jay Leno emceeing a "launch" presentation at Microsoft's headquarters in Redmond, Washington.[5]

Persuasive events usually involve more than a single medium. Political campaigns rely upon speeches, rallies, bumper stickers, posters, radio, television and print media ads, personal appearances, direct mail, door-to-door canvasses, and so on. As political analyst Dan Nimmo wrote, "most campaigns that achieve success blend diverse media into a balanced, total persuasive appeal."[6]

Third, persuasive campaigns take place over an **extended period** of time. Campaigns are won or lost over an extended period of time.

It is axiomatic that persuasive efforts must be conducted over an extended period of time. While a sales agent may be seeking to reach closure in a given interview, the company that the agent represents plans longer-term advertising campaigns to pave the way for the agent. Before a president can deliver an inaugural address, the candidate must get elected by convincing the voting public that he or she is the best potential president with a series of persuasive efforts over an extended period of time. Before a social movement can gain sufficient power to effect a change, it must provide a series of persuasive efforts over weeks, months, or even years to gain and maintain its membership.

Public approval throughout the campaign will rise and fall. With the technology to assess public opinion through polls, campaigns can be fine-tuned to respond to variations in public opinion as they occur. Consequently, the specific form and focus of a campaign is malleable and a function of its ongoing effectiveness in achieving its overall goal.

The final characteristic of campaigns is that they are directed toward a **goal.** Determining the goal of a campaign is a matter of identifying the strategic position to be obtained. For example, a campaign may seek to create an image of a product or person in the minds of the receivers.

The goal may be subdivided into a series of objectives. For example, in order to achieve the overall goal of electing a candidate, a political campaign must seek to accomplish the more limited objectives of (1) surfacing, that is, emerging as a viable candidate and announcing candidacy; (2) primaries, in other words, narrowing the field of candidates and focusing the issues, (3) nomination, that is, legitimizing the candidate and the political platform in the minds of the public; and (4) election, the ultimate objective of securing more votes than the opponents.[7]

CONSTRUCTING CAMPAIGNS

With the preceding perspective in mind, we can explore two major forms of persuasive campaigns: marketing campaigns and social movement campaigns. Marketing campaigns seek to achieve specific objectives involving persuading receivers to take some action. Social movements seek ongoing objectives to persuade the receiver toward a particular viewpoint.

MARKETING CAMPAIGNS

Marketing campaigns have features that distinguish them from social movements; they differ in terms of the objectives they seek to achieve, the leadership, and the developmental stages. In brief, marketing campaigns are aimed at the limited goal of influencing the receivers, whereas social movements are ongoing efforts with the objective of bringing receivers into the movement. Marketing campaigns employ leadership in terms of management whereas social movements have leaders that display group leadership characteristics. Finally, marketing campaigns go through specific stages designed to accomplish the objective of the campaign but social movements have different stages that serve the interests of the movement. We shall consider each of the three elements—objectives, leadership and stages—in our consideration of marketing campaigns.

Objectives

Marketing campaigns include political campaigns in which the main objective is to secure votes on a ballot, charity campaigns in which the

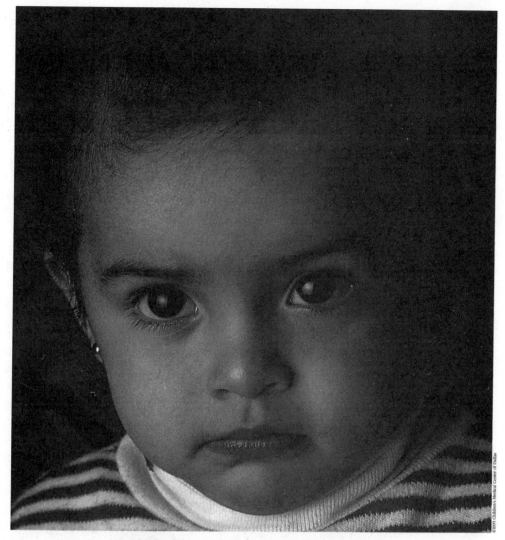

While Many Hospitals Answer To Stockholders And Financial Holding Companies, We Answer To A More Concerned Audience.

There's a difference between Children's Medical Center of Dallas and other hospitals. It's children. As a fully dedicated not-for-profit children's hospital, we've committed ourselves to preserving the value of our most sacred resource. A commitment that's deeply rooted in every nurse,

doctor and staff member. You won't find our executives pouring their energies into some multi-million dollar merger. They have a bigger gain to be concerned with–the betterment of the lives of children. We've had this mission for more than 80 years, and it continues today. Children come first.

children's
MEDICAL CENTER OF DALLAS

For The Love Of Children.

This image-oriented ad seeks to enhance the reputation of the Children's Medical Center of Dallas.

objective is to garner contributions for the cause, product campaigns in which the objective is to sell products or services, and image-oriented campaigns in which the objective is to influence the reputation of the person, company, or product.

As indicated earlier, the objectives of marketing campaigns are limited. Generally there is a specific deadline for accomplishing the objective. A presidential political campaign, for example, is geared toward the election in November. In addition to having a limited time objective, marketing campaigns have a narrowly restricted objective in terms of the receiver response sought. A charity campaign, for example, seeks to get the receivers to send in pledges, and a product campaign seeks to get the receivers to purchase the product.

The objectives of a marketing campaign, like those of a persuasive presentation, should be objectively defined in advance of launching the campaign. Campaign planners spend considerable time and effort on this phase of the process because figuring out what needs to be accomplished determines who must be persuaded, when they must be persuaded, and what means are available to persuade them.

Public relations expert Quentin Heitpas recommended that an objective should meet six criteria.[8] (1) The objective must be "related to overall objective(s) of the organization." In other words, the campaign should be aimed at contributing to the client's success. (2) The objective should be "improvement oriented." This should always be stated as positive enhancement. For example, an objective that meets this criterion would suggest the charity campaign result in an increase of donations by 10 percent. (3) Objectives must be "clearly defined." This criterion means an objective must be unambiguous. (4) Objectives must be specific. In other words, an objective must be precise. As Heitpas put it, "Generalities have no place in a good objective." (5) A good objective is measurable. As we shall see, a campaign must be evaluated at the end of the effort. If the objective sets measurable, quantifiable targets, the success or failure of the campaign is easy to define. (6) Finally, an objective should be attainable. Idealistic goals lead to frustration. If the objective is unrealistic, the campaign is doomed from the outset.

Box 12.1 illustrates these criteria applied to a fund-raising campaign for a local public television station. Note that this hypothetical example clearly and measurably defines the objective of the campaign.

Leadership

Campaigns are conducted by organized groups of people. Therefore issues of leadership become relevant to planning and implementing any

Box 12.1

CAMPAIGN OBJECTIVE

"To raise $30,000 in new membership pledges during the fall membership drive."

- **Related to organizations's objectives:** As a part of the annual membership drive, this objective is clearly a part of the overall designs of the station.
- **Improvement Directed:** Since the objective is aimed at *new* members, this will be an improvement over current levels.
- **Clearly defined:** The objective is unambiguous.
- **Specific:** The objective avoids imprecise language.
- **Measurable:** As worded, the objective identifies quantifiable amounts and time frames.
- **Attainable:** Assuming that the campaign will seek $60 membership levels and that it will reach a sufficiently large population, the objective is attainable. In a sparsely populated region, it would be unrealistic.

campaign. There are specific duties that must be met for the group to accomplish the objectives of the campaign. In this section, we shall consider the organizational structure of two types of campaigns, a political campaign and an advertising campaign, and the effects of that structure on leadership.

Professor Steven J. Wayne has written a series of books on the politics of presidential campaigns. In one of these works, he wrote, "Running a campaign is a complex, time-consuming, nerve-racking venture. It involves coordinating a variety of functions and activities. These include advance work, scheduling, press arrangements, issue research, speech writing, polling, media advertising, finances, and party and interest group activities. To accomplish these varied tasks, a large, specialized campaign organization is needed."[9]

The organizational chart for a presidential campaign appears in Figure 12.1. Note that the various offices and duties are covered at national, state, and local levels.

Advertising campaigns also require organizational structure. There are four departments that are generally involved in an advertising agency.[10] These are the account services department, the creative department, the media department and the research department.

Figure 12.1
Organizational Chart of a Presidential Campaign

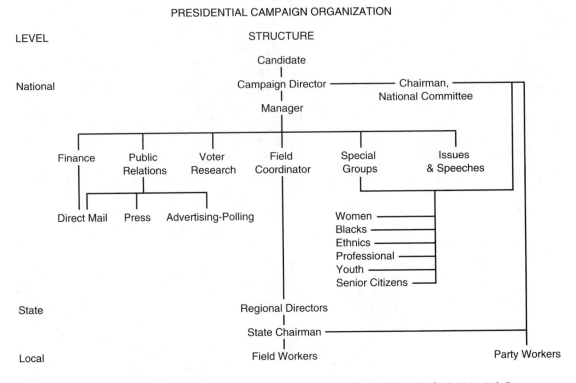

PRESIDENTIAL CAMPAIGN ORGANIZATION

SOURCE: Stephen J. Wayne. *The Road to the White House,* second edition. (New York: St. Martin's Press, 1984.) Copyright © 1984 by Stephen Wayne.

First, the account services department serves as the liaison between the client and the agency. The account executives are people who deal directly with the client who has a product or service to advertise. The account executive must interpret the ideas of the other departments and present those concepts for approval by the client.

Second, the creative department consists of the copywriters, commercial artists, and other individuals who actually generate the advertisements. The writers and artists are central to any campaign. Depending on the type of media to be used in the campaign, this department may involve radio and television production crews and/or print production specialists.

Third, the media department is made up of the people who keep track of the costs, availability, and the audiences reached by the various media in which the ads will be placed. This department has two responsibilities. The first is to develop a media plan for the client that will identify media that will reach the clientele for the product. The second responsibility is to purchase the advertising space or time from the various newspapers, magazines, or broadcast stations that have been selected.

Finally, there is the research department. These individuals conduct research on the needs, wants and values of target audiences; track the market environment including competing products or services; and conduct tests of the potential impact of ads.

In small agencies, all of the roles may be filled by one or two people. Whether in a large agency or a small agency, the roles described are all critical to the success of an advertising plan.

Stages

A marketing campaign must go through stages to meet its objectives. These stages have been defined in a variety of ways, depending on the type of campaign being explored. We will examine two general frameworks and three specific models.

The broadest description of campaign stages was described by Michael Pfau and Roxanne Parrott. They wrote, "[t]he essential components of persuasive communication campaigns include planning, implementation, and evaluation."[11] Planning involves determining the objectives of the campaign, identifying the target audience, and identifying the essential issues to be covered. Implementation is the stage of a campaign in which the persuasive messages are actually executed. Evaluation is a careful critique of the effectiveness of the planning and implementation stages.

A more elaborate general mode of a persuasive campaign was developed by Herbert Simons. The stages of the Simons model can be found in Figure 12.2.

In Simons' Campaign Stages and Components Model, the first stage involves planning, including the types of goal setting and audience analysis we have stressed throughout the book. The mobilization stage is concerned with determining and implementing the various resources necessary for the campaign. The third stage of the model is the legitimation stage. In this phase of the campaign, the object of the campaign gains acceptability as a matter to be taken seriously through one or more means identified in the model. The promotion stage involves the development of recognition and credibility through the persuasive messages and events of the campaign. Finally, the activation stage involves

Figure 12.2
Herbert Simons' Campaign Stages and Components Model

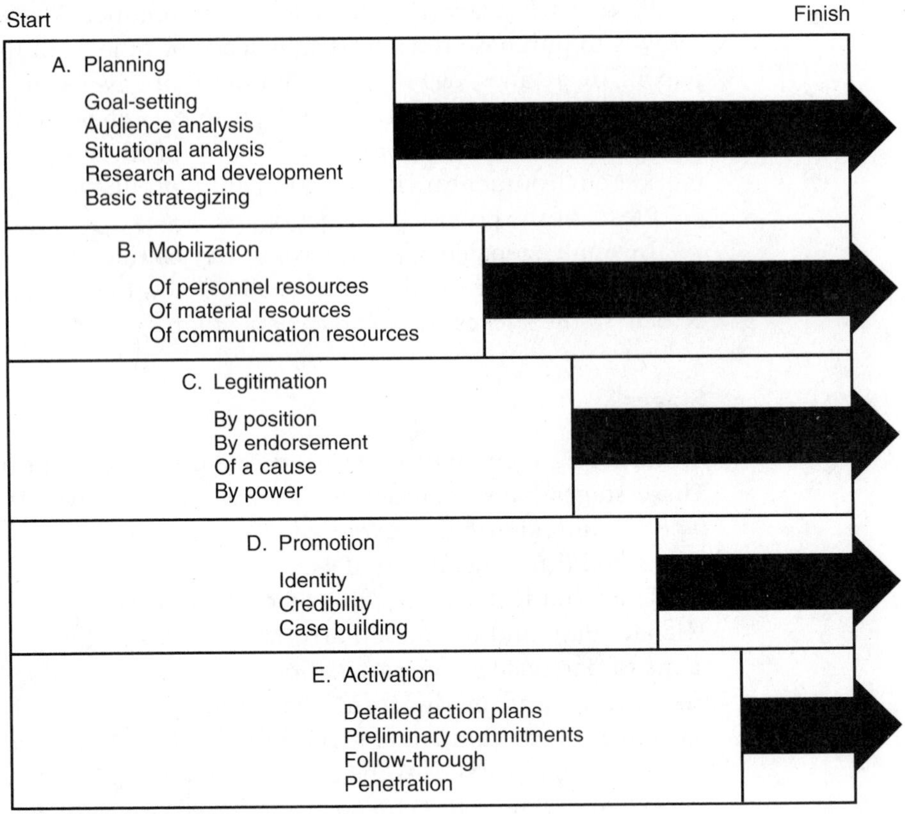

Start   Finish

A. Planning

  Goal-setting
  Audience analysis
  Situational analysis
  Research and development
  Basic strategizing

  B. Mobilization

    Of personnel resources
    Of material resources
    Of communication resources

    C. Legitimation

      By position
      By endorsement
      Of a cause
      By power

      D. Promotion

        Identity
        Credibility
        Case building

        E. Activation

          Detailed action plans
          Preliminary commitments
          Follow-through
          Penetration

SOURCE: Herbert W. Simons, *Persuasion: Understanding, Practice, and Analysis* (New York: Random House, 1986), p. 229.

actions and follow-through in hopes of achieving penetration which Simons defined as the situation in which "those reached directly become persuaders themselves."[12]

More specific models have been developed for particular types of campaigns. In *The Making of an Advertising Campaign*, Jaye S. Niefeld described four essential steps in an advertising campaign.

1. Defining the target group
2. Determining the appeal or creative strategy that will be most effective with the target group
3. Executing the creative strategy in the most arresting and appealing fashion

Figure 12.3
A Model of Political Marketing

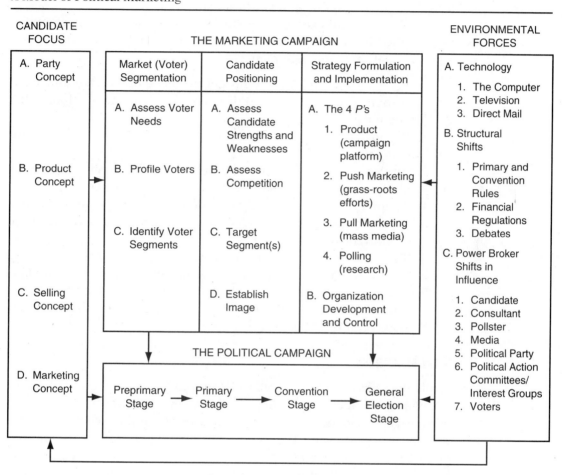

SOURCE: Bruce I. Newman, *The Marketing of the President,* p. 12. (Copyright © 1994 by Sage Publications.) Reprinted by permission of Sage Publications, Inc.

    4. Selecting the most effective and cost-efficient media to reach the target group.[13]

    A marketing campaign model was applied to a political campaign by Bruce I. Newman (See Figure 12.3).

    Newman suggested that the focus or objectives of the various parties involved in the campaign constitute the candidate's focus. He also indicated that the elements of a marketing campaign (market segmentation, positioning, and strategy formulation and implementation) are directly applicable to the traditional stages of a political campaign. Finally, he noted that various environmental forces constrain the candidate focus as well as the marketing and political campaign.[14]

Finally, we shall examine the stages in a public relations campaign as described by Baskin and Aronoff. They suggested seven guidelines in a public relations campaign plan.

1. Problem Statement "should define the scope of the effort and recognize any special requirements of the organization, target audiences, and media."
2. Purpose Statement provides an outline of the objectives of the campaign.
3. Audience Analysis details the nature of the target audience including appeals that are likely to affect the audience.
4. Actions Recommended offers a description of tactics, describes expected outcomes, and identifies the media and activities to be employed.
5. Time Frame schedules the activities of the campaign.
6. Projected Costs lays out a proposed budget for the campaign.
7. Evaluation Design explains how the campaign will be assessed to determine "the extent to which the objectives of the campaign have been reached."[15]

Social Movements

While the terms campaign and social movement are sometimes used interchangeably, there is a difference between the concepts. As we indicated earlier, a social movement is a broader term that refers, according to Stewart, Smith, and Denton, to "an organized, uninstitutionalized, and large collectivity that emerges to bring about or to resist a program of change in societal norms and values, operates primarily through persuasive strategies, and encounters oppositions in a moral struggle."[16]

This definition highlights that, while a social movement may engage in a persuasive campaign, a social movement seeks to create or resist social values and norms rather than focus the persuasive efforts on "pitching" a person, product, or service. For example, an environmental protection group may develop a campaign to oppose the building of a specific nuclear power plant, but also has broader, ongoing objectives of resisting environmental pollution.

Our exploration of social movements will focus on objectives, leadership, and developmental stages. These three topics will provide a basis for contrast with a persuasive campaign designed to market a product or person.

What if you and the Twain never met?

Well, my huckleberry friend, like two Mississippi riverboats passing in the night, we would have missed some of the most vivid adventures of our childhood. Like travels with Twain and all the great books that opened up whole new worlds via our imagination. And from our imaginations, a dream for a better future. Help kids love to read and learn to imagine. Simply by writing to Reading Is Fundamental, the nation's largest children's literacy organization, today.

Give children a good read on a better future.℠
Write: Dept W, Box 23444
Washington D.C. 20026.

RIF.
Reading Is Fundamental.

Photo by
William G. Wagner
Make-up by
Kathleen Murphy
Ad created by
Gianettino & Meredith
Advertising, NJ

Social movements tend to focus on belief and value systems.

Objectives

Social movements seek to indoctrinate receivers into the movement. A political movement, for instance, may seek to create institutional change in the status quo or to resist changes in the status quo. Sometimes movements will seek to accomplish all of those objectives. The animal rights movement, for example, may seek to expand its membership, pass laws to prohibit animal testing of cosmetic products, and resist efforts to loosen the restrictions on killing seals.

Three features distinguish the objectives of a social movement from the objectives of a campaign. The objectives of a social movement are ongoing and range beyond the accomplishment of short-term objectives. The objectives of social movements focus more on the receivers' beliefs and values than on their behaviors. Finally, the objectives of social movements are based on a sense of morality.

The objectives of a social movement are not narrowly circumscribed in the way that a campaign's objectives are restricted. The objectives of the women's rights movement, for example, are not limited to the passage of an equal rights amendment to the Constitution. As we discovered earlier, marketing campaigns operate within set time frames and have specifically defined outcomes. Social movements, in contrast, are **ongoing** and may operate for generations.

The objectives of social movements also differ from campaign objectives in their focus. The focus of a campaign is behaviorally oriented, but a social movement, although it may elicit behaviors from its membership, will focus more on the receiver's **belief and value systems.** Social movements are aimed at broader objectives of developing or resisting societal values. The new right movement, for example, aims at instilling and preserving conservative political values while the Republican party's congressional campaigns are aimed at securing the votes of the American public.

Finally, the objectives of a social movement are based on a sense of **morality.** Leland Griffin argued that "all movements are essentially moral—striving for salvation, perfection, the 'good.'"[17] Campaigns are essentially amoral, that is, they are neither moral nor immoral but ethically neutral. While morality may be used as a persuasive appeal in a campaign, the campaign itself is merely a tool, a means to an end rather than the end itself. The leaders and members of a social movement, on the other hand, "assume the power to distinguish right from wrong, good from evil, and ethical from unethical motivations, purposes, characters, choices, and actions."[18]

We have noticed, then, that a social movement uses persuasive tactics including persuasive campaigns, to accomplish its broader objectives. Social movements have ongoing, generalized objectives that have a moral tone and seek to influence the beliefs and values of the receivers.

Leadership

The leadership of social movements also differs from campaign leadership. While campaign leaders function like managers, social movement leaders function like guides. Social movement leaders can be defined along a type continuum and by the roles that they fill.

Social movement leadership ranges from moderate to militant. Moderate leaders tend toward the rational forms of persuasion and seek conciliation rather than confrontation. Militant types of leaders tend to prefer the more emotional forms of persuasion and seek to confront the opposition, to clash with alternative views.[19]

Herbert W. Simons extended the militant to moderate continuum in his analysis of movements. He suggested that militants serve purposes that are in contrast with the purposes of moderates:

1. Militant tactics confer visibility on a movement; moderate tactics gain entry into decision centers. . . .
2. Militants thrive on injustice and ineptitude by the larger structure. . . . The moderate, by contrast, requires tangible evidence that the larger structure is tractable in order to hold followers in line. . . .
3. Militant supporters are easily energized; moderate supporters are more easily controlled. . . .
4. Militants are effective with "power vulnerables"; moderates are effective with "power invulnerables"; neither is effective with both.[20]

Whether militant or moderate or somewhere in between, the leaders of social movements must fulfill various and sometimes conflicting roles in the group. The leader's major roles include:

[Reprinted by permission of Waveland Press, Inc., from Charles Stewart, Craig Allen Smith, and Robert E. Denton, *Persuasion and Social Movements*, 3rd Edition. (Prospect Heights, IL: Waveland Press, Inc., 1994). All rights reserved.]

1. must adapt to different audiences at once but not appear to be a political chameleon;

2. produce short-run successes but not preclude long-run successes;
3. use militant tactics to gain visibility for the movement but use moderate tactics to gain entry into decision-making centers;
4. foster strong convictions in the movements principles but control the implication that their attainment justifies any necessary means;
5. strive for organizational efficiency without dampening the enthusiasm and spontaneity generated during the early, less-structured days of the movement;
6. understand that militants are effective with power vulnerables such as elected and appointed officials and moderates are more effective with power-invulnerables such as judges, business owners, and much of the "silent majority";
7. vilify established orders but be willing and able to work with them when it is to the movement's advantage; and
8. grasp at opportunities to deal with an established order on its own turf without appearing to be "selling out" or "going soft."[21]

Stages

Social movements, like campaigns, pass through various stages of development. Scholars have examined social movements from a variety of perspectives. In this section we shall explore two views of how social movements develop.

The first perspective, described by Blumer,[22] suggested that movements begin in a state of agitation. Because a social movement is a reaction against the status quo, there must be a perception of initial dissatisfaction that is sufficiently severe to create concern for the issues of the movement. The next stage is the development of esprit de corps, or a coming together of individuals as a collective to address the issues. The third stage is morale development. Members must not only be attracted to the movement, they must also be periodically reinforced. Eventually, claimed Blumer, the movement will develop a group ideology, or doctrine, to identify the group's purpose, develop arguments against the opposition, and establish the ideals of the movement. Finally, Blumer argued that movements develop a tactical stage in which new members are recruited, existing members are maintained, and the overall objectives are sought.

Communication scholars Stewart, Smith, and Denton suggest an alternative view of the stages of a movement. Their five stages are genesis, social unrest, enthusiastic mobilization, maintenance, and termination.

In the genesis stage, the movement identifies some imperfections that must be addressed. By the social unrest stage, people are drawn together in a growing concern for the issues identified by the movement. During the enthusiastic mobilization stage, the movement becomes legitimized and the group grows in cohesiveness. In the maintenance stage, a "social movement returns to more quiet times . . . as institutions, media, and the public turn to other, more pressing concerns."[23] Finally, a movement faces a termination stage in which it either disbands or evolves into a new movement.

CAMPAIGNS AND CONSUMERS

Campaigns may fail for a variety of reasons.[24] Sometimes the target audience is simply unreachable. Despite the concern for the impact of media on receivers, empirical studies indicate that the media alone are relatively powerless in motivating receivers. John Ledingham, for example, conducted a telephone survey of 501 randomly selected respondents to a United Way campaign. He concluded that "mediated messages need to be supplemented by interpersonal communication in order to motivate behavior."[25]

Sometimes the campaign fails to fit in with the expectations of the receivers. Summarizing the literature on this issue, Edwin Diamond and Stephan Bates wrote, "academic research now suggests that people pay attention principally to messages that reflect their preexisting views. . . ."[26] Social movements are also aimed at broader objectives of developing or resisting societal values. Researchers Bartlett, Drew, Fahle, and Watts examined voter responses to a political campaign and found empirical support for the selective exposure principle that "people seek consonant information that supports or reinforces their previous beliefs and avoid dissonant, or challenging, information."[27] Another study found that in a U.S. Senate campaign, voters inoculated against attacks in advance were significantly more resistant to persuasion than voters who had no inoculation preparation.[28]

Sometimes campaigns fail because receivers use selective perception. In "Mass Media and Political Persuasion," Sears and Kosterman found that "de facto selectivity was a relatively common phenomenon; that is, audiences did tend to be biased in favor of the message they heard."[29]

Another reason why campaigns fail is that receivers may have differing interpretations of the persuasive appeals. Because campaigns must appeal to a wide variety of receivers, some knowledgeable and others

Counterpersuasion is one means of resisting social movements.

less knowledgeable, the decision about which appeals to use becomes complex. In a study of a health campaign, John Pavlik found that "audience complexity affects the outcome of a campaign and thus should be one of the factors taken into consideration in campaign planning. . . ."[30]

Campaign consumers may also find that there is insufficient appeal to actually alter attitudes. Both political and product campaigns abound with examples of insufficient appeal. The Dukakis campaign of 1988, the Bush campaign of 1992, the IBM Adam computer campaign, and the New Coke campaign are all examples of failures to significantly affect audiences.

Movements, like campaigns, may be resisted.[31] One type of resistance is evasion. The members of the status quo will avoid exposure to the movement's messages and may actively seek to prevent the expression of the movement's appeals.

Another type of resistance is counterpersuasion. To counter the impact of a movement's persuasion, the existing institution may launch its own effort at persuasion—a tobacco company official testifying, for example, that cigarettes are not addictive.

Still another form of resistance is adjustment. Sometimes the status quo may modify its position to accommodate the social movement. While total capitulation is rare in any situation short of a successful revolution, sometimes a modest adjustment by the existing institution defuses the momentum of a movement. As a more moderate position is reached and accommodations are made, the wide disparity that initially fueled the movement is dissipated.

Finally, the status quo may utilize some form of coercion. Especially when confronted with militant tactics, the existing institutions may respond with coercion rather than persuasion. The tragedy of National Guard members killing protesters at Kent State University is a tragic example of the response of the status quo to the peace movement during the Vietnam War.

Summary

We defined campaigns as a systematic series of persuasive events conducted over a period of time and designed to achieve a predetermined objective. Campaigns apply to the two major realms of persuasion: commerce and politics.

Marketing campaigns have clear objectives that must be related to the sponsoring organization, aimed at improvement, clearly defined, specific, measurable, and attainable. Leadership in campaigns is defined as the organizational chart of the group running the campaign. In advertising agencies the structure includes account services departments, creative departments, media departments, and research departments. Commercial campaign stages were defined in terms of Simons' Campaign Stages and Components model: planning, mobilization, legitimation, promotion, and activation. In addition, we noted Baskin and Aronoff's description of campaign stages: problem statement, purpose statement, audience analysis, actions recommended, time frame, projected costs, and evaluation design.

Next we examined persuasion in social movements. Social movements differ from marketing campaigns in terms of objectives, leadership, and stages. The objectives of social movements are broader and ongoing in comparison to the more narrowly constrained objectives of a marketing campaign. We noted that in contrast to the organizational management model of leadership in a marketing campaign, the leadership of a social movement is defined in group leadership characteristics such as militant and moderate leadership. Finally, we found that social movements appear to grow through stages like genesis, social unrest, enthusiastic mobilization, maintenance, and termination rather than the more formal structures of a marketing campaign.

In looking at campaigns from the consumer's perspective, we noted the reason why campaigns fail. They may fail to fit the expectations of the consumer. They may fail because receivers use selective perception. Differing interpretations of the persuasive appeal is another reason why campaigns may fail. Finally, campaigns may fail because there is a lack of sufficient appeal.

Social movements also may be resisted. The members of the status quo may avoid exposure to the movement's messages. Counterpersuasion is another form of resistance to movements. Adjustment is still another form of resistance. Coercion appears to be the ultimate form of resistance to a social movement.

Notes

[1] Paul F. Boller, *Presidential Campaigns* (New York: Oxford University Press, 1985), pp. 358–359.

[2] William A. Watts and William J. McGuire, "Persistence of Induced Opinion Change and Retention of the Inducing Message Contents," *Journal of Abnormal and Social Psychology*, 68 (1964), pp. 233–241; Thomas Cook and Chester Insko, "Persistence of Attitude Change as a Function of Conclusion

Reexposure: A Laboratory–field Experiment," *Journal of Personality and Social Psychology*, 9 (1968), pp. 322–328.

[3] Dan Nimmo, "Election as a Ritual Drama," *Political Persuasion in Presidential Campaigns*, L Patrick Devlin, ed. (New Brunswick, NJ: Transaction Books, 1987), pp. 164–165.

[4] Leland M. Griffin, "The Rhetorical Structure of the Antimasonic Movement," *The Rhetorical Idiom*, Donald C. Bryant, ed. (New York: Cornell University Press, 1966), pp. 145–160; Leland M. Griffin, "The Rhetoric of Historical Movements," *Quarterly Journal of Speech*, 38 (April 1952), pp. 184–188.

[5] "'Start Me Up': CEO Prepares for Carnival," *USA Today*, (August 25–27, 1995), pp. 1–2.

[6] Dan Nimmo, *Political Communication and Public Opinion in America* (Santa Monica, CA: Goodyear Publishing Company, 1978), p. 163.

[7] Judith Trent and Robert Friedenberg, *Political Campaign Communication*, third edition (Westport, CT: Praeger Publishers, 1995), pp. 17–50. Reprinted with permission of Greenwood Publishing Group, Inc., Westport, CT.

[8] Quentin Heitpas, "Planning," *Precision Public Relations*, Ray Eldon Hiebert, ed. (New York: Longman, 1988), p. 178.

[9] Stephen J. Wayne, *The Road to the White House*, second edition (New York: St. Martin's Press, 1984), p. 171.

[10] Jan Greenberg, *Advertising Careers* (New York: Henry Holt and Company, 1986), pp. 11–12.

[11] Michael Pfau and Roxanne Parrott, *Persuasive Communication Campaigns* (Boston, MA: Allyn & Bacon, 1993), p. 14.

[12] Herbert W. Simons, *Persuasion: Understanding, Practice, and Analysis* (New York: Random House, 1986), p. 241.

[13] Jaye S. Niefeld, *The Making of an Advertising Campaign* (Englewood Cliffs, NJ: Prentice-Hall, 1989), p. 8.

[14] Bruce I. Newman, *The Marketing of the President* (Thousand Oaks, CA: Sage Publication, 1994), pp. 11–14.

[15] Otis Baskin and Craig Aronoff, *Public Relations: The Profession and the Practice* (Dubuque, IA: William C. Brown Publishers, 1992), pp. 146–147.

[16] Charles Stewart, Craig Allen Smith, and Robert E. Denton, *Persuasion and Social Movements*, third edition (Prospect Heights, IL: Waveland Press, 1994), p. 17.

[17] Leland Griffin, "A Dramatistic Theory of the Rhetoric of Movements," *Critical Responses to Kenneth Burke*, William Rueckert, ed. (Minneapolis: University of Minnesota Press, 1969), p. 456.

[18] Stewart, Smith, and Denton, *Persuasion and Social Movements*, p. 11.

[19] Edward P. J. Corbett, "The Rhetoric of the Open Hand and the Closed Fist," *College Composition and Communication*, 20 (December, 1969), pp. 288–296.

[20] Herbert W. Simons, "Requirements, Problems, and Strategies: A Theory of Persuasion for Social Movements," *Quarterly Journal of Speech*, 56 (February 1970), pp. 1–11.

[21] Stewart, Smith, and Denton, *Persuasion and Social Movements*, p. 102.

[22] H. Blumer, "Social Movements," *Studies in Social Movements: A Social Psychological Perspective*, Barry McLaughlin, ed. (New York: The Free Press, 1969).

[23] Stewart, Smith, and Denton, *Persuasion and Social Movements*, p. 81.

[24] See, for example, Herbert H. Hyman and Paul B. Sheatsley, "Some Reasons Why Information Campaigns Fail," *Public Opinion Quarterly*, 11 (1947), pp. 412–423.

[25] John Ledingham, "The Kindness of Strangers: Predictor Variables in a Public Information Campaign," *Public Relations Review*, 19 (Winter 1993), p. 381.

[26] Edwin Diamond and Stephan Bates, *The Spot: The Rise of Political Advertising on Television* (Cambridge, MA: The MIT Press, 1992), p. 347.

[27] Dorothy L. Bartlett, Pamela B. Dress, Eleanor G. Fahle, and William Watts, "Selective Exposure to a Presidential Campaign Appeal," *Public Opinion Quarterly*, 38 (Summer, 1974), p. 264.

[28] Michael Pfau and Michael Burgoon, "Inoculation in Political Campaign Communication," *Human Communication Research*, 15 (Fall 1988), pp. 91–111.

[29] David Sears and Rick Kosterman, "Mass Media and Political Persuasion," *Persuasion: Psychological Insights and Perspectives*, Sharon Shavitt and Timothy Brock eds. (Boston, MA: Allyn & Bacon, 1994), p. 263.

[30] John Pavlik, "Audience Complexity as a Component of Campaign Planning," *Public Relations Review*, 14 (Summer, 1988), p. 12.

[31] Stewart, Smith, and Denton, *Persuasion and Social Movements*, pp. 147–157.

For Further Thought

1. What are the differences between campaigns and social movements? What must a persuader do to adapt campaign tactics to a social movement? to adapt a social movement to a campaign?

2. Review the news accounts of a recent political campaign. Were the campaign objectives clearly defined? What did the leadership do to improve the structure of the campaign? to meet the challenges of opposing campaigns?

3. Use Herbert Simons' campaign stages to outline a campaign for getting people to donate blood to the Red Cross.

4. Identify a social movement that you are a part of or that you would like to become a part of. Explore the qualities of the leaders of that movement. Are they militant or moderate? What do they do to fulfill the roles of leadership described in this chapter?

5. Examine a failed campaign. Explain why the campaign failed. What could the leaders have done differently to have a better chance of success?

For Further Reading

Eyerman, Ron and Andrew Jamison. *Social Movements: A Cognitive Approach.* University Park, PA: The Pennsylvania State University Press, 1991.

Lyman, Stanford, ed. *Social Movements: Critiques, Concepts, Case Studies.* New York: New York University Press, 1995.

Manheim, Jarol B. *All of the People, All of the Time: Strategic Communication and American Politics.* Armonk, NY: M. E. Sharpe, 1991.

Merelman, Richard M. *Language, Symbolism, and Politics.* Boulder, CO: Westview Press, 1992.

Nimmo, Dan D. and Keith Sanders, eds. *The Handbook of Political Communication.* Beverly Hills, CA: Sage Publications, 1981.

Pfau, Michael and Roxanne Parrott. *Persuasive Communication Campaigns.* Boston: Allyn & Bacon, 1993.

Stewart, Charles J., Craig Allen Smith, and Robert E. Denton, Jr. *Persuasion and Social Movements,* second edition. Prospect Heights, IL: Waveland Press, 1989.

CREDITS

1-4   Urban Alliance on Race Relations. Toronto, Canada;

3-2   Reprinted with permission from The Humane Society of the United States, Washington, D.C. 20037

4-2   Friends of Animals

4-3   National Archives

5-1   Spike Lee © National Fluid Milk Processor Promotion Board. Reprinted with permission Bozell Worldwide, Inc.

6-1   © 1958 Turner Entertainment Co., Weingarten Dec. 12, 1967 Trust

8-2   © Bill Mayer Inc. 1986

10-4   Photographer—Paul Bevitt (U.K.)

10-7   Courtesy, CIGNA Corporation

12-2   Children's Medical Center

12-4   © Robert Brenner/PhotoEdit

Literary Credits

BYTE Magazine, July 1994 © by The McGraw Hill Companies, Inc.

Chaim Perelman and L. Obrechts-Tyteca, *The New Rhetoric,* trans. John Wilkenson and Purcell Weaver (Notre Dame, IN: University of Notre Dame Press, 1969). From *The New Rhetoric: A Treatise on Argumentation* by Chaim Perelman. © 1969 by Chaim Perelman.

Excerpt from *Guerrilla Selling.* Copyright © 1992 by William K. Gallagher, Ph.D., Orvel Ray Wilson, and Jay Conrad Levinson. Reprinted by permission of Houghton Mifflin Company. All rights reserved.

Ferdinand F. Fournies, *Why Customers Don't Do What You Want Them to Do—and What to DO about It.* Copyright 1994. Reprinted with permission of The McGraw Hill Companies.

Japan Business (San Rafael, CA World Trade Press) © 1994 World Trade Press.

Judith Trent and Robert Friedenberg, *Political Campaign Communication.* Reprinted with permission of Greenwood Publishing Group, Inc., Westport, CT. Copyright © 1991.

Kim Baker and Sunny Baker. *How to Promote, Publicize, and Advertize Your Drowning Business.* Copyright © 1992, John Wiley and Sons. Reprinted by permission of John Wiley and Sons.

M. Fishbein/I. Ajzen, *Belief, Attitude, Intention and Behavior,* © Addison-Wesley Publishing Company, Inc.

Reprinted with permission from the *World Almanac and Book of Facts 1996.* Copyright © 1995 Funk & Wagnalls Corporation. All rights reserved.

Stephen J. Wayne, *The Road to the White House,* 2nd edition. St. Martin's Press, Inc., New York, NY, copyright © 1984 by Stephen Wayne.

The Nature of Human Values by Milton Rokeach. Copyright © 1973 by The Free Press, a division of Simon & Schuster.

INDEX